A Chanticleer Press Edition

Taylor's Guide to Vegetables & Herbs

Houghton Mifflin Company Boston 1987

Based on Taylor's Encyclopedia of
Gardening, Fourth Edition, copyright © 1961
by Norman Taylor, revised and edited by
Gordon P. DeWolf, Jr.

Library of Congress
Cataloging-in-Publication Data
Taylor's guide to vegetables & herbs.
(Taylor's guides to gardening)
Based on: Taylor's encyclopedia of gardening.
4th ed. 1961.
Includes index.
1. Vegetable gardening. 2. Herb gardening.
3. Vegetables—Dictionaries. 4. Vegetable
gardening—Dictionaries. 5. Herbs—Dictionaries.
6. Herb gardening—Dictionaries. I. Taylor's
encyclopedia of gardening. II. Title: Taylor's
guide to vegetables and herbs. III. Title:
Guide to vegetables & herbs. IV. Title:
Guide to vegetables and herbs. V. Series.
SB321.T37   1987   635   86-20018
ISBN 0-395-43092-5 (pbk.)

Prepared and produced by Chanticleer Press,
Inc., New York

Designed by Massimo Vignelli

Color reproductions made in Italy
Printed and bound in Japan

First Edition.

DNP   10   9   8   7   6   5   4   3   2   1

Contents

Gordon P. DeWolf, Jr., Ph.D.
Coordinator of the Horticulture Program at Massachusetts Bay
Community College in Wellesley Hills, Massachusetts, Gordon P.
DeWolf revised and edited the fifth edition of *Taylor's Encyclopedia of
Gardening,* upon which this guide is based. DeWolf previously
served as Horticulturist at the Arnold Arboretum at Harvard
University and is a frequent contributor to *Horticulture* magazine.

Jim Wilson
Editor of the vegetable and herb descriptions in this guide and
author of most of the gardening essays, Jim Wilson is a co-host of
The Victory Garden, a public television program. Along with his
wife, he owns and operates Savory Farm, a nursery that supplies
herbs to restaurants nationwide. He coauthored *How to Grow a
Thriving Vegetable Garden.*

Thomas E. Eltzroth
General consultant for this guide, and one of its major contributing
photographers, Thomas Eltzroth is a professor of horticulture at
California Polytechnic State University. Eltzroth has an extensive
horticultural photo library, and is coauthor of *How to Grow a
Thriving Vegetable Garden.*

Katharine D. Widin
Author of the essay on pests and diseases, Katharine Widin holds an
M.S. and Ph.D. in plant pathology. Currently she operates a private
consulting firm, Plant Health Associates, in Stillwater, Minnesota.

Preface

Growing vegetables and herbs is in many ways the most rewarding kind of gardening. There's no denying that harvesting and eating fresh vegetables and herbs from your own garden brings enormous satisfaction. Not only do these plants provide tangible results in a single growing season, but also they let you, your family, and even your neighbors enjoy the pleasurable bounty of a home garden almost immediately.

Throughout this book, the emphasis is on growing more produce in less space—and with minimal effort. In contrast, a large garden means more work and increased demands on time and energy. By following the practical advice in this guide, you will discover efficient skills that will help you enjoy gardening as a relaxation. Beginners will find easy-to-grow favorites, while experienced gardeners can select many unusual or newly introduced crops. The how-to-grow section tells you which plants are simple to raise and offers valuable pointers about some of the more challenging vegetables and herbs that require a lot of care or a special environment to succeed.

Many food trends have shaped the selection of crops featured here. As more and more Americans have become interested in health, new vegetables and herbs have found their way to the table. Along with the garden classics—tomatoes, lettuce, corn, cucumbers, snap beans, watermelons, and mint—are some unusual and exotic vegetables and herbs—arugula, radicchio, Persian melons, and black salsify—that were once consigned only to the gourmet produce section or restaurant menus. Not forgotten are the latest imports brought by new Americans from faraway homelands; among these are tomatillo, small greenish-yellow fruits from Latin America; jicama, a root crop from Mexico; and Chinese cabbage, a leafy staple of the Orient.

No matter where you live—country, suburbs, or in an apartment surrounded by concrete, bricks, and asphalt—you can grow vegetables and herbs successfully. Many of the plants recommended in this book are highly suitable for container gardens. Whether your garden is a large plot, small bed, or tub, this book offers a wonderful selection of vegetables and herbs and tells you exactly how to grow and harvest them. It will help you increase your success in growing food crops and give you the confidence to try new cultivars and new gardening methods. Your efforts will be rewarded with satisfaction in knowing you have the skills needed to grow food. Moreover, you will experience a unique pleasure when you taste fresh-grown food from your own garden.

How to Use

There are few rewards in life as gratifying as the fresh flavor of home-grown vegetables, straight from the garden. Lucky is the person who can provide family and friends with the matchless taste of juicy tomatoes, mouth-watering sweet corn, crisp salad greens, tangy peppers, or tender beans. And nothing enhances the pleasure of eating well like the delicate aroma and flavor of fresh-grown herbs—so subtly, but infinitely, superior to their store-bought counterparts.

With a little effort, all these rewards can be yours. This guide will tell you all you need to know to grow and harvest a luscious bounty of fresh vegetables and herbs. For beginners and experts alike, this book provides a wealth of information and insights. If you have never grown so much as a tomato before, you will find here all the basic tips that will take you from start to finish—from planning and starting a vegetable garden to the final harvest of the season. For more experienced gardeners—those with adventurous gardening styles or appetites—the book provides advanced techniques and information about challenging additions to the kitchen garden.

How This Book Is Organized

This guide contains 3 types of material: color plates, an encyclopedia of plants, and how-to gardening tips to guide you through every aspect of growing a cornucopia of vegetables and herbs.

The Color Plates

More than 400 of the most popular vegetables and herbs are illustrated in full-color photographs. Here you will find choice varieties and cultivars as well as unusual plants, divided into 2 main groups—vegetables and herbs. Within these groups, the vegetables are arranged in 7 sections according to basic type—all the tomatoes, for instance, are in one group; squashes, melons, and other vining crops appear in another section; beans and peas in another group, and so on. The herb photographs are organized according to plant color and shape, to simplify identification and help you plan a decorative herb garden.

Visual Key

The color section begins with the Visual Key, which shows how the photographs are arranged and provides an overview of each of the major groups of vegetables and herbs.

Plant Chart

Immediately following the Visual Key is the plant chart, which is divided into 2 sections—one for vegetables and one for herbs. The chart summarizes the chief growing requirements and characteristics of all the plants in the book, including the average number of days to maturity for the vegetables, and recommended uses for each of the herbs.

This Guide

Captions
Each color photograph of a vegetable or herb is accompanied by a
detailed caption that gives the common and scientific name of the
plant plus important growing information at a glance. The vegetable
captions tell you what kind of plant it is and how it is grown; its
hardiness; its light requirements; and the number of days to
maturity. The herb captions inform you about the plant height;
whether it is an annual, perennial, or biennial; its hardiness; its light
requirements; and the amount of moisture required in the soil.
Finally, all the captions refer you to the page in the Encyclopedia of
Vegetables and Herbs where you will find a full and detailed account
of the plant.

Encyclopedia of Vegetables and Herbs
This section gives you an in-depth description of each of the
vegetables and herbs in the book, based on the authoritative *Taylor's
Encyclopedia of Gardening,* revised and updated for this guide. The
accounts are divided, like the photographs, into 2 main groups,
vegetables and herbs; within these groups, they are arranged
alphabetically according to the common name of the plant, and
cross-referenced by page number to the color plates. Individual
vegetables that are members of large groups appear together, rather
than separately—thus you will find lima beans, string beans, and
broad beans all under the superheading Beans.
Each description begins with a list of alternate common names given
to the plant. Next comes information of historical and general
interest: where the plant originated, how long it has been in
cultivation, and what it will look like as it grows in your garden.
The descriptions are accompanied by a black-and-white illustration
showing the edible part of the plant, its habit of growth, or some
other detail.

How to Grow and Harvest
In the How to Grow section you will find all the most important
directions for growing. Generally, this section tells you how to start
the plants—indoors or out, from seed or from seedlings; the best
season in which to plant; optimum temperature for growth; and any
other special conditions that should be met. Information on how to
harvest the plant follows the How to Grow section. Here you will
also learn how to use or store vegetables and herbs.

Varieties
Most popular vegetables and a few herbs are available in a wide array
of scientifically developed, tried-and-true varieties. Varieties may
differ in a single characteristic—color, shape, size, disease resistance,
days to maturity, flavor—or all of these characteristics. When there
are many varieties on the market, the plant account covers the most
important ones in cultivation today.

How-to Gardening Tips

Written by experts, these articles explain every aspect of growing vegetables and herbs. Basic Botany discusses the reproductive cycle, the development of hybrids, and the meaning of scientific names. Getting Started tells you step-by-step how to prepare your property for growing vegetables—choosing a site, evaluating and amending the soil, tilling, fertilizing, and ensuring good drainage. The essay Planting provides guidelines for buying seeds and seedlings, starting seedlings indoors and transplanting them to the garden, and sowing seeds outdoors. The frost date map included here tells you the frost zone in which you live; it is important to know your zone so you can make a planting schedule based on the spring and fall frost dates in your particular area. Garden Care discusses the pros and cons of different kinds of mulches, when and how much to water, and how to keep your vegetables weed-free.

A Garden Plan

Presented here is a sample design for a long, productive season of vegetables and herbs. The illustration shows how you can employ the techniques of succession planting to make the most of your garden—by producing a carefully timed sequence of spring, summer, and fall crops, even within a limited space.

Harvesting and Container Gardening

The essay on harvesting explains when to pick crops at their peak and offers tips on the various ways to store and preserve vegetables, as well as tips on drying and using herbs. Gardeners with only limited space need not be disappointed; the section on growing plants in containers presents alternative solutions and provides all the facts you need to have your own successful crop of vegetables and herbs.

Handy References

The appendices follow the encyclopedia. Included here is a buying guide, which describes how to buy plants and seeds and provides a list of some seed and plant sources around the country. The essay on pests and diseases describes ailments that can cause your vegetables and herbs to falter; an illustrated chart tells you how to recognize and cure some of the most common garden problems. Finally, a glossary defines for you any terms that may be unfamiliar.

Basic Botany

A beginner could read and understand this book without consulting this section, because the meanings of new and different terms can usually be deduced from the context. But to spare you that struggle, these few pages will tell you much of what you need to know to sail through the text and produce a bountiful crop of fresh vegetables.

What Is a Vegetable?

Vegetables are usually herbaceous (not woody) plants grown for food: Leaves, fruits, buds, tubers, roots, or flowers may be eaten. Plants grown principally for their seeds are usually considered grains; if used for seasoning, they are herbs or spices. Vegetables are easy to distinguish from fruits that grow on trees or bushes, but there is some overlap in the small herbaceous fruits, such as strawberries.

Herbs

A vegetable differs from an herb in that it can be used alone, either cooked or raw; herbs are used chiefly to flavor and season dishes. Most herbs are herbaceous, but a few are woody shrubs. Herbs may be grown among vegetables, in a special herb garden, among flowers in landscapes, or in containers. The line between herbs and spices is blurred, but spices are usually considered to be the dried fruits, nuts, leaves, roots, seeds, or bark of tropical or semitropical trees, shrubs, or vines. Virtually all spices are imported.

Life Span

Botanists classify vegetables and herbs as annual, biennial, or perennial, depending on their life cycle. Most vegetables and herbs are annuals. These plants live for one growing season, then flower, set seeds, and die, having completed their reproductive cycle. Most annuals are frost-tender, which means that they germinate and grow in spring and summer, and die in fall. A few are winter-hardy—in the wild, they germinate in the fall and grow a bit in the winter, then in spring they quickly grow, flower, and set seeds. They dry up and die with the first hot days of summer.
Biennials make up a minority of vegetables and herbs. In nature, biennials germinate in spring, grow into sizable plants, overwinter, and bloom the following spring. All are frost hardy, especially species native to northern Europe.
Many herbs and a few vegetables—such as rhubarb and asparagus— are hardy perennials; many more are tender perennials grown as annuals. In general, perennial vegetables and herbs flower and set seeds each year and, having done so, resume vegetative growth.

Family, Genus, Species

Botanists categorize plants according to certain commonalities; this convenient method of classification makes it possible to identify a plant and recognize its close relatives.
Families are groups of plants with a common ancestor and some

Basic Botany

common characteristics. Some families are very large; the Compositae, or daisy family, for example, has thousands of members. Others may include just a few species, or even a single species. A family is made up of genera (singular, genus); genera are more narrowly defined groups of plants that share a certain level of similarity and often have a fairly recent common ancestor. Genera are more significant to gardeners than families; the genus *Brassica,* for example, contains all the cole crops.

A species (plural, species) is a naturally occurring population of plants that can reproduce true to type from seed. Plants within a species display a certain degree of variation—nature's way of ensuring survival of the species. Subspecies are groups of plants that develop in isolation from the main population and, in so doing, have evolved distinct differences from the typical population. These differences persist if the subspecies is grown from seeds.

Pollination

Most vegetable and herb species must be pollinated before fruits and seeds can form; that is, the male germ plasm, or pollen, must be brought into contact with the female stigma. The term pollination is used interchangeably, if not entirely accurately, with fertilization, which occurs when male and female reproductive cells unite.

Close- or self-pollinated species have the male and female parts arranged so that pollination and subsequent fertilization occur without pollen from outside; tomatoes, peppers, and beans are self-pollinated. The activity of insects or manipulation by the gardener can disturb this process by introducing pollen from another plant.

Open- or cross-pollinated species rely on wind, insects, or gravity to transfer pollen between blossoms or between plants; when the outside agent, or vector, is absent, plants bear blossoms but no fruit.

Hybridization

When plants with different traits interbreed, the process is called hybridization; the offspring of such a cross are known as hybrids. Crosses between species are possible, but the offspring are usually sterile (mules are an example of this). Most hybrids represent a cross between cultivars or strains of the same species.

Hybridization may be deliberate or accidental. Hybrids occur almost exclusively between open-pollinated varieties of the same species. Super-sweet corn, for example, can cross with standard sweet corn hybrids, and sweet corn can cross with popcorn; these crosses can result in diminution of sweetness or poor flavor. But, except for corn, the effects of most such accidental crosses are never manifested.

Man-made Hybrids

The object of hybridization is to improve plants—that is, to harness genetic traits, such as vigor or hardiness, that make it possible for a plant to be more productive in adverse circumstances. Vegetable hybrids often incorporate several desirable traits, such as enhanced flavor, increased disease resistance, or greater productivity. Plants grown from hybrid seeds are usually more uniform and vigorous than those from open-pollinated varieties.

Gynoecious and Parthenocarpic Hybrids

Garden catalogues sell a range of hybrids with special attributes. Gynoecious hybrids set only or mostly female blossoms; they are usually interplanted with a few seeds of a standard male/female variety. Gynoecious cucumbers are more productive than standard cucumbers because they can set a fruit at every node.

Parthenocarpic hybrids form fruits without pollination occurring. This apparent defiance of the laws of nature comes from an internal stimulation of the embryonic ovules of cucumbers. The fruits that form contain no true seeds; this proves a real advantage, because the fruits are edible at larger sizes.

Varieties and Cultivars

A variety is a group or class of plants occurring naturally within a species with constant traits that distinguish them from the typical form and from other varieties within the same species. Varieties grow from seeds. Breeders select one or a few similar and desirable plants from the same species and breed them for a few generations, all the while weeding out off types and guarding against accidental cross-pollination. At least every 7 years, breeders start over with new but true-to-type selections.

Cultivars are man-made forms or selections within a species. A cultivar, like a variety, is set apart from typical members of a species by the traits it possesses. Plants within a cultivar are very similar but not always identical; they are subject to genetic flukes, and mutations can occur. If you save and plant seeds from cultivars, you may get considerable, and not always desirable, variation in the progeny.

Plant Names

Every species has a scientific ("Latin") name, composed of 2 parts and written in italics. The first part, with the first letter always capitalized, tells you what genus the plant belongs to; the second part, usually not capitalized, is known as the specific epithet. Cultivar names, never italicized, usually are set off by single quotation marks.

Terms such as "class" and "group" are used to describe varieties or cultivars within the same species that have one or more common characteristics. All the creeping rosemary cultivars, for example, are a class. This terminology is trade jargon rather than botanical language.

Getting Started

No matter what climate you live in, finding a site where a vegetable and herb garden will grow successfully involves both common sense and a few scientific factors.

Sunlight Requirements
Vegetables and herbs need at least 6 hours of full sun per day, all season long. Adequate sunlight is especially crucial during spring and fall, when plants most need it to warm the soil.

To determine the areas that receive the most sun, go out early one sunny spring morning and later that evening and stake off the parts of your property that are shaded by trees and structures. Areas that receive full sun for more than half the day are where very early spring vegetables and warmth-loving, long-season vegetables belong. Garden sites that don't enjoy as much full sun can still produce good vegetables and flowers, however. Areas on the east and north sides of a house, fence, or other structure are in shade for perhaps half the day in the morning and generally receive only reflected light during early spring. Because the soil is too cold and moist, these are not good places to direct-seed early spring crops, but you can set in transplants of cool-loving crops. For example, cole (cabbage family) crops have broad leaves, which gather sunlight more efficiently. Follow the cole crops with root vegetables that also prefer cool soil. Areas receiving afternoon shade are suitable for vegetables that tend to burn out in full summer sun, such as parsley, scallions, and Swiss chard. Follow these with a fall crop of leafy or root vegetables that will benefit from the afternoon shade.

The amount and intensity of sunlight your garden receives varies according to season, atmospheric quality and climate, and latitude. If you live in a cloudy, foggy, or smog-laden climate, your garden will perform differently from one in the Southwest where the sun is so intense that some shade is needed to keep plants cool and prevent the sun from bleaching them.

Bear in mind that in the Sun Belt, midsummer days are relatively short and nights are long, while in the far North, midsummer days are very long. This extra light is one reason vegetables and herbs grow so fast in the northern states.

It is extremely difficult to grow a good vegetable or herb garden in the shade except in very hot climates. If you don't have a sunny spot on open land, consider growing plants in portable containers placed here and there in sunny areas. If shade is caused by a tree and there is no alternative but to cut it down, the return may justify the cost in the form of valuable wood chips and cords of firewood. Another approach is to move the food garden to a sunny side or front yard, or scout around for a vacant lot or community garden.

Other Factors to Consider
Beyond locating your garden where there is adequate sunlight, you must also consider a few practical points. Vegetables can't compete

successfully with the roots of trees or other plants for nutrients and water; isolate the garden from invasive or toxic plants such as bamboos and other aggressive grasses, blackberries, black walnut trees, and surface-rooted maples. Every garden needs good drainage; avoid planting in the path of concentrated runoff water or where water from storms collects. Good air movement is also important; it helps to decrease frost damage and foliage diseases. Fences should be open to let wind pass through; tame wind tunnels with baffle fences. Since you can't always rely on the weather for sufficient rainfall, plant the garden near a water source to make watering a manageable chore.

You may have to plan for a wire fence to protect against destructive pets and wildlife. Arches of chicken wire may have to be readied to discourage birds from pulling up seedlings until the plants can fend for themselves. If possible, plant the garden where you can see it from your house windows so you can measure its progress daily and watch for destructive pets and wildlife. A few flowers or flowering herbs will brighten up the view. If the only site available for your garden is within a few feet of a busy city street, where lead from gasoline, other toxic metals, and tire dust may have been accumulating in the soil for years, consider growing plants in containers of potting soil. Alternatively, you can lay a sheet of plastic on the ground, surround it with a wooden frame, and build up beds using potting soil.

Garden Soil

Vegetables and herbs grow best in healthy, living soil that drains moderately fast, retains nutrients, and contains a fair amount of organic matter.

Soil is composed of clay, sand, and silt. These components all consist of particles; clay particles are the smallest, sand the largest. Loam, the most desirable type of soil, contains up to 25 percent clay, up to 50 percent silt, and less than 50 percent sand, plus organic matter.

Regardless of its immediate condition, your soil will probably require some modification to bring its productivity up to a level at which a vegetable garden can thrive. Generally this means incorporating organic matter and other important nutrients.

Dense clay soil bakes hard, sheds water, and drains slowly. Because it holds so much water, clay soil is also slow to warm up in spring. To correct this situation, incorporate organic matter and sand when you till the soil. In some cases it is better simply to build raised beds on top of the tenacious clay.

Sandy soil warms up fast in spring but drains quickly and dries out rapidly; add copious amounts of organic matter. Sandy soil usually also requires frequent applications of lime. Do not add clay, which will solidify in a layer below the sand particles and form a "hardpan" that will interfere with the passage of air and moisture.

Loamy soil usually needs the same modification as clay but less of it. When amended with organic matter, loam offers the best of both worlds: It drains and warms up faster than clay and stores moisture and nutrients better than sand.

Organic Matter

Productive garden soil should contain 2 to 5 percent organic matter, or humus—garden compost, pasteurized cattle manure, peat moss, pulverized pine or hardwood bark, or other finely chopped, decayed vegetable matter. Organic matter helps water penetrate the soil and stores nutrients. It also activates beneficial soil organisms, which break down soil particles and fertilizers to release the plant nutrients.

Fresh (unpasteurized) manure, tankage, sewage sludge, and similar forms of organic matter are so high in nutrients, salts, and ammonia that they can do more harm to plants than good. Such materials should be thoroughly composted before use. Fresh manure is particularly undesirable because it contains large amounts of weed seeds.

Composting

The easiest, most economical way to have a ready supply of usable organic matter is to make your own compost heap. Coarse organic matter must be composted to reduce the size of the particles for garden use. Wood chips, pine needles, leaves, dried lawn clippings, garden trimmings, hay, straw, and kitchen waste are all possible materials. Avoid using raw sawdust or shavings, which contain tannin and phenols that break down during composting and are toxic to vegetables and herbs. Do not use disease- or insect-infested vegetation or grass clippings from lawns treated with herbicides. Don't use weed plants loaded with seeds. And be sure any kitchen waste you add is free of meat, grease, or bones, which attract unwanted animals.

Ingredients

You can make a working compost heap on your first try and have rich, brown organic matter within 1 to 2 months. The right blend of ingredients is the secret. By volume you should include 2 or 3 parts of green matter, 1 part dry matter such as leaves, and 1 part garden soil. In compost piles built later in the season, substitute half-decomposed compost for the garden soil to generate faster action. The decomposition process should be aerobic, with oxygen-loving microbes predominating. When the pile packs down and becomes wet, it ferments and generates bad odors; when it contains too much coarse, dry material, it stays loose and dry and does nothing.

Dry leaves pack down, shed water, and cause dry spots in the pile, so use a rotary mower to reduce them to a particle size that will decompose faster. To break down green matter, place it in plastic bags for 2 or 3 weeks. This will reduce the volume, soften heavy stems, and spoil any seeds that may have emerged as weeds in the garden. If you plan to add lawn clippings to the compost heap you must dry them first or allow them to ferment in plastic bags. When you pour this semi-digested material onto your compost heap, cover it with soil so that it will not draw flies and will quickly decompose to humus.

Building a Compost Heap
Compost heaps need not be elaborate. The best arrangement is 3 cylinders of strong wire mesh fencing or snow fence, each 3 to 4 feet in diameter, placed side-by-side. Wire the cylinders together where they overlap. (Alternatively, you can build bins of treated lumber lined with plastic or plastic bags.) Material will decompose faster in these medium-size piles, eliminating frequent turning. Large piles can develop anaerobic problems in the center where oxygen can't reach.

By layers, add 6 inches of green matter, 2 inches of dry material, an inch or so of garden soil, and a sprinkling of garden fertilizer or chicken manure as a starter. Wet this layer and repeat the layers. When the cylinder is full, cover it with plastic secured with twine. This not only keeps the rain out, but also concentrates heat. Soak the pile every 2 weeks; when it has settled considerably, fill it to the top and cover it again. Set aside a few forkfuls of the old compost to add as a starter to the new material.

Aim to have all 3 compost heaps filled and largely decomposed by autumn so that you can utilize fallen leaves. To empty the cylinders, snip apart the wires holding the 3 together and remove the wire mesh from around the pile. Save 3 or 4 bushels of compost to use for starting new piles and spread the rest on the vegetable garden.

Shred dry leaves and layer them in the cylinders with leftover compost plus some garden soil, lime (to counteract the acidity of the leaves), and a sprinkling of fertilizer to aid decomposition. Cover the cylinders with plastic sheeting and let them "cook" in full sun during the winter. Come next spring, the piles will be only about half decomposed. As dried grass clippings become available, mix them with the old compost to get the decomposition "fired up." When the material is brown and crumbly, it is ready to use.

Green Manure
If your garden plot is already established, consider growing green manure crops—grasses or legumes that eventually are turned under as an economical source of organic matter. Annual ryegrass is the favorite in the North; in the South, winter legumes such as crimson clover are preferred. Seeds are sown among standing vegetables late in the summer and form a green mat by winter. This valuable open

Getting Started

To have a ready supply of organic matter, build your own compost heap. By layers, add 6 inches of green material such as garden clippings, 2 inches of dry material such as dead leaves, an inch of garden soil, and sprinkle with fertilizer. Wet the pile and repeat the layers; when the container is full, cover it with plastic.

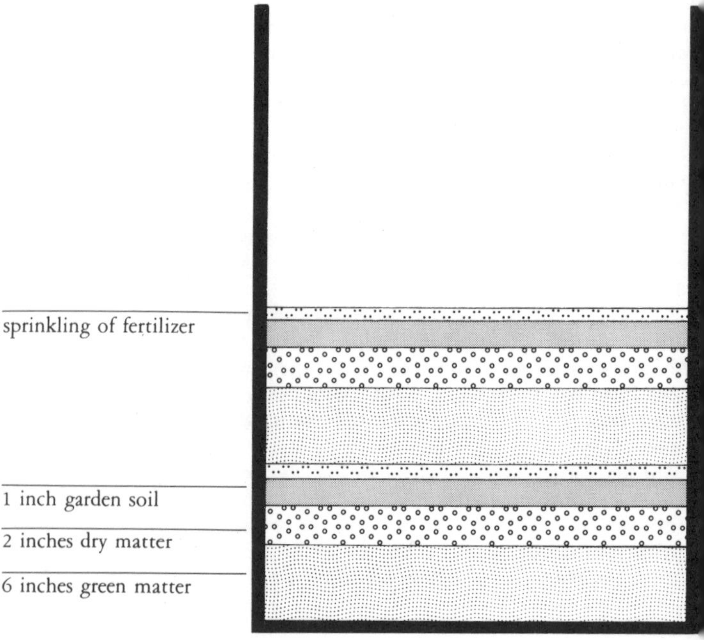

sprinkling of fertilizer

1 inch garden soil

2 inches dry matter

6 inches green matter

sod conserves nutrients that otherwise leach out of the soil during winter and early spring, inhibits the growth of weed seeds, and reduces erosion. Before the spring sowing, this crop is first mown down and then tilled under.

Fertilizer

The major nutrients plants require are nitrogen, phosphorus, and potassium; a complete fertilizer contains all 3 elements. The amounts of each of these nutrients are expressed by the 3 numbers on the package; they may be 10-5-10, 10-10-10, or some other formula. The first number refers to the percentage of nitrogen the fertilizer contains, the second to its phosphate, and the third to its potash. "Simple" fertilizers contain only 1 of the major nutrients.

Fertilizers in dry, granular form are designed to be either tilled into the soil, side-dressed, drilled into a furrow alongside a row of plants, or mixed with compost used for mulching. Liquid fertilizers are designed to be poured onto the soil around plants. Manure tea, one kind of liquid fertilizer, is an extract made from a solution of water plus fresh or pasteurized manure. Some others can be sprayed on and absorbed by plant foliage, but they must be applied with care. They cost more than granular dry fertilizer but act faster to correct nutrient deficiencies. Other fertilizers are sold in the form of water-soluble crystals. These dissolve better in warm, slightly acid water; if your water is alkaline, try adding 1 cup of vinegar per gallon of water.

Time-release fertilizers distribute plant nutrients over a gradual, fairly predictable period and save the gardener much work. Some are triggered by soil temperature to release plant nutrients; others act in response to water, slowly degrading by hydrolysis; still others are activated by bacteria in the soil. Time-release fertilizers are generally unnecessary on moderately fertile to fertile soil, but work wonders if you are growing vegetables on sandy soil or in containers, where nutrients leach away rapidly. Because they don't work well if scattered on the surface of garden soil, they should be applied by drilling into furrows no farther than 3 inches away from planting rows. For container plants they work best when mixed thoroughly with the potting soil before planting.

Organic versus Chemical Fertilizers

There is no evidence that organic fertilizers are superior to manufactured ones and no consistent evidence of differences in food value or flavor. It is possible to grow vegetables in the home garden without using chemical fertilizers. Some gardeners do it very well using compost plus concentrated natural sources of phosphorus and potassium in the form of unrefined minerals such as rock phosphate, granite dust, and greensand marl. Natural fertilizers, usually byproducts, include blood meal, bone meal, fish emulsion, tankage, soybean or cottonseed meal, and bird or bat guano.

pH Levels

Garden experts judge the acidity or alkalinity of soil by measuring the pH level—the hydrogen-ion concentration. Acidity and alkalinity influence the plants' uptake of nutrients such as calcium, magnesium, and sulfur, and of micronutrients such as iron, zinc, boron, copper, and cobalt. pH is rated on a scale from 1 to 14, with 7 representing a neutral level, the level of pure water. The lower numbers indicate acidity, the higher ones alkalinity.

Where you live can help determine the pH level of your soil. If you live in the East and have oak trees and azaleas on your property, you probably have acidic soil and should add lime to it. Soils in the arid West and Southwest, and in areas where they are derived from limestone, seldom need liming. Much of the Midwest has alkaline soil; adding the agricultural grade of sulfur will make it more acidic.

Testing the Soil

Before working up the soil, many gardeners like to have the soil tested by their local county Cooperative Extension Service. These tests analyze the presence of the 3 major plant nutrients: nitrogen, phosphate, and potash. Levels are rated as very low, low, medium, high, or very high. These ratings tell you how much fetilizer and what type to use to bring the nutrients up to levels needed to grow food crops. The test report will probably also note the percentage of organic matter in your soil and the pH level, so you will know whether to apply lime.

To take a soil sample, dig a half-dozen holes 6 to 8 inches deep at various spots around the garden. Make the sides of the holes more or less vertical. Then, take a thin slice from the side of each hole, slicing from top to bottom. Mix the soil from all holes to make a composite sample. If the soil is wet or frozen, dry it before sending it in.

Start taking soil samples early; during the spring rush, results may require 3 to 4 weeks. The cost for this service is modest, and the information is extremely useful.

Incorporating Phosphate Sources

In most areas of the United States it is necessary to supplement fertilizers with additional phosphate sources (usually as superphosphate). Because phosphate stays where you place it, be sure to mix it thoroughly into the deep layers of soil so it will be available to plants where they need it—in their root zone. A single preplant application in spring should suffice for a full season. Slow-release rock phosphate, preferred by organic gardeners, may be used on relatively acid soils but becomes almost completely insoluble on alkaline soils.

Supplementing Nitrogen

Plants can get some of the nitrogen they need from the

decomposition of organic matter. The higher the organic matter content of your soil, the less nitrogen fertilizer you will need to apply during planting. In a vegetable garden, managing nitrogen in the soil is a bit complex. If you apply too little, your vegetables will be yellow and stunted. If you apply too much, the fruiting vegetables will grow lush foliage and set fruit sparsely. Straight nitrogen sources can burn plant leaves or roots, so use complete dry fertilizers: Buy 2 formulations, one high in nitrogen, such as 20-10-10, and one with a medium amount, such as 10-10-10. Use the high-nitrogen formulation for leafy vegetables and the medium formula for fruiting vegetables. Don't worry about putting on too much phosphate or potash. Within reasonable limits these are either stored in soil particles or leached into the subsoil by percolating water. Advanced gardeners occasionally custom-blend their own formulations.

Preparing the Site

There is more to preparing a new site than spading and raking the soil smooth. After carefully choosing where to place your garden, divide the plot into long, narrow strips the width of a square-pointed shovel. Next, carefully skim off the top 1 to 2 inches of soil or sod and put it aside into a wheelbarrow or onto a plastic sheet. This top layer can be composted and used as fill later. By meticulously stripping off the top layer, you will reduce the weed problem for years to come.

If the plot contains deep-rooted spreading grasses such as Bermuda, quack, centipede, or Johnson grass, kill them with an herbicide specially formulated to eradicate perennial grasses. (Do not use a soil sterilant or it will take months before anything will grow in the soil. Turning these grasses under doesn't eradicate them; they will soon come up plentifully from pieces of roots and rhizomes.) In about 7 to 10 days the grasses will have died. Skim off the top 1 to 2 inches of dirt, and you are ready to prepare the soil for your garden.

Testing Soil Moisture

Before preparing the soil for planting, check whether it has the right moisture content for tillage. Turn over a spadeful of soil and squeeze the soil into a ball. If the soil is so sticky that the ball holds its shape, it is too wet to work. Wet soil will form dense clods or balls that will require years of root action to granulate and break apart. If given 3 or 4 days, wet soil should dry enough for working.

If the soil is too dry to form a ball, don't even attempt to spade it and definitely do not run a tiller through it. Working dry soil will destroy the structure built up over the years and turn it into powder. Soak dry soil deeply with a sprinkler and work it after 3 or 4 days. If the ball of soil crumbles when pinched, it is just right to be worked. Sandy soil can be worked virtually any time because it doesn't have much structure.

Getting Started

To till soil by hand, drive a spade into the ground to full depth. Lift and overturn each spadeful of dirt; break up any solid pieces and remove stones and other debris. Work in installments. Mix in amendments after the soil has been spaded.

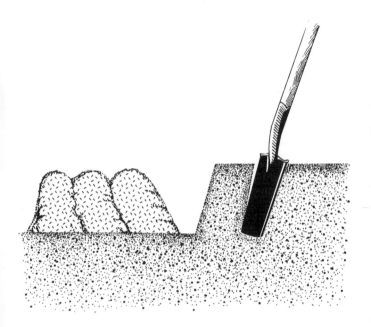

Preparing the Soil

Spread the amounts of lime and phosphate called for by your soil tests. If you plan to rent a tiller, ask for a big one if your soil is heavy; a rear-tined 5 or 8 horsepower model should do the job. An alternative method is to turn over the soil with a spade or a spading fork, but this requires a strong back. Drive the implement into the ground to full depth; lift and overturn each spadeful. Break apart any solid pieces with the back of the spade. Be sure to remove stones, sticks, and other debris as you go. For a large plot, dig in installments because this is heavy work. Back up as you spade, and work in straight lines back and forth across the plot. This method ensures uniform tillage.

After you have spaded or tilled the soil, spread a 2- to 3-inch layer of organic matter over it. (Don't use coarse organic matter such as half-rotted compost, raw wood chips, or chunks of manure.) If your soil is clayey, add a 1-inch layer of sand. Mix these amendments thoroughly to spade or tiller depth. The soil level will rise because of the bulky material added.

Establishing Drainage

There is one more step before you plant. Excavate soil to create aisles in the garden and pile it on the beds, raising their height to 2 to 4 inches above the surrounding soil. If your terrain slopes, make the beds level by running them across the slope rather than up and down it. If the terrain is flat, you may have to run a ditch or a sunken drainpipe from the garden to a lower spot to improve drainage. If these methods are not possible, you can create a dry well. Dig a deep hole at the lowest corner of the garden. Fill it with coarse stones or masonry rubble and cap it off with gravel; cover it with a screen to keep it from being clogged with soil. The dry well will absorb a lot of runoff while allowing water to percolate into deep soil layers.

Double-digging

In recent years, some gardeners have advocated double-digging to till the soil. The point of this technique is to improve the drainage and aeration of the subsoil as well as the topsoil. First you dig and lay aside the topsoil. Then you get into the trench and dig the subsoil to spade depth. Next you incorporate organic matter and fertilizers to open the soil up and make it more fertile. Finally, you return the topsoil to the trench, while incorporating more organic matter and fertilizers. The result is an enriched soil to a depth of 18 to 24 inches.

Double-digging is exceedingly hard work. It is not always recommended, especially when good topsoil overlays poor subsoil. But if despite your best growing techniques your garden is giving only mediocre yields, then try this method. Do one bed and analyze the improvement before you invest a lot of time and effort.

Getting Started

Double-digging improves drainage and aeration of the subsoil as well as the topsoil. First dig a section of topsoil to 1 spade depth and lay it aside. Loosen the subsoil to another spade depth, adding amendments. Then dig another section of topsoil, incorporate amendments, and place it atop the first trench of amended subsoil. Work in installments.

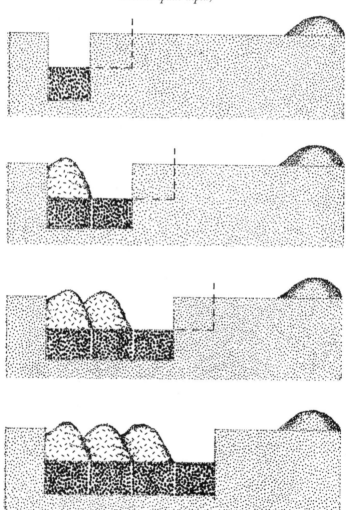

Preparing an Existing Site

Have your soil tested every year or two. If you grow a green manure crop or have grasses or weeds on the plot, run over it with a rotary mower before tilling or spading to lessen the chance of the clumps sprouting in the prepared soil. Respect the same guidelines for soil moisture content as indicated for preparing a new garden. Think back to the previous season; if your fruiting plants were lush and bore light crops, you probably shouldn't add more organic matter. Otherwise, work in a 1-inch layer along with the now-composted mulch from the previous season. At the same time incorporate lime and phosphate sources as called for by soil tests. If your soil is clayey and has stubbornly refused to granulate when amended with organic matter, try adding gypsum at the manufacturer's recommended rate (on dense soils, you may need as much as 100 pounds per 1000 square feet). Work it in very thoroughly to spade depth; gypsum is effective only if very well mixed with the soil. Gypsum (calcium sulfate) won't change the pH of your soil but will gradually cause it to "flocculate"—loosen into particles like coffee grounds. The effect can last for 2 or 3 years.

If you begin garden preparation early, the green material worked into the soil will have had time to decompose by the time you must plant summer vegetables. Experienced gardeners work up one-third of their gardens in the fall and mulch with compost to decrease leaching of nutrients. Fall is also a good time to remove roots of perennial grasses that have invaded the garden.

When the time comes to plant early vegetables in the spring, rake aside the compost you applied the previous fall. If your soil needs chemical fertilizers, now is the time to drill the granular forms into it. First, dig a furrow about 3 inches deep 3 to 5 inches to the side of the place where your planting row will be. Then trickle a narrow band of fertilizer down the bottom of the furrow. As a rule, drill in 1 to 2 pounds of fertilizer per 100 feet of row on fertile soil and up to 3 pounds on poor soil. Cover the fertilizer with soil and level it. This method of drilling, or banding, reduces the exposed surface area of the fertilizer and slows the release rate. Covering the fertilizer with soil reduces the loss of nitrogen.

Now you are ready to dig a shallow planting furrow or planting holes to the side of the drilled fertilizer. As the plants grow, they will absorb nutrients from the band of fertilizer.

Getting Started

Drilling, or banding, fertilizer into the soil is done before planting. Dig a furrow 3 inches deep, 3 to 5 inches to the side of where the planting row will be.

Trickle fertilizer down the bottom of the furrow and cover it with soil. As plants grow, their roots will reach out to absorb the nutrients.

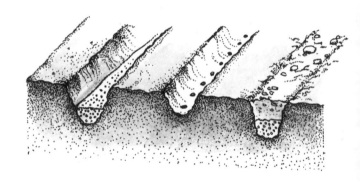

Planting

Most vegetables and herbs can be grown from seeds. Some choice cultivars are planted as seedlings, and a few kinds are grown from roots, tubers, corms, or offsets. The chart on page 72 tells you how to start each plant featured in this book.

Your county Cooperative Extension Service publishes a list of vegetable varieties recommended for growing in your area. This is a good starting point for making up your seed shopping list. Certain states also sponsor Master Gardeners, who volunteer their time and skills to conduct courses in gardening and trouble-shooting when the County Agent is unavailable.

Most states also publish bulletins on herb gardening. These give good instructions on how to plant and what will and will not grow in your state. They are not allowed to publish lists of sources, however, because they have to be noncommercial.

Choosing Seeds

When choosing seeds, most gardeners like to be a little adventurous. They try to go by the County Agent's list, but it takes 2 to 3 years for new varieties to be evaluated and pronounced fit for inclusion. So, many people succumb to the lure of the brand new varieties described in seed catalogues. They enjoy studying the catalogues during the winter and ordering seeds to arrive well before planting time. If you order new varieties from established seed companies, who subject new introductions to rigorous performance trials, you should not have any problem. Beware, however, of the quick-buck artists who come out each spring with flamboyant ads promising amazing plants. These people operate just inside the law. They don't publish catalogues, and they don't run performance trials.

You may prefer to wait and shop for seeds from a display at a local garden center. Seeds are sold at retail in packets or cartons. Seed packets must, by law, be imprinted with the gardening season in which they are to be sold. Selling outdated seed packets is illegal, but you will sometimes see them at flea markets. They are no bargain at any price. Seeds are living organisms with a finite life span—sometimes quite short.

Hybrids versus Nonhybrids

If you order seeds, you can often choose between hybrids and nonhybrids—called open-pollinated varieties. Hybrid seeds are more reliable, because they have been produced under controlled conditions to incorporate disease resistance, productivity, and uniformity into new vegetables. Most of the major vegetable hybrids now offer disease resistance so strong and dependable that it is risky to plant a more susceptible open-pollinated variety just because it is an old favorite. However, there is a vocal segment of gardeners who not only espouse the old open-pollinated varieties, but even offer seed exchanges to keep heirloom varieties in circulation.

Planting

Disease Resistance

Abbreviations are often used in catalogues, seed packets, and even plant names to describe disease resistance. They are becoming so pervasive and complicated that you can hardly tell the players without a program. Here are a few to look for:

TM	Resistant to tobacco mosaic virus; applies to tomatoes and peppers
VFN	Resistant to verticillium root rot, fusarium wilt, and nematodes; applies to tomatoes
A	Resistant to alternaria (early blight); applies to tomatoes
MR	Resistant to common bean mosaic; applies to all beans
PMR/DMR	Resistant to powdery mildew or downy mildew; applies mostly to melons
CMV	Resistant to cucumber mosaic virus
WR	Resistant to wilt; applies to watermelons

Most garden catalogues describe the resistances of each variety listed. Be wary of catalogues that simply claim "disease resistance," which is meaningless.

Treated Seeds

Some vegetable seed catalogues that serve both small-scale commercial growers and home gardeners offer treated seeds and tell you so in their listings. Seed treatment involves applying a coating of a chemical fungicide to protect the seeds from disease between planting time and emergence from the ground. These protectants also contain dyes to alert people that they shouldn't nibble the seeds or feed them to animals. Organic gardeners prefer not to use chemically treated seeds, but the treatments do improve seed germination and emergence, particularly in cold soil. Often, seeds that do not emerge have actually germinated but then suffered from "pre-emergence damping off," caused by fungal attacks.

Seed Tapes and Pellets

Seed tapes are a relatively new product, designed to ensure proper spacing and uniform planting depth. They consist of a narrow strip of water-soluble plastic or fiber material folded over precisely spaced seeds to make a tape. To use a seed tape, just make a furrow to the recommended depth, cut the tape to the length of the row, and lay it in the furrow. Cover with soil or sand to the depth directed.

Pelleted seeds also provide easy handling and uniform spacing, and they can incorporate seed treatment as well. Pelleting is usually limited to fine, costly seeds. They work best in soil that is kept uniformly moist. In dry soil they will germinate erratically.

Bulk Seeds

Some garden centers and, bless 'em, old-fashioned seed stores offer bulk seeds. They will weigh and bag for you quantities of large-seeded vegetables, such as peas, beans, and corn, for planting sizable areas. Beware of buying bulk seeds late in the season unless the seed store is air-conditioned. Hot, humid air is deathly to seeds.

Ordering Early and Storing Seeds

Catalogue companies often sell out of desirable varieties and hybrids late in the season, and if the planting weather is good, seed packet displays will be stripped of popular kinds. It pays to order or buy early. When you have all the seeds needed to fill your garden plans, group the packets together with rubber bands by planting season. There should be 3 groups: those to be planted as soon as the ground can be worked; those to plant 2 to 3 weeks before the frost-free date in your area; and those that must wait until any danger of frost is past. Store your seeds in the refrigerator, sealed in a wide-mouth jar. Also seal in some pouches of desiccant. A few tablespoons of powdered milk wrapped in a paper towel will also dry the air. At the usual 40° F refrigerator temperature, sealed in dry air, seeds will keep until planting time. Such careful storage is not so crucial for seeds shipped in laminated foil and plastic packets, which are impermeable to moisture vapor. Any seeds left over after planting should be promptly sealed and stored cool and dry. The cool-weather crop seeds will come in handy for fall planting.

Buying Seedlings

For some varieties of vegetables—tomatoes, for example—you may want to buy started plants, sometimes called seedlings or bedding plants. These are usually free of diseases and insects, but they can be neglected on display shelves in mass markets where the clerks don't know much about plants. Sometimes, a prolonged cold, wet spring can depress sales and keep plants on the shelf weeks longer than is good for them. They may grow lanky, hard, or wiry, and even form buds prematurely, especially brassicas such as cauliflower and broccoli. These plants are doing what is called "buttoning," and they will never form normal heads when transplanted.

Plants coming by mail from an herb specialist may suffer in transit. Set them in a lightly shaded area, out of the wind, and water them with a weak solution of liquid fertilizer. After a day or two, move them to full sun, but cover them in the event of a hard frost. When the plants have fully hardened, transplant them to your herb garden.

Planting

Starting Plants from Seeds Indoors

Once you have selected your seeds, the next step is to start them indoors so that sturdy seedlings will be ready for transplanting at the proper time.

The equipment you need is fairly inexpensive and consists of:

1. Two 40-watt fluorescent daylight tubes and a reflecting fixture
2. Two lightweight chains for raising and lowering the fixture
3. Two or 3 shallow pans, 15 to 16 inches long and 12 inches wide, to use as trays for holding pots
4. A package of 2½-inch peat pots
5. A package of seed-starting medium—not regular potting soil
6. A rubber bulb syringe with sprinkler head, for dampening seeded pots without washing the seeds away
7. Several 4- to 6-inch plastic pots

Using Fluorescent Lights

Certain seeds are too valuable to risk starting in the garden or on a windowsill. Instead, place the fluorescent lights where daytime temperatures average 70° to 80° F and nighttime temperatures 55° to 60° F. No supplementary sunlight is necessary, since the tubes will cast the equivalent of strong sunlight on an area of 12 by 40 inches. In a cool room, how can you raise the temperature of the growing medium to the 70° to 80° F recommended for sprouting many species? You can either use a heating cable, sprouting boxes heated by grounded incandescent lights, or place the seeded pots, covered with clear plastic, in a warm spot, such as the top of a refrigerator or on top of a water heater, until the seeds sprout. Then, at the first hint of green sprouts, move the pots to a cool room and put them under fluorescent lights.

Hang your lights on chains so that they can be lowered to within 2 inches of the top of seeded pots. The slight warmth and strong light from the tubes will make seedlings grow in a hurry. When the seedlings are the size of a dime, raise the lights so that they hang about 6 inches above the seedlings. If you start some seed containers late, you can still use the same light distance by setting the new containers on empty pots, thereby raising the individual pots closer to the tubes. If seedlings start to stretch, lower the lights and, if possible, the room temperature as well.

Special Seed-starting Mixtures

Garden soils are not satisfactory for starting seeds in containers. Plant diseases can flourish in garden soil, especially damping-off, a malady that can run through seedlings like wildfire. It is particularly serious under cool, damp, low-light conditions.

The best seed-starting media are special mixes of high-grade sphagnum peat moss and vermiculite, or horticultural vermiculite

When you start seeds under lights, lower the chains so the light tubes are within 2 inches of the top of the seeded pots. Raise the lights to 6 inches as soon as seedlings sprout.

If seedlings start to stretch, lower the lights again. Place shallow trays under the pots. To prevent root rot, do not allow water to stand in trays.

alone. Using these mixes substantially lessens the chances of damping-off disease. In addition, a topping of shredded, milled sphagnum moss (not peat) can prevent most disease pathogens from developing.

Recommended Sprouting and Growing Temperatures

Seed packets and catalogues will give you the recommended range of temperatures for seed sprouting. Some seeds will sprout at relatively low temperatures, 50° to 60° F. A few prefer temperatures of 75° to 85° F. A fact that escapes many gardeners is that certain vegetable and herb seeds sprout best in complete darkness. Seed packets may not tell you this, but the better seed catalogues will.

As a rule, optimum growing temperatures are 10° to 15° F below sprouting temperatures. If you fail to lower the temperature as soon as the seeds have sprouted, the seedlings may stretch, become leggy, and succumb to disease.

Planting Indoor Seedings

Most gardeners use shallow, clean, 4- to 6-inch plastic pots for sprouting seeds. Fill each pot to the brim with seed-starting mix just as it comes from the package, then tamp it down with the bottom of another clean pot. Next, set the filled pots in a tray of warm water and let the water soak up from the bottom through the essential drainage holes. Once the surface is moist, scatter the seeds evenly over the surface and cover lightly with vermiculite, milled sphagnum moss, or sharp, gritty sand that has been heated at 150° F for an hour to kill disease organisms and weed seeds.

Now, place your seed pots in shallow pans under the fluorescent light fixture, which is adjusted to the proper height. You should rotate the pots occasionally because those on the ends receive less intense light than those in the center. When the tiny seedlings have sprouted, you will need to transplant them to 2½-inch peat pots. Place 1 or 2 seedlings in each pot. This will expand your space requirements, and you will soon run out of room, even if you move pots to windowsills and heated porches.

Another option is to grow fewer kinds of plants and to seed them directly into peat pots or peat wafers. The space requirements are then the same at the start and finish, and transplanting is avoided. However, far fewer plants can be started in a given area.

When seeding a large number of vegetables or herbs, transplanting seedlings from seeded flats or pots is virtually essential. The seedlings are growing close together and have sparse root systems. Although individual plants can be carefully pricked out and reset into small pots indoors, attempting to transplant them directly into the garden usually fails because the root system is not yet strong enough. Indoor transplanting permits a dense, compact root system to form, which will support the little plant through the rigors of adjustment to the garden.

Cold Frames and Hotbeds

A cold frame is a homemade or ready-made structure covered with a glass sash, clear fiberglass sheet, or clear plastic film. The frames are designed to seal out cold while admitting sunlight, and their cover is pitched or arched to shed rain. Some cold frames have reliable heat-actuated opening and closing devices. Do-it-yourself frames can have a lining of rigid plastic foam insulation, painted black for heat absorption. All frames should drain well if sunk into the ground, to prevent their becoming a bathtub when it rains. Moreover, the cover should prop open securely.

Gardeners use cold frames for several purposes. Early in the spring, the cold frame acts as a halfway house and parking lot for indoor-started, transplanted seedlings of frost-hardy species. Later in spring, the frost-tender species can be moved to the cold frame. Always keep a weather eye out for cold or windy nights, and cover the frame to prevent drastic drops in temperature or freezing inside the frame. In the fall, the frame can be left open during the day but closed at night to prolong the growing season.

Cold frames heated with electric cables or a grid of hot-water pipes are called hotbeds, and they act as small greenhouses. Electricity for heating can be expensive, so hotbeds are usually well insulated. They should not be bottled up too tight or condensation will occur, which can encourage the spread of plant diseases.

Caring for Indoor Seedlings

Beginning gardeners have a tendency to kill seedlings with kindness. Plants should be inspected daily and watered only when the container feels light, not when the soil surface looks a little dry. If seeds fail to emerge and seedlings pinch off at the base or topple over, damping-off has occurred. Move the seeded pots into strong, direct sunlight, reduce the watering frequency, and drench with a special seedling fungicide.

The best way to water seeded pots or flats is from the bottom, or by spraying them from above using a very fine, low-pressure spray of tepid water. The rubber bulb syringe with a small sprinkler head is ideal for this purpose. If the containers feel light when lifted, water them from below. Evening watering should be done early enough to let the foliage dry before nightfall.

As a rule, seedlings should not be fertilized while growing in a seeded pot or flat. Even indoor transplanting shocks seedlings, and they must develop new feeder roots before being fed. The regular potting soils formulated for transplanting contain enough plant nutrients to sustain seedlings for 3 to 4 weeks.

Slow-growing species are usually kept in seeded pots for 5 to 6 weeks and small individual pots for another 6 weeks before they are set into the garden. Only 1 or 2 feedings would be needed during this procedure, and these only near the end of the indoor period.

Fast-growing kinds may spend as little as 3 to 4 weeks in seeded pots

Planting

The lid of a cold frame should prop open securely to 3 positions: slightly open, half-open, and fully open. Sink the frame into the ground or build a bank of soil part way up the sides. Many cold frames also have rubber insulation around the inner rim.

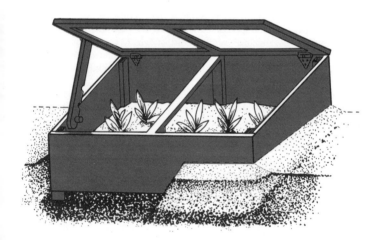

and another 4 weeks in individual pots. One feeding would suffice for them. Soluble plant foods with a 1:2:1 ratio of nitrogen, phosphate, and potash (10-20-10, for example) are good for seedlings, especially if the formulation also contains micronutrients. Use fertilizers at only one-quarter to one-half the rates recommended for mature plants.

Hardening Off Seedlings

The last step in preparing seedlings for the harsh outdoor environment is to harden off, or acclimatize them. Their major adjustment will be against drying winds, more than to cold or to strong sunlight. The tissues of seedlings grown indoors are soft and succulent, and the cell walls thin. Thrusting seedlings into the garden at such a vulnerable stage is asking for damage or loss. Hardening off is simple. A week before the safe transplanting date, find a corner of a porch, patio, or garage that is protected from strong winds yet open to sunlight and temperature changes. Move your transplants there. Watch them closely; they may need twice-daily watering, depending on the ratio of top growth to root ball size. After 3 to 5 days, set them in a fully exposed outdoor location but still in their pots. Be wary of cold nights; even though it may not frost, a warm-weather species can be severely shocked by near-freezing temperatures. Move the plants back inside at night rather than risk such damage or loss.
A cold frame is an ideal hardening-off site because the cover can be propped open by degrees to gradually accustom plants to wind, dryness, and cold.

When to Plant

One of the keys to successful gardening is to know when to plant the varieties, hybrids, and cultivars you want to grow. Use the frost date map on page 36 and the descriptions in the encyclopedia to find the best planting dates for each vegetable and herb in this book.
The map divides the country into 7 areas according to length of growing season and prevailing climate during the growing season. After you determine which zone you are in, it is a good idea to check with your county Cooperative Extension Service about average dates of the last spring and first fall frosts in your area. This information could contradict the map, in which case you should take the agent's word as gospel. Your town may be on a high ridge or in a low valley, near a moderating body of water, or within a zone of urban warming, all of which could affect frost-free dates. The importance of pinpointing these dates cannot be overstressed.

Transplanting Seedlings

Seed packets and catalogues will suggest the necessary spacing between plants. It may seem like a lot of room at first, but the

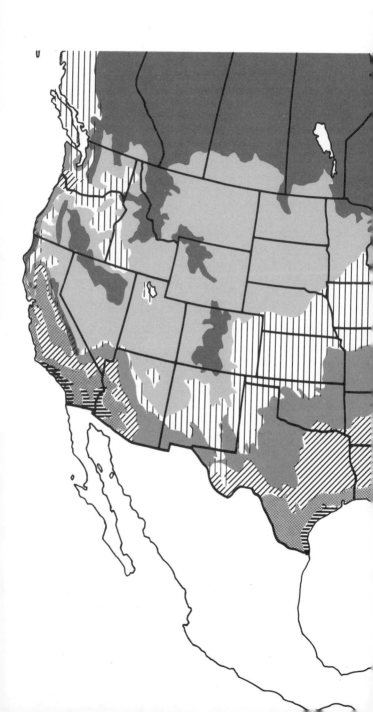

The key below shows the average dates of the last spring frost and the average length of the growing season in 7 frost zones. The growing season is the period between the spring and fall frosts, often referred to as the frost-free days.

This map is based on freeze data tabulations made by the United States Weather Bureau.

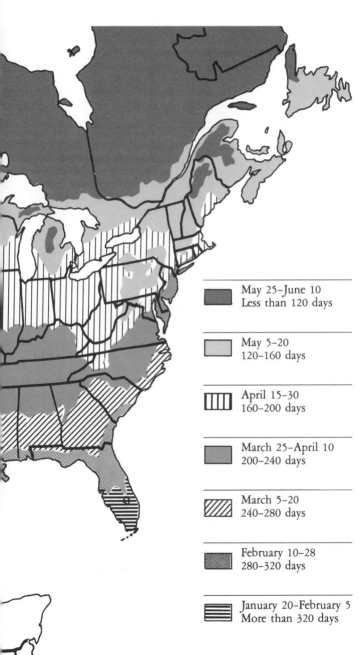

May 25–June 10
Less than 120 days

May 5–20
120–160 days

April 15–30
160–200 days

March 25–April 10
200–240 days

March 5–20
240–280 days

February 10–28
280–320 days

January 20–February 5
More than 320 days

plants will spread or billow out to nearly touch each other at maturity. If you crowd plants, the result may be poor performance as well as problems with diseases and insects.

Prepare the soil and work phosphate and lime into it, if needed. A low-nitrogen complete fertilizer, such as 5-10-10, can be substituted for the phosphate. Some gardeners swear by high-phosphate starter fertilizers, which are dissolved in water and then used to water-in the transplants. These are most effective on soils with adequate nitrogen, for neither phosphorus nor nitrogen works well alone. Although some gardeners claim vitamin concoctions help in transplanting, no scientific data support their use. Fish emulsion, dissolved at half the normal rate, gets transplants off to a fast start.

A tried-and-true method of transplanting is to dig planting holes and fill them with water. Let the water soak in, and then add more. It is much easier to supply a reservoir of soil moisture before transplanting than after, because many types of soil seal over and shed water.

Inspect your seedlings as you take them out of individual pots. The soil should be moist. Ordinarily, seedlings have enough vigor to outgrow a minor pot-bound condition. But if roots circle around and create a mat, draw a sharp knife up one side, across the bottom, and down the other side. New feeder roots will form at the cut line. They will grow out into the surrounding soil instead of being trapped inside the cage of girdling roots.

Direct-Seeding

Some vegetable seeds—either large seeds or the small seeds that sprout and grow quickly—can be sown directly into your garden. Direct-seeding is a quick, easy, and economical way to grow vegetables. With many kinds there is no advantage to transplants over direct-seeding—peas, beans, and corn, for example.

Experienced gardeners know that "broadcasting," or scattering seeds randomly, is not wise. It is virtually impossible to cover broadcast seeds to a uniform depth. Seeding in rows or bands works much better. Rows are long, straight furrows made with walking space in between. Bands are like broad furrows, 6 to 12 inches wide. A band should not be so wide as to prevent you from reaching its center to harvest the plants. In either case, planting uniformly helps you to tell the seedlings from the weedlings.

With only a little practice you can master the ages-old art of direct-seeding and get predictably good results. Just keep these pointers in mind:

1. Plant during the recommended span of dates.
2. Prepare a seedbed so that the top surface is raked free of clods, stones, and debris and is composed of fine particles.
3. Tie a string between stakes to line off planting rows or bands.
4. For large seeds, use a triangular hoe or the corner of a

Rows are long, straight furrows with walking space in between. Bands are like broad furrows, 6 to 12 inches wide; they work well for smaller vegetables.

square-bladed hoe to open a furrow about 2 inches deep, lined up with the string. If you are band planting, make 2 or 3 closely spaced parallel furrows or 1 broad furrow.

5. For small seeds, use the edge of a 1-inch-wide board to press a furrow 1 inch deep in the seedbed, lined up with the string. Take a pinch of seeds and dribble it thinly down the furrow to get the desired spacing.

Covering the Seeds

Now for the covering. More planting failures are caused by improper coverage than by any other shortcoming. Here is a method that always works well. Make up a container of disinfected sand and cover it tightly to exclude dust and other contaminants. A small plastic garbage can is ideal. Disinfect the sand with a 10 percent solution of household bleach, roughly 1 cup to a gallon of water. Use enough solution to wet the sand. After an hour or so, pour off the solution and spread the sand thinly on a clean sheet of plastic to let the chlorine evaporate. The sand will dry partially. Return the sand to the covered container. Dip it out with a clean bottle. Use this disinfected sand to cover seeded furrows.

The old guideline of covering to 3 times the thickness of the seed still works for large seeds. With small seeds, scatter sand over them until you can no longer see the seeds. The next step is to firm the sand over the seeds. Take the back of a clean square hoe and tamp down each planted row just enough to make an imprint.

Because water accumulates in the soil during winter, direct-seeded vegetables and herbs usually germinate in spring with no problems. Seeds sown in dry soils, however, may need a boost to germinate. If there is no rain in sight, use a sprinkler to wet the soil to a depth of 1 foot or more. Seeds that take more than a week to germinate require more than one sprinkling.

Finally, put a fine spray nozzle on your hose and moisten the soil. Stop when you see water running off. Sprinkle at least daily unless rains do the job for you. Discontinue sprinkling when you see the first seedlings emerge. Begin watering more deeply and less often.

The advantage of using disinfected sand for covering seeds is severalfold. Unlike soil, sand won't crust or blow, it warms quickly, it bonds with the soil when you firm it down, and it conveys moisture to the seeds. Disinfecting kills damping-off organisms. Using disinfected sand is a bit more work but will result in improved germination. Even sprinkling untreated sand over seeds ensures a more uniform depth of coverage than pulling garden soil over the seeds with a hoe.

A Few Options

Experienced gardeners have discovered that slight alterations in the general direct-seeding method can improve the stand of vegetables

Plastic gallon jugs with the bottoms cut out can be placed over frost-tender seedlings such as tomatoes to protect them until the weather warms up.

You can protect a row of seedlings with a tunnel made from a sheet of corrugated fiberglass arched over the row and held in place with stakes.

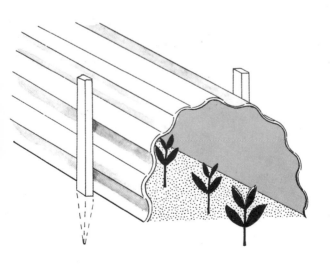

Planting

and herbs in less-than-ideal conditions. If the weather is dry but relatively cool, make your furrows 6 inches deep and flood them 2 or 3 times with water. Then replace the soil excavated from the furrow and make a new furrow to the proper depth. Seeds then planted and covered as previously described will germinate better due to the soil moisture "subbing," or rising from below by capillary action.

In hot, dry weather, make and flood a deep furrow without replacing the soil as above. Plant seeds in the bottom of it and cover them with sand, but don't tamp it down. Lay a board over the furrow to shade the seeds and keep them from drying out. Remove the board at the first sign of emerging seedlings.

Finally, in cold weather, cover the direct-seeded beds with clear plastic trenched in at the edges to keep the wind from tearing it off. Germination will be speeded and more seeds will escape damping-off. You must remove the plastic at the first sign of emerging seedlings, however. For this reason, don't try to cover a row of parsley and a row of mustard greens under the same sheet. Parsley requires 14 to 21 days to come up. Mustard needs only 3 to 5 days.

You can sometimes add many days fore and aft of the accepted planting season in your area by covering direct-seedings and young transplants with bottomless plastic milk jugs, fiberglass tunnels, cloches, and other heat-saving devices that offer protection from frost.

Planting in Hills
An alternative to direct-seeding in furrows is planting large seeds in hills—low, flattened mounds of soil. Hill planting is sometimes used for sweet corn and often for cucumbers, squash, and melons. Prepare the seedbed as usual and simply space 3 to 5 seeds around the top of each hill. Poke the seeds 1 to 1½ inches deep into the soil, using your forefinger. Don't cover. Down in the bottom of the hole the conditions are just right for a seed to sprout. In dry weather the planting depth can be increased to 2 inches.

Protecting Seedlings from Wildlife
Several kinds of critters relish seedlings. Crows, pigeons, jays, and other birds will pull up fleshy young plants such as corn, beans, and peas. Toy owls and dummy snakes used as scarecrows provide some deterrence, but lightweight arches of chicken wire give absolute protection. Burrowing rodents such as chipmunks, gophers, and mice may have to be trapped or poisoned.

Perhaps the most mysterious villains are slugs and snails—they can "disappear" a row of seedlings the first night after they emerge. Cutworms are about as sneaky. These plump worms will curl around the base of the stem at night, topple the seedling, and move on to another, just like clear-cutting timber.

You can kill slugs and snails with metaldehyde bait in frozen juice cans laid on their sides and flattened to exclude dogs and cats. Collars made of bottomless tin cans do a good job of keeping cutworms away from seedlings.

Intensive Gardening—Growing More in Less Space
With a few gardening seasons under his or her belt, an observant gardener can manipulate a garden to produce an incredible amount and variety of food. Here are some of their secrets:

1. Plan the garden in detail—what, when, and where to plant—well ahead of planting time. Dividing the garden into small units helps you plan and control everything that goes on.
2. Modify the soil to achieve maximum response.
3. Make raised beds, either freestanding or enclosed by frames of lumber.
4. Mulch aisles—the spaces between rows—with coarse organic matter. Aisles are not all lost space. Vegetable roots invade them for water and nutrients, and foliage overhangs them.
5. Plant only adapted, productive, disease-resistant varieties, whether open-pollinated or hybrid.
6. Use fluorescent lights to grow seedlings.
7. Cover direct-seedings with disinfected sand.
8. Plant as close together as the particular variety can stand but not so close as to cause malformed root crops or stunted leaves or fruit. This takes practice.
9. Plant smaller-growing vegetables in bands rather than in single rows.
10. Use protective shelters such as cloches, bottomless jugs, tunnels, and cold frames.
11. Mulch with organic material or plastic sheeting.
12. Install drip/trickle irrigation in lieu of sprinklers.
13. Use vertical structures—cages, arbors, trellises, and fences—to grow vines on rather than letting them ramble.
14. Anticipate the completion of harvest by interplanting a new crop.
15. Practice preventive pest control.
16. Fertilize plants frequently and lightly.
17. Harvest fruiting crops promptly. Letting them hang on the plant depresses further production.
18. Shade leafy vegetables during hot weather.
19. Practice succession planting—replanting as soon as a crop is harvested.
20. Utilize containers to expand restricted planting areas.
21. In cold climates, cover or bank-up crops in the fall to extend the harvest, and plant green manure crops such as annual ryegrass.
22. In warm-winter areas, start fall/winter crops early enough for them to grow to a good size before cold weather comes.

Garden Care

No one can promise a maintenance-free vegetable and herb garden. But the time needed for watering, mulching, and weeding can be kept at a minimum if you consider your options from the beginning and choose the methods that suit you best.

Maintenance Watering

No matter where you live, your garden is sure to require some irrigation. Even with normal rainfall, you will have to water occasionally. Maintenance watering begins after transplants have taken and direct-seeded vegetables and herbs have emerged. Vegetables need a lot of water to grow rapidly; most herbs (except mint and basil) can get by on less.

On the average, gardens need 1 to 3 inches of rainfall or irrigation water per week. One inch of water will wet a loam soil to a depth of about 5 inches (less in clay soil and somewhat more in sand).

There are 3 principal ways to irrigate—sprinklers, drip/trickle irrigation, and flood or basin irrigation. Sprinkling is the simplest method, but it tends to encourage foliage diseases and causes weed seeds to sprout like mad. Place a water glass near the sprinkler head; when 2 inches of water has collected in the glass, move the sprinkler. If water runs off, move the sprinkler after an initial watering and come back to the original position after the water has soaked in. Sprinkle in the morning so the foliage will dry in the sun.

Drip/trickle irrigation is the coming thing. It conserves moisture, increases production up to 30 percent, does not encourage foliage diseases, and leaves most of the soil surface dry. You can run drip tubes underground or cover them with mulch, but aboveground tubes are easier to repair and unclog.

You don't need an engineer to install a drip/trickle system; you can order a system readymade or as components, or purchase one at a large garden center or hardware store. Talk to your local nursery specialist for advice.

The oldest irrigation method is flooding. Flood irrigation helps to reduce the accumulation of salts in the soil, especially in parts of the West, but this method is inefficient because much water is lost to evaporation. Flooding also encourages weed seeds to germinate. To flood between plant beds, dam the ends of walkways and make a little pond of water that will soak in. You can also build a basin of soil around larger plants and fill this basin with water.

Flood irrigation can be used only for narrow beds, because water doesn't move far horizontally. Flooding pathways between wide beds does not work; capillary action will pull water up the shoulders of the bed but won't wet the middle.

Using Organic Mulches

Throughout most of the country, organic mulches are widely used to keep down weeds, conserve moisture, and reduce soil temperature. Organic mulches also provide an important secondary benefit, because they decompose into humus—fine, dark organic particles that retain moisture and nutrients and enrich the soil. Some parts of the West Coast, however, have large populations of snails, slugs, earwigs, and sowbugs, which shelter beneath mulches and come out to feed on vegetables and herbs.

Materials

One very popular organic mulch is also simple to make. It consists of a layer of moistened cardboard or newspaper, topped with 2 to 6 inches of dried grass clippings, leaves, vegetable trimmings, and other organic refuse. After a few days the mulch settles down and looks tidy.

Weed-free straw also makes a good mulch. Some gardeners maintain a year-round layer 4 to 6 inches deep, pulling aside just enough to open rows or set in transplants, and adding to it each spring. You can rake off straw mulches in early spring so the soil can absorb the sun's warmth, then replace the straw as plants reach 4 to 6 inches. Hay is not recommended for mulching, as it contains many grass and weed seeds.

Sawdust, shavings, and pulverized pine bark, composted for at least 1 to 2 months, can be used to mulch vegetables. Used fresh, however, these materials cause "nitrogen drawdown," and may cause plants to turn yellow. Before mulching with raw wood products, apply 1 to 2 pounds of nitrogen fertilizer per 100 square feet. Raw wood products also contain tannins and phenols detrimental to plants, but these will leach away harmlessly if the mulch layer is only 1 to 2 inches deep. The fibrous material called "hardwood bark mulch," available in parts of the southern and central United States, is an excellent mulch. It does not cause nitrogen drawdown, allows water to penetrate, and won't wash or blow away.

Peat moss makes a poor mulch; it tends to go dry and stay that way, repelling water or blowing away. It is best used as a soil amendment, incorporated during tillage.

Using Plastic Mulch

Plastic mulches are unsightly but very effective. You can buy black plastic sheeting in various thicknesses, and it is usually sold in rolls 4 feet wide and 100 feet long. Build up flat-topped beds, 4 to 6 inches high and about 30 inches across at the top. Apply fertilizer and lime as needed and work it in. Rake the bed smooth, walk over it to firm it down, and rake it level again, making sure to remove stones and sticks that might puncture the plastic.

Install a drip irrigation tube or a soaker hose down the center of the row. Lay down the plastic and bury the edges with soil; work your way down the length of the row, pulling the plastic tight as you go. Use organic mulch in the dirt walkway between beds to keep down

Garden Care

weeds and to keep your shoes clean. To insert transplants, make slits or cookie-cutter holes in the plastic, 6 to 8 inches from the drip tube.

Black plastic mulches combined with drip irrigation are very good for heat-loving, long-term vegetables such as peppers, eggplants, tomatoes, and melons. Plants grow faster, produce more, are cleaner and free of weeds. In the South, where the temperature beneath black plastic can rise too high for plants, growers spray-paint white areas around each planting hole. White plastic is available, but it can encourage weeds to grow. In the Far North, clear plastic mulches work better than black plastic to accumulate solar heat early in the season. In late spring, scatter compost or straw over the clear plastic to block out sunlight and to stop the greenhouse effect, which promotes weeds and grass.

Weeding

Every now and then some philosophical gardeners come up with a "holistic gardening" concept supporting growing vegetables and weeds together. You can't blame them. Weeding is onerous and neverending. Certain vigorous vegetables may be able to tolerate an understory of small, inoffensive weeds but most weeds are not inoffensive: Many are big, aggressive plants that suck up the water and nutrients needed by adjacent food plants.

To keep weeds in check, you can either choose to weed on a regular basis or to mulch so that weeds cannot grow at all.

Hand Weeding

Try to weed on a warm, dry day. If the soil is moist, weed around noontime so that the pulled weeds will wilt rather than re-root. Use a long, sharp-edged dandelion digger or a narrow spade to dig deep underneath the weed. Remove completely the long roots of perennial weeds such as dock, pokeweed, or nightshade. If you cut these off at the surface, the roots will regrow and branch.

Go over the garden with a lightweight push/pull scuffle hoe. Slide the blade just beneath the surface of the soil and work it back and forth. The serrated cutting edges at the front and back of the hoe will cut off weeds as you pull the tool. For greater efficiency, keep the upper and lower surfaces of the blade clean. Near small plants, do not use a hoe; hoeing may injure plants. Instead, use a small hand implement such as an L-shaped "Cape Cod Weeder." This tool cuts on the pulling stroke, snagging and pulling out weed seedlings that are growing close to your small vegetable plants.

Using a Tiller

Some gardeners arrange their row-and-bed spacing in order to accommodate a small, lightweight power tiller. However, tillers are best for large gardens with rock-free soil. They are not labor savers for small gardens and they cannot operate well in rocky soil.

Using Herbicides

Although herbicides are quick and easy to use, they are not very safe around vegetable and herb gardens. Commercial growers use them, but with great discretion. Sprayed directly, contact herbicides kill weeds or grass, and sometimes both. Pre-emergent herbicides keep weed and grass seeds from germinating. Either type of herbicide can stray into the food garden and kill desirable plants. However, if used extremely carefully near the garden border, contact herbicides are great labor savers. But if you use a herbicide, be sure to wash your sprayer with a strong ammonia solution and rinse it several times to remove any trace of herbicide. If not thoroughly clean when you next spray with insecticides, it could damage food plants.

Although weeds are inevitable, you can decrease the number of weeds each year by following several commonsense procedures: Never let weed plants go to seed; never throw weed seed heads into the compost; always direct the blast from your mower away from your garden; and put cardboard or newspapers underneath your organic mulch to prevent weeds.

Equipment and Supplies

Having the right equipment can make gardening much easier and more pleasurable. If you are a beginner, the initial cost of the supplies you will need to start a garden may seem high, but investing in the best you can afford will pay off.

Good tools are expensive. You can rationalize their purchase by amortizing the cost over a 5-year period. Good tools will keep going strong for years if they are routinely cleaned and painted or oiled to preserve the wood.

Garden Tools

A basic set of garden tools consists of 5 items:

1. Round-pointed shovel or spade for turning the soil. A round-pointed shovel can be used for both spading and shoveling; a spade has a straight blade and is essential for bed preparation.
2. Iron rake about 14 inches wide. Distinct from the flexible lawn rake, an iron rake has rigid teeth for leveling the soil.
3. Square-bladed hoe or combination hoe with a square blade on one end and a pointed blade on the other. This invaluable tool is used for chopping weeds, scraping or cultivating soil, and making furrows or planting holes.
4. Push-pull scuffle hoe for quick weeding. The blade is equipped with sharp, serrated edges for cutting weeds as this tool is pulled back and forth.
5. Sprayer, either 2 or 3 gallons

Also helpful but not strictly necessary for a small garden are the following tools:

Garden Care

6. Heavy-duty wheelbarrow or cart
7. Garden hose, about 50 feet
8. Trowel, weeder, dandelion digger, shears, and other small hand tools
9. Loppers
10. Pickaxe for hard soil
11. Fluorescent light fixture for starting seeds indoors

Tillers, shredders, composters, and other expensive items are hard to justify except for large gardens. If you can afford them, these tools certainly do take a lot of the toil out of gardening.

Soil Amendments
For the first year, you will need to spend more on soil amendments than ever again. A 3-cubic-foot bale of peat moss spread 2 inches deep will cover about 20 square feet of land. For a garden that is 300 square feet, you will need 15 bags. Local forest or farm byproducts such as pulverized pine bark, redwood compost, or composted rice hulls are less expensive and can be used in lieu of peat moss.

Seeds
For a 300-square-foot garden, seeds are a nominal annual expense. Perennial plants such as asparagus crowns and perennial herbs represent a one-time investment that will last for years. For a small garden you can usually buy a few plants of a certain kind as cheaply as you can buy seeds, although seeds offer a greater choice of varieties.

A Garden Plan

Planning your vegetable or herb garden on paper helps you make the most of your time, space, and efforts. Unless you have a lot of spare time to devote to gardening, it's prudent to plan a plot that, once established, will require no more than 4 to 6 hours of care per week. Preparations during the first few weeks will demand more time, of course, but if they are made according to a well-considered plan, you'll be rewarded with good eating at harvest time.

Drawing a Map

Let's work through the planning of a hypothetical vegetable garden. A good size for a beginner is 15 by 20 feet, the size of a large room. From this you can harvest enough vegetables to more than pay for materials and plants. Your own garden may be smaller or larger, but the principles involved are the same.

Use graph paper and set a scale of 1 inch = 2 feet. The outline of the garden will be 7½ by 10 inches. Mark off 4 beds lengthwise, each 3 feet wide, with 1-foot aisles between them. Then, divide each bed into five 4-foot lengths using dotted lines. Dividing the garden into these 20 "squares" makes planning easier. (See page 52.)

It doesn't make much difference whether your beds are oriented east-to-west or north-to south unless you live in the northern part of the country. There, a slight advantage lies with north/south orientation because the sun's path will cross the rows at right angles. If it were to parallel the rows, every plant in the row would be shaded by its neighbor during part of the day.

In northern gardens, tall plants and garden structures—corn, sunflowers, bean arbors, tomato cages, and so forth—should be concentrated along the east side so that their shadows will not fall on the garden during the afternoon and evening. Over the rest of the country, put the tall plants where they won't block your view of shorter plants.

Assigning Space

As a rule of thumb, our 300-square-foot garden can accommodate about 10 vegetable crops per planting season. But remember, in all but short-season areas you can have 2 or 3 crops on the same ground in one year. Here's a way to match your aspirations to your vegetable garden space:

1. List all the vegetables you'd like to plant and give each a priority·
2. Make 3 columns next to your list and label them "Early Spring," "After Frost-free Date," and "Late Summer/Fall." Read the description in the encyclopedia section of this book for each vegetable on your list to learn the best time to plant it. Experience will teach you that you'll need to set aside about two-thirds of your garden space for warm-weather crops. Then, when your spring crops are harvested, you can plant either a late warm-weather crop or hold the space open for a fall crop.

A Garden Plan

3. Assign bed space in each season according to mature plant size. Beside each vegetable on your list note the approximate size of the mature plant: small, medium, or large. Now figure out how many linear feet of vegetable beds are in your garden. For example, our 15 by 20 space contains 4 beds 20 feet long, or 80 linear feet of bed. Just as a rough guide, for such a garden assign about 10 to 12 feet to each large vegetable—corn, pole beans, tomatoes, bush squash, and okra, for example. Assign 6 to 8 feet of bed to each medium-size crop—eggplant, peppers, cabbage, broccoli. Assign 4 feet to each small vegetable or root crop: lettuce, radishes, carrots, and dwarf peas, for example.
4. Now you can make planting lists for 3 gardens: spring, summer, and fall. Plan for about 50 to 55 linear feet of bed for summer crops and 25 to 30 feet for spring and fall crops in succession.

Your first garden will probably produce too little of some kinds and too much of others. Save your planting chart and make notes of adjustments needed for the coming year.

A Sample Plan
Every gardener's "top 10" list will of course be different, but here is an example of how one list could be fit into our plan. Start by setting aside 2 of the squares in the back of the garden for asparagus, a long-term crop. You would soon tire of walking around it if you placed it in the front.

The Spring Garden
Use a transparent colored marker to shade the 5 squares in the front bed and 1 in the second bed. These 6 squares represent 24 linear feet, or one-third of the space remaining after planting asparagus. They will become the spring garden.
Assume you would like to have these early-planted vegetables in the spring garden: broccoli, cabbage, kohlrabi, leaf lettuce, parsley, radishes, onions, peas, spinach, and potatoes. This is a good, manageable list—with one exception. You may want to rethink the potatoes. They take up a lot of space, and the home-grown product is only slightly better than what you can buy in the stores. Drop potatoes and see if you can work the other 9 kinds into the plan. See the illustration for these space-maximizing techniques:

1. Reserve 2 blocks for peas for a good yield.
2. Run the peas up strings and edge the pea beds with parsley.
3. Interplant 1 row of broccoli between 2 rows of spinach.
4. Interplant 1 row of midget cabbage between 2 rows of leaf lettuce.
5. Plant 1 square solid with onion seedlings to grow bulbs.
6. Plant 2 bands of kohlrabi and scatter radish seeds thinly in the same square.

The Summer Garden

Color 12 more squares with a different colored transparent marker. These are your 48 linear feet of summer garden. Assume you'd like to plant pole snap beans, pole lima beans, beets, carrots, tomatoes (an early and a midseason variety), peppers, Swiss chard, zucchini, corn, and cucumbers. That's 10 kinds. Some of the crops are vines and can be run up arbors, stakes, or cages to conserve space.

1. Reserve 2 squares in the back for tall sweet corn, in 4 rows forming a block for better pollination.
2. Take 2 squares for the zucchini; put 4 plants in each square.
3. Put in 1 square of main-crop tomatoes and 1 of an early hybrid. You might be able to squeeze in 4 cages.
4. Put up an arbor over 2 squares. Plant pole limas on one side, pole green beans on the other. Down the center, plant Swiss chard.
5. On 2 squares put up a frame and run vines of cucumbers up it. Edge the cucumber bed with rows of beets.
6. Plant 4 pepper plants in 1 square. That's plenty.
7. Plant the last square with 2 wide bands of carrots.

The Fall Garden

This is the point where most gardeners stop planning, because the plan is full. But remember, the spring garden will be empty by midsummer and can be followed with crops for fall harvest. Try these: broccoli, cauliflower, cabbage (late, red, or Savoy), Chinese cabbage, endive or escarole, kale, collards, rutabaga, turnips, kohlrabi, spinach, and winter radish. There are more prospects, but of these you could probably fit in nine. That's 28 kinds of vegetables in a 300-square-foot garden.

This complex plan, typical of intensive gardening, doesn't require any more labor than a loosely managed garden with lots of wasted space.

Planning an Herb Garden

A simple arrangement for a beginning herb garden is a rectangular plot, 12 by 16 feet. This can produce a sizable amount of the major herbs for fresh use or drying.

On your plot plan, divide the garden into 12 squares, each 4 feet by 4 feet. The garden will be 4 squares long and 3 wide. Let your walkways cut through the beds.

In the 2 center beds plant the large summer herbs, such as sweet basil, lemon verbena, and sesame. You can plant 4 to 12 herb plants in each square of the herb garden. Put the trailing, creeping herbs in groups of 3 plants along the outside border. Plug the perennials in here and there, and plant the quick-maturing cool-weather herbs between them.

Banish all the mints and pennyroyal to containers. They spread invasively and make bad neighbors for the other herbs.

A Garden Plan

Here is a 15-by-20 foot garden with 4 beds (dark gray) separated by aisles. Each bed is divided into 5 squares.

Long-term crops fill 2 squares at the back; summer crops occupy 12 squares, and spring crops 6 squares. After you harvest spring crops, you may wish to plant cool-weather crops

Long-term and Summer

1. Asparagus
2. Zucchini
3. Sweet corn

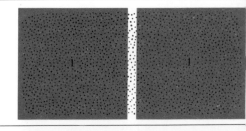

Summer

4. Pole lima beans
5. Swiss chard
6. Pole snap beans
7. Early tomatoes
8. Main-crop tomatoes
3. Sweet corn

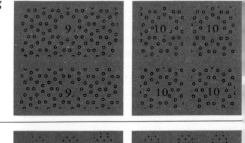

Summer and Spring

9. Carrots
10. Peppers
11. Beets
12. Cucumbers
13. Kohlrabi
14. Radish

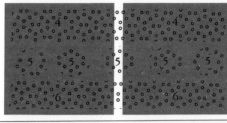

Spring

15. Parsley
16. Peas
17. Spinach
18. Broccoli
19. Leaf lettuce
20. Cabbage
21. Onions

Late Summer–Fall

22. Cauliflower
23. Escarole or endive
24. Rutabaga
25. Collards
26. Turnips
27. Winter radish
28. Chinese cabbage

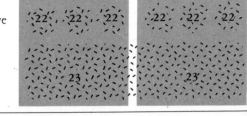

for fall (light gray) and repeat a favorite vegetable in 2 squares.

Long-term crops

Summer crops

Spring crops

Late Summer–Fall crops

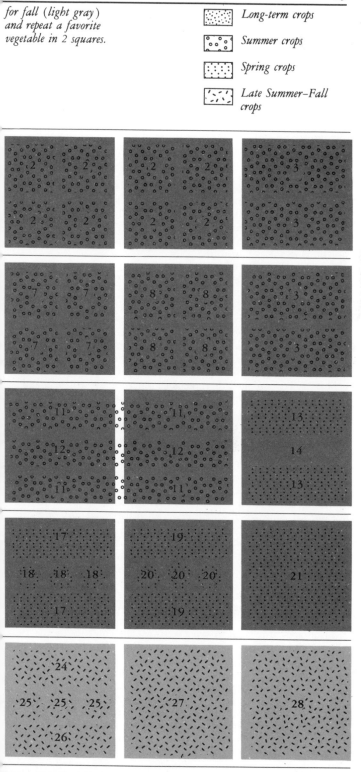

Harvesting

Before you set out to harvest, it is useful to know when your crops are at maximum flavor and freshness. Refer to the accounts in the Encyclopedia of Vegetables and Herbs for any additional harvest directions or tips.

As a rule, it is wise to begin harvesting fresh vegetables when they are on the young side and pick them heavily at prime maturity; the few that grow to be slightly overripe will still be fine for eating. It is better to harvest fruiting vegetables frequently—rather than to pick larger quantities less often—because overly mature fruits that hang on the vine will debilitate the plant.

When to Harvest Vegetables and Herbs

Harvest most vegetables early in the morning, when they are still cool from the night. (Beans are one of the few exceptions: Handling bean foliage when it is wet can spread diseases from one sick plant to others.) Bring along a bucket of cold water, and as soon as you pick the vegetables, plunge them into the bucket. Let them sit for several minutes, discharging heat into the water; then change the water, and repeat the dunking process 2 or 3 times to flush out the field heat. Trim or shell the vegetable, put it in a plastic bag, and refrigerate. (Do not refrigerate okra, which can turn black when cold.)

This treatment helps many vegetables stay sweeter. As soon as you pick corn, dunk it in cold water and refrigerate it to stop the conversion of sugar to starch. Refrigerating actually increases the sugar content of some greens, such as collards and kale.

The time to harvest herbs for drying is midmorning, before the heat comes up and after the dew has dried. The best stage of maturity for harvesting is when the flower buds have begun to form but have not opened. Unless herbs are muddy when harvested, do not wash them before drying; the excess moisture slows the drying process and takes away some of the strength of the herb. Harvesting with these points in mind should maximize flavor and aroma.

Saving Seeds

As you harvest your vegetables and herbs, you may want to save the seeds from them for next year's planting. However, unless you are preserving heirloom or rare plants that are difficult to replace, the disadvantages of relying on saved seeds usually don't justify the effort. Hybrids grown from saved seeds will not breed true, but will revert to less desirable plants. Vegetatively propagated herb cultivars also usually won't breed true. And seeds can harbor certain bacterial and viral diseases, as well as seed-eating insects, their larvae, and their eggs.

If you do decide to save seeds, here are a few tips. The seeds of beans, peas, and corn can be air-dried, shelled, and stored in sealed jars with a desiccant and an insect repellent. Fruiting vegetables must first ripen and begin decaying; then they must be mashed, washed, and spread out to dry so the shreds of pulp and skin can be winnowed out. Biennials must complete their full life cycle before they will flower and set seeds. In cold-winter climates, pull cabbage and other half-hardy biennials in the fall and store them over winter in a cool cellar, then replant in the spring to flower and set seeds. Vine-crop seeds are long-lived and will germinate after 5 years or more if stored in the proper conditions. Lettuce seed also keeps well, but onions, chives, and parsnips have notoriously short-lived seeds; germination drops significantly after less than 1 year.

Storing Vegetables

If you want to store some of your crop for later use, here are a few general rules that you can apply.

Root vegetables should go into cool, moist storage for winter. It is hard to find a spot between 32° and 40° F that doesn't occasionally drop below freezing, so you may have to settle for a cold corner of the basement that stays at 40° to 45° F. Root vegetables store well in boxes of damp sand; trim the tops, leaving a 3-inch stub. Onions and potatoes will store well at temperatures between 32° and 40° F; they should be kept dry on racks, not touching each other.

Sweet potatoes and winter squash will hold well at 55° to 60° F. Certain varieties of winter squash will keep for up to 12 months at room temperature, although they may shrivel somewhat.

Use sealed containers for dried shelled beans and peas as well as for seeds such as poppy and sesame. Store at around 40° F. This treatment helps keep the oils and proteins from going rancid. Seeds may carry a few uninvited guests, such as weevils, the seed-eating larvae of moths, beetles, and eggs of flies and wasps. Place a few dried hot peppers or dried, insect-repellent herbs such as pennyroyal in the container to eradicate bugs.

Preserving Vegetables

You can preserve most vegetables (except for a few, such as lettuce, endive, and chard) in cans or jars. Many people prefer home canning to freezing, since a power failure can cause the loss of everything in a freezer. The process of canning relies on heat, pressure, and salt to kill organisms that can cause spoilage or severe poisoning. If you decide to can your vegetables, be very careful, and do not cut corners. In some rural areas, Home Demonstration Agents sponsor food preserving training, complete with equipment, to teach safe, sanitary techniques.

Freezing vegetables is quick and easy, especially for smaller amounts. Frozen vegetables taste fresher, retain more nutritional value, and need no salt for preservation. Home gardeners now can enjoy the legacy of nearly half a century of work that resulted in better varieties for freezing.

Some vegetable varieties, however, don't freeze well. For example, certain hybrid corn varieties pick up the taste of the cob when whole ears are frozen. Some green bean varieties have cavities around the immature seeds and the pods are flabby when frozen. The whole pods of certain snap peas must be blanched (boiled rapidly for no more than 2 minutes) before freezing, or the pods will go limp. The descriptions in garden seed catalogues generally indicate whether a variety is suitable for freezing.

Today, not as much pickling is done as in former years. The pickling process depends either on vinegar or salt, or both, to preserve vegetables. Cucumbers, peppers, beets, and cabbage (kraut) are the vegetables most commonly pickled, but this process will preserve almost any vegetable. Pickled daikon radishes, for example, are relished in Japan, and pickled gourds and melons in other countries. Pickling is not costly and requires little equipment. But it is destructive to vitamins and minerals and can contribute heavily to salt intake.

Dehydration deserves more importance than it has achieved in food preservation. Dehydrated vegetables make delicious, nutritious snacks and, when reconstituted, have good taste and texture in cooked foods. You pay high prices at gourmet food stores for such items as dried tomatoes, corn, carrots, squash, and onions. But home dehydration units are moderately priced, long lasting, fast, and simple to operate. An unused cold frame makes an excellent solar dryer; add a small fan to draw off warm, moist air.

Drying Herbs

In drying herbs the object is to retain as much as possible of the color, aroma, and flavor. Permitting too much sunlight in the drying room can fade colors. Bunching thickly or stacking herbs too deep on drying racks can encourage mold.

Herbs are usually air-dried. The traditional way is to hang them in small bunches, secured with twist-ties that can be tightened as the bunches dry and shrink. It is best to dry herbs in a dark area at 75° to 90° F. A small fan helps to speed the process. In a clean, dust-free room, you don't need to wrap the herbs, but if you hang them in a barn or garage, wrap each bunch in an open-ended paper cylinder and hang it head down to dry. Almost all herbs dry well, although some—such as lemon balm—lose most of their fragrance.

Microwaving is an increasingly popular way to dry small quantities of herbs. This method is used chiefly for quick-drying ornamental herbs for wreaths and swags. Home dehydration units are another alternative.

Basil, the most popular culinary herb, must be dried rapidly, or else an enzyme that it contains will turn the foliage black. As a general rule, if you are oven-drying basil or any other herb, avoid heat of more than 120° F.

After herbs have dried completely, place them with a desiccant in a sealed jar to maintain the maximum potency. Do not rub or grind them until just before use.

Herbs dried at home are superior to most commercial dried herbs. Many commercial dried herbs are imported, some from countries with few or no regulations on insecticides and herbicides. A lot of these products are ground into powders or small fragments. Home-dried herbs, if kept in the whole-leaf stage and stored with desiccants, will keep longer than small cans or bottles from the grocery store; if the herbs were properly dried, they will deliver more flavor and aroma.

Using Herbs

Herbs get their flavor and aroma from oils and volatile chemicals in the leaves, stems, buds, flowers, and seeds. The flavor and aroma are more subtle and complex in fresh herbs than in the dried product. Whenever possible, chefs at fine restaurants use fresh herbs because they impart a richer flavor with more overtones.

The leaves of fresh herbs are usually stripped off the stems, chopped, and added at the last stage of cooking to preserve as much of the flavor and aroma as possible. Certain herbs have a warm, spicy flavor best suited for use in cooked dishes. Others have a sweet, tart, or fruity character and go better with salads, sauces, fruits, desserts, and drinks. Some, such as mints, serve both purposes. The rule of thumb for comparing quantities of fresh and dried herbs is to use 2 or 3 parts fresh to one part dried. Rosemary, however, is used on a 1-to-1 ratio.

When cooking with dried herbs, try putting a measured amount into a stainless steel tea caddy or cheesecloth square. Insert the caddy or cheesecloth into the liquid 2 minutes before cooking is complete, and remove it before serving. Dried herbs are not particularly attractive in foods, and this is an easy method to remove spent leaves and stems.

Once you get the feel of which herbs go best with which foods, you will gain the confidence to mix herbs. Food experts with acclaimed "noses" and palates have a vocabulary to describe the way the subtle flavors and aromas work together, but the art is even more subjective than wine tasting. You don't have to be able to describe why you mix certain herbs with others; suffice it to say that you tried it, and it worked.

Gardening in

With only a few exceptions, any vegetable or herb that will grow in a garden will also grow in a container of appropriate size. Container gardening is more expensive, so the challenge is to find and learn how to grow the vegetables and herbs that produce lots of relatively valuable greens, roots, or fruits in a small space.

Types of Containers
The size and type of containers you can use is limited only by your imagination. Some people like decorative redwood boxes and tubs, half-barrels, or planter boxes; others use basic containers like plastic buckets, garbage cans, and foot tubs. Large terra-cotta or concrete pots also work, as do heavy plastic bags, crates lined with plastic sheeting, and hanging baskets. Do not use galvanized containers for growing plants.

Most vegetable containers range in capacity from 3 to 30 gallons; plants grown in smaller containers dry out too quickly and the pots provide too little rooting area. Containers larger than 30-gallon capacity tend to hold too much water and give rise to root-rot problems. The soil in large pots warms up slowly.

In containers, good drainage is a must. Holes smaller than three-eighths of an inch often clog and restrict drainage. If your potting mixture tends to find its way out of holes, place a double layer of newspaper in the bottom. The paper will quickly deteriorate, but by that time, the soil will have packed down and bridged over the holes. It is not necessary to put gravel or pot shards in the bottom of the container.

In warm climates, light-colored containers are better. Black ones can absorb too much heat on the side facing the afternoon sun, and roots proliferate heavily on the shaded or east side of the root ball.

Soil for Containers
Unamended garden soil is not suitable for container gardening. It is heavy, can contain disease organisms and insects, and tends to dry out. You can use packaged potting soil in containers; buy it in large bags or bales to reduce the cost. Or, make your own soil.

The object in making your own soil for container growing is to provide a mix or "medium" that is economical, moderately fast draining yet moisture retentive, and lightweight, with a pH of 5.6 to 7.0. Most packaged potting mixes, except those sold for azaleas, fall in that range.

The mixture should be composed of about two-thirds coarse particles, no larger than a pea or bean, to one-third fine particles. Peat moss is the best source of small, moisture-retentive particles, but screened, fully decomposed compost comes a close second.

Fertilizers and Lime
Most components, or simples, used in artificial soil media have no inherent fertility and tend to be acid. (Pasteurized manure is an

Containers

exception; it tends to be alkaline.) Therefore, you will usually need to add lime and fertilizers.

Adding lime is simple; use half an ounce of pelleted dolomitic limestone per gallon of soil mix. The best way to fertilize is to mix in the recommended amount of one of the new time-release fertilizers. Mixes must be used promptly; allowing the fertilized mix to sit longer than 10 to 14 days before using can cause salt problems. Supplement with weekly feedings of liquid fertilizer.

Moisture and Drainage
Hanging baskets dry out rapidly, especially those of 16 inches or less in diameter. Line hanging baskets with ropy sphagnum moss to help keep them cool and to soak up and hold water. Keep them where there is no danger that high winds will snap supporting wires. Shade from the afternoon sun is recommended.

Set freestanding containers on bricks or blocks to improve drainage and to keep water from standing underneath and accumulating algae. Window boxes should have drainage holes on the front edge to keep them from dripping on walls.

Placement
Freestanding containers do well placed in groups on sunny patios, porches, wide stone walks, or low walls—always near a water faucet, and never under the drip line of eaves. Mixed or matched for type and size, containers look good in groups of 3 or 5, with blocks to raise them to various elevations.

Starting Container-grown Plants
It is better to start container vegetables and herbs from plants rather than seeds, because growing seeds can add days or weeks to the time to maturity. It is simple to transplant into containers. There are 3 major precautions: Leave a 1- to 2-inch headspace so you can water heavily without washing soil out of the top of the containers; be sure to firm down soil around the roots of plants when you set them in; and set plants back at least 2 inches from the edge of the container to decrease the chance of the roots' drying out.

Buy a water-breaker nozzle for your hose; it turns a heavy stream of water into a soft rain of droplets that won't blast soil away. Water-breakers come with a long, rigid extension so you can reach hanging baskets.

What Vegetables Should You Choose?
Certain kinds of vegetables seem born to be grown in containers. They are productive, and they are expensive when purchased at produce stands. The best kinds of vegetables are small, quick-maturing salad greens (leaf lettuce, midget cabbage, mustard or turnip greens, kale, kohlrabi, Swiss chard, and Malabar or New Zealand spinach); root vegetables that will grow close together

Gardening in Containers

(scallions grown from sets or seedlings and baby carrots); and fruiting vegetables that will produce over an extended period (tomatoes, peppers, eggplant, and summer squash).

Most of the larger vegetables will grow fine in containers but produce relatively little for the space occupied, or can be purchased reasonably at the grocery store. There are exceptions: Compact-vined muskmelon hybrids will produce 2 or 3 melons from a 7-gallon tub—marginal production but mighty good eating.

Many vegetables come in miniature or midget varieties. The seeds are costly and the little plants are not always as vigorous as standard varieties. You have to decide whether to grow them; usually the deciding factor is whether you have the space for growing larger and more productive varieties in larger containers.

Some gardeners place fast-growing salad greens and herbs around slower-growing container vegetables. This technique works best if the slow-growing vegetables are erect, rather than spreading— peppers, eggplant, and broccoli, for example. Around them plant seeds of radishes, lettuce, cress, dill, coriander, chervil, and others—respecting recommended planting dates, of course.

Growing Tomatoes in Containers

The most popular vegetables for containers are tomatoes. Hybrid tomatoes with large determinate or indeterminate vines produce the big slicing tomatoes, but they require 25- or 30-gallon containers. Some of the dwarf or compact hybrid tomatoes will grow in 3-gallon buckets, but the fruits are small and some have tough skins.

If you opt to grow the large-plant tomatoes, you will need a tall, strong support for the heavy vines. A good arrangement is a sturdy wooden platform, 30 inches square. Equip it with industrial casters. Make 2 arches of conduit or 1-inch PVC pipe, 6 feet high, and connect them where they cross at the top. Plug the pipes into holes bored into the platform, or into reinforced brackets. The connections must hold up under considerable stress. Run 2 or 3 stout strings down to the base of the tomato plant. As it grows, remove all "suckers" growing in the leaf axils to encourage the plant to grow tall. When the plant begins to reach, tie one of the strings loosely around the trunk of the tomato and twine the string around the stem higher up. When the plant is 1 to 2 feet tall, allow one or two suckers to grow and form "leaders," then begin removing suckers from them. Train the plants up the strings. Your plant will be rather tall and slender, and it can be reached from all sides for care and harvesting. Eventually, the vines will reach the top of the arches and begin to flop. Leave them alone; let them cascade.

Tomatoes in containers frequently suffer from blossom-end rot, which is caused by a shortage of calcium and by wet-to-dry cycles in the growing medium. Be sure to use quickly available pelleted limestone in the soil mix instead of slow-release ground limestone. Also, water the container every morning. Flow water into it until

Here is a convenient way to grow tomatoes if your garden space is limited. The 30-gallon tub is roomy enough for 2 plants; the stout twine and double arches form a sturdy vine support. Casters make the platform movable for easy harvesting. Two large plants can yield up to 60 pounds of tomatoes.

you see it draining out the bottom. During hot, dry weather, water 2 or 3 times daily. Despite this tender care, you may see leaf-rolling. Leaf-rolling isn't fatal—ignore it. Don't confuse leaf-rolling with the drooping that comes naturally during hot, dry weather.

Yield

Some extraordinary yields have been recorded from container vegetables. It is not unusual to harvest 30 pounds of tomatoes from one standard vine hybrid grown in a 25- or 30-gallon plastic garbage can and trained up a frame. A 7-gallon plastic tub with 3 green pepper plants can produce 25 to 30 peppers for stuffing or salad use. An orange crate lined with plastic sheeting, perforated for drainage and filled with potting soil, can produce 2 dozen long, sweet carrots, provided that you pull some of them when they are half-grown.

Container-grown Herbs

Herbs are quite popular as container plants. Most are decorative, and they require smaller containers than vegetables.

Containers of 3- to 7-gallon capacity are adequate for all except basil, which needs a 10-gallon container to develop to full size. The wide, shallow terra-cotta or concrete basins of 3- to 5-gallon capacity display herbs well, especially the trailing kinds. The trailers also do well in hanging baskets, as they can tolerate the minor drying out that sometimes is unavoidable. Creeping rosemary, lemon thyme, and curly mint are superb hanging basket specimens.

Hanging baskets have to be watered so often that nutrients and lime leach out. Feed them with time-release fertilizer pellets and supplement with liquid fertilizer every week. In midsummer, add half the original rate of pelleted limestone to pots of rosemary, lavender, oregano, and tarragon.

Except in mild-winter climates, the herbs most popular for containers are the fast-growing annuals. However, perennials such as the various thymes, lemon verbena, rosemary, lavender, and the mints make such lovely container plants that they are worth growing as annuals. The most popular herb for container growing is chives. They will grow best in 1-gallon pots, but these small pots tend to dry out and blow over. A good solution is to group three 1-gallon pots in attractive containers filled halfway with sand. Plunge the pots into the sand to anchor them and to retard drying out.

Container Vegetables for Apartment Dwellers

Rooftops, balconies, and terraces are good sites for container gardens, but lightweight potting media must be used; omit sand and garden soil, which are twice as heavy as lightweight artificial media when wet.

These elevated sites always suffer more wind damage than ground-level gardens, and gardeners learn to use see-through baffles or screens of flowering vines to take the bite out of the wind.

Residential roof surfaces are not designed to take much foot traffic, so it is not a bad idea to make board walkways with padded cleats to protect the seal. Residents on the north or east sides of apartment buildings often are faced with a lack of sun. Growing anything other than shade-tolerant ornamentals in such locations is practically impossible.

Indoor Gardening

It is possible to grow herbs or vegetables indoors in containers, given strong sunlight coming in west or south windows, but only from spring through fall. During winter the light loses intensity, and days are short and often cloudy as well; under these conditions, herbs and vegetables become spindly. Rather than fight such difficult conditions, experienced apartment gardeners take cuttings or divisions of choice perennial plants and grow them under fluorescent lights during the winter. Come spring, they shift the plants to larger pots and place them in direct sunlight.

Leaf lettuce is probably the favorite vegetable for indoor growing, and sweet basil the most popular herb.

Plants in air-conditioned apartments have a hard time of it, due more to the dry air than to cool temperatures. One way to decrease the problem is to grow small plants under fluorescent lights, concentrating them in gravel-filled trays that serve as humidifiers.

Postage-stamp Gardens

Some dwellings have tiny back or side yards, usually fenced or walled in. These are too small and intimate for the conventional vegetable or herb garden. And, since they are usually the only garden space for the home, the emphasis should be on beauty as well as food production.

A good plan is to select some choice ornamentals that will remain small, and place them where they look best, in the soil or in containers. Then, plant a few pots of flowers from bedding plants. Put these pots on a tray and move them around until you find a spot that looks right, then set them in the ground. Use the balance of the space for food plants; try using ornamental ones, like red chard, bronze lettuce, and scarlet runner beans. Run vines up strings stapled to the fence, and contain the whole layout with edgings of chives or parsley. Buy a few good-looking planters of various sizes and shapes; pieces of terra-cotta flue liners used as plant stands will give them height.

Consider every plant in your garden as expendable or portable. If it doesn't look right where you placed it, harvest the plant or move it. Not even landscape architects leave all plants where they put them.

The Color Plates

The plates on the following pages are divided into eight groups: roots and tubers; berries, corn, and others; tomatoes and peppers; beans and peas; melons, squash, and cucumbers; cabbages; salad greens; and herbs.

Visual Key

The visual key on pages 66–71 shows the range of vegetables and herbs included in each of the eight groups.

The first group represents crops whose edible parts develop underground, including such popular vegetables as carrots, potatoes, and onions, as well as the less familiar celeriac and Jerusalem artichoke. The second group contains a broad range of plants, among which are strawberries, edible cactus, asparagus, and sweet corn. In the third group are fruitlike vegetables, including eggplants, tomatoes, and peppers. The fourth group encompasses leguminous vegetables—numerous kinds of beans and peas. The fifth group consists of vining crops that include melons, summer and winter squashes, gourds, pumpkins, and cucumbers. Cabbages and their kin—broccoli, cauliflower, and more—constitute the sixth group. The last of the vegetable groups represents a wide array of lettuce varieties and other leafy crops, from spinach to radicchio; celery, Florence fennel, and a few other stalky vegetables are included here as well. The herbs follow; grown for aromatic leaves, stems, flowers, or seeds, they include many versatile plants.

Plant Chart

The plant chart is divided into the vegetables and the herbs. Each plant is listed alphabetically by common name, or occasionally under the common name of a group, such as the beans. The names are followed by the page numbers of the text descriptions. Each vegetable is evaluated in five ways: how grown—as an annual, biennial, or perennial (indicated by A, B, or P); when grown; how planted; light requirements; and the number of days to maturity. Herbs are also evaluated in five ways: how grown, soil pH, light requirements, uses, and parts used.

Visual Key

Roots and Tubers

The vegetables in this group are all grown for their edible underground parts—roots, as in carrots and radishes; tubers, as in potatoes and Jerusalem artichokes; and bulbs, as in onions and garlic.

Berries, Corn, and Others

This diverse group includes both the familiar—strawberries, asparagus, artichokes, sunflowers, and corn—and the unfamiliar, such as prickly pears, rape, and the grain crop quinoa.

This chart shows the range of plants in each group of color plates.

Pages 86–115

Pages 116–125

Visual Key

Tomatoes and Peppers	Featured here are colorful, fruitlike vegetables—eggplants, tomatoes, and peppers, as well as tomatillos, cape gooseberries, and garden huckleberries.	
Beans and Peas	Snap beans, limas, black-eyed peas, and green peas are among the legume crops in this section.	
Melons, Squash, and Cucumbers	Included here are vine crops: sweet muskmelons to juicy watermelons, ornamental gourds, cucumbers for slicing and pickling, tender summer squashes to hard-skinned winter squashes, and festive Halloween pumpkins.	 
Cabbages	In this group you will find cole crops—cabbage family members that include cabbages, kale, cauliflower, broccoli, kohlrabi, and Brussels sprouts.	

69

Pages 126–153

Pages 154–167

Pages 168–195

Pages 196–209

Visual Key

Salad Greens

Numerous varieties of lettuce belong to this group, as do Chinese cabbages, spinach, leaf chicory, and radicchio; several potherbs, such as amaranth and stinging nettle; and stalky crops like celery and Swiss chard. Also included are the lush ornamental vines of winged and Chinese yams, which have edible tubers.

Herbs

Herbs constitute a wide range of plants grown for culinary use, aroma, and beauty. Among them are chamomile, a soothing ingredient in teas; dill, its seeds used for pickling and its leaves for seasoning fish and other dishes; fragrant lavender; refreshing mint; and marjoram and rosemary, used to flavor meats.

Vegetables

	Page Number	Grown As
Vegetables		
Amaranth	292	A
Artichoke	292	A
Arugula	293	A
Asparagus	294	P
Beans		
Azuki Bean	295	A
Broad Bean	296	A
Butterbean	297	A
Dry and Horticultural Beans	297	A
Garbanzo Bean	299	A
Lima Bean, bush	299	A
Lima Bean, pole	299	A
Mung Bean	300	A
Scarlet Runner Bean	301	A
Snap Bean, bush	302	A
Snap Bean, pole	302	A
Soybean	303	A
Winged Bean	304	A
Yard-long Bean	305	A
Beet	306	A
Broccoli	307	A
Sprouting Broccoli	308	A
Brussels Sprouts	309	B
Great Burdock	309	B
Cabbages		
Cabbage	310	A
Chinese Cabbage, heading	311	A
Chinese Cabbage, nonheading	312	A
Ornamental Cabbage	313	A
Cactus	313	P

Cool Season	Warm Season	Spring to Fall	Direct-Seed	Transplants	Roots/Crowns	Sets/Tubers	Full Sun	Light Shade	Days to Maturity
□	▧	■	■	▧	▧	▧	▧	□	
	▧		■				▧		45–60
		■			▧		▧		150–180
□			■				▧	□	45–60
□			■		▧		▧		2 years
	▧		■				▧		120–150
□			■				▧		75–90
	▧		■				▧		60–80
	▧		■				▧		60–80
	▧		■				▧		90
	▧		■				▧		60–65
	▧		■				▧		70–80
	▧		■				▧		90–120
	▧		■				▧		70–80
	▧		■				▧		50–60
	▧		■				▧		60–70
	▧		■				▧		60–80
	▧		■				▧		120–150
	▧		■				▧		90–120
		■	■				▧		50–70
□			■	▧			▧		70–95
□			■	▧			▧		80
□				▧			▧		90–120
□	▧	■	■	▧			▧	□	150–180
□			■	▧			▧	□	70–80
□			■	▧			▧		65–80
□			■	▧			▧	□	60
□				▧			▧	□	60–80
		■		▧	▧		▧		2 years

Plant Chart

	Page Number	Grown As
Cardoon	314	A
Carrot	315	A
Cauliflower	317	A
Celeriac	318	A
Celery	318	B
Celtuce	319	A
Chayote	320	A
Leaf Chicory	321	A
Collards	322	A
Corn		
Ornamental Corn	323	A
Popcorn	324	A
Sweet Corn	324	A
Common Corn Salad	327	A
Cress		
Curled Cress	328	A
Upland Cress	328	A
Watercress	329	P
Cucumber	329	A
Dandelion	331	A
Eggplant	331	A
Curly Endive	332	P
Escarole	332	P
Florence Fennel	333	A
Garlic	334	A
West Indian Gherkin	335	A
Ginger	335	A
Good-King-Henry	336	P
Cape Gooseberry	337	A
Dwarf Cape Gooseberry	337	A
Gourds		
Balsam Apple	338	A

Cool Season	Warm Season	Spring to Fall	Direct-Seed	Transplants	Roots/Crowns	Sets/Tubers	Full Sun	Light Shade	Days to Maturity
□	▨	■	■	▨	▨	▨	□	□	
		■		▨			□		150–180
		■	■				□		50–70
□				▨			□		50–70
		■		■			□		90–120
□				▨			□	□	90–110
□			■	■			□	□	90
		■	■				□		120–150
□			■	▨			□	□	70–110
□			■	▨			□	□	80–90
	▨		■				□		120
	▨		■				□		95–110
	▨		■	▨			□		60–90
□			■	■			□	□	45–60
□			■				□	□	45–60
□			■				□	□	45–60
		■	■	▨				□	60
	▨		■	■			□		50–75
		■	■	■			□		90–100
	▨			▨			□		60–80
□			■	■			□	□	90–100
□			■	■			□	□	80–90
□		■	■				□		90–110
		■				□	□		90
	▨		■	■			□		60–70
	▨				□		□	□	150–180
		■	■				□		70–90
		■		▨			□		70–80
		■		▨			□		70–80
	▨		■	▨			□		120–150

Plant Chart

	Page Number	Grown As
Gourds continued		
Balsam Pear	338	A
Bottle Gourd	339	A
Hercules' War Club Gourd	340	A
Serpent Gourd	340	A
Groundnut	340	A
Horseradish	341	A
Garden Huckleberry	342	A
Jerusalem Artichoke	342	P
Jicama	343	A
Kale	344	A
Ornamental Kale	344	A
Kohlrabi	345	A
Lamb's-Quarters	346	A
Leek	346	A
Lettuce		
Butterhead Lettuce	347	A
Cos or Romaine Lettuce	348	A
Crisphead Lettuce	349	A
Leaf Lettuce	349	A
Miner's Lettuce	350	A
Melons		
Casaba Melon	351	A
Chinese Preserving Melon	352	A
Crenshaw Melon	352	A
Honeydew Melon	353	A
Muskmelon	353	A
Watermelon	355	A
Mustard Greens	356	A
Tendergreen Mustard	357	A or B
Stinging Nettle	357	A
Okra	358	A

Cool Season	Warm Season	Spring to Fall	Direct-Seed	Transplants	Roots/Crowns	Sets/Tubers	Full Sun	Light Shade	Days to Maturity
□	■	■	■	■	■	■	□	□	
	■		■	■			□		120–150
	■		■	■			□		90–100
	■		■	■			□		90–100
	■		■	■			□		90–100
		■	■			■	□	□	120–150
		■			■		□		120–150
	■		■	■			□		120–150
		■				■	□	□	120–150
	■		■			■	□		180–210
□		■	■	■			□	□	60–70
□			■	■			□	□	70–90
□			■	■			□		50–60
		■	■				□		60–70
		■	■	■			□		80–110
□			■	■			□	□	90–100
□				■			□	□	90–100
□				■			□	□	90–100
□			■	■			□	□	45–50
□			■				□	□	45–60
	■		■	■			□		110
	■		■	■			□		150–180
	■		■	■			□		110
	■		■	■			□		80–90
	■		■	■			□		65–90
	■		■	■			□		75–95
□			■				□	□	40–50
□			■				□		30–45
		■	■	■				□	60–90
	■		■	■			□		55–70

Plant Chart

	Page Number	Grown As
Onions		
Onion	359	A
Bunching Onion	360	A
Egyptian Onion	361	P
Orach	361	A
Root Parsley	362	A
Parsnip	363	A
Peas		
Edible-Podded Pea	364	A
Green Pea	365	A
Southern Pea	366	A
Winged Pea	367	A
Peanut	368	A
Peppers		
Hot Pepper	369	A
Ornamental Pepper	370	A
Sweet Pepper	370	A
Perilla	371	A
Pokeweed	372	A
Potato	373	A
Pumpkins		
Pumpkin	375	A
Mammoth Pumpkin	376	A
Purslane	376	A
Quinoa	377	A
Radicchio	378	A
Radishes		
Spring Radish	378	A
Winter Radish	379	A
Rape	380	A
Rhubarb	381	P
Rutabaga	382	A

Cool Season	Warm Season	Spring to Fall	Direct-Seed	Transplants	Roots/Crowns	Sets/Tubers	Full Sun	Light Shade	Days to Maturity
□	▦	■	■	▦	▦	▦	▦	□	
		■	■	▦		▦	▦		75–100
		■	■	▦			▦		60–70
		■				▦	▦		100
	▦		■				▦		60–90
		■	■	▦			▦		80–95
		■	■				▦		120–150
□			■	▦			▦		60–70
	▦		■	▦			▦		55–70
	▦		■				▦		65–90
□			■	▦			▦		60–70
	▦		■				▦		120–150
	▦		■	▦			▦		70–80
	▦		■	▦			▦	□	70–80
	▦		■	▦			▦		60–70
	▦		■				▦	□	60–90
		■	■				▦	□	45–60
□			■			▦	▦		90–120
	▦		■	▦			▦		95–120
	▦		■	▦			▦		110–120
	▦		■	▦			▦		45–60
	▦		■				▦		90–120
		■	■	▦			▦	□	365–390
□			■				▦		27–35
		■	■				▦		60–80
□			■				▦		60–70
		■	■	▦			▦	□	2 years
□			■				▦		90–120

Plant Chart

	Page Number	Grown As
Salsify	383	A
Black Salsify	383	A
Shallot	384	A
Skirret	385	A
Garden Sorrel	386	P
Spinach	386	A
Malabar Spinach	387	A
New Zealand Spinach	388	A
Squashes		
Summer Squash	389	A
Winter Squash	390	A
Strawberry	392	B or P
Alpine Strawberry	393	P
Sunflower	393	A
Sweet Potato	394	A
Swiss Chard	396	A
Tomatillo	396	A
Tomatoes		
Tomato	397	A
Cherry Tomato	401	A
Pear Tomato	401	A
Tree Tomato	402	A
Turnip, greens	403	A
Turnip, roots	403	A
Chinese Yam	404	A
Winged Yam	404	A

Cool Season	Warm Season	Spring to Fall	Direct-Seed	Transplants	Roots/Crowns	Sets/Tubers	Full Sun	Light Shade	Days to Maturity
□	▦	■	■	▦	▦	▦	▦	□	
		■	■				▦		110–130
		■	■				▦		110–130
		■				▦	▦		90–120
		■	■			▦	▦		120–150
		■	■	▦			▦	□	90
□			■	▦			▦	□	45–55
	▦		■	▦			▦	□	90–120
		■	■	▦			▦	□	60–90
	▦		■	▦			▦		50–55
	▦		■	▦			▦		90
		■			▦		▦	□	240–420
		■		▦	▦		▦	□	240–420
	▦		■	▦			▦		100–120
	▦					▦	▦		150–175
		■	■	▦			▦	□	55–65
	▦		■	▦			▦		90–110
	▦		■	▦			▦		55–80
	▦		■	▦			▦		60–70
	▦		■	▦			▦		60–70
	▦			▦			▦		210–240
□			■				▦	□	45
□			■				▦	□	70
	▦			▦			▦		210–240
	▦			▦			▦		210–240

Herbs

Herbs	Page Number	Grown As
Alexanders	408	B
Angelica	408	P or B
Anise	409	A
Anise Hyssop	409	A
Anyu	410	A
Basil	410	A
Holy Basil	412	A
Bay	412	P
Sweet Bay	412	P
Bergamot	413	P
Wild Bergamot	414	P
Borage	414	A
Salad Burnet	414	P
Calendula	415	A
Caper	416	P
Caraway	416	B
Catnip	417	P
Leaf Celery	417	A
Roman Chamomile	418	A
Sweet False Chamomile	419	A
Chervil	419	A
Chive	420	P
Garlic Chive	421	P
Sweet Cicely	421	P
Clove Pink	422	P
Coriander	423	A
Costmary	424	P
Black Cumin	424	A
Dill	425	A
Sweet Fennel	425	P or B
Scented Geraniums	426	A
Hyssop	427	P

pH 5.5–6.5	pH 6.5–7.5	Full Sun	Light Shade	Culinary	Tea/Tisane	Scent/Ornament	Leaves/Stems	Seeds	Flowers
□	▨	▨	■	■	▨	▨	▨	▨	□
□		▨		■			▨		□
□		▨		■			▨	▨	
□		▨		■			▨	▨	
□		▨			■		▨		
□		▨	■	■					□
□		▨		■			▨		
□		▨		■					
□		▨		■			▨		
	▨	▨	■	■			▨		
□		▨	■	■	▨	□	▨		□
	▨	▨	■		▨		▨		
□		▨		■	▨	□	▨		□
	▨	▨	■	■			▨		
	▨	▨	■	■	▨	□			□
	▨	▨				▨			□
□		▨		■		□	▨	▨	
	▨	▨	■		▨		▨		□
	▨	▨	■	■			▨		
□	▨	▨			▨	□			□
	▨	▨			▨				□
□		▨	■	■			▨		
□	▨	▨		■		□	▨		
□	▨	▨		■		□	▨		
□			■	■		□	▨	▨	
□	▨	▨		■		□			□
	▨	▨		■		□	▨	▨	
□	▨	▨	■	■		□	▨		
□		▨		■				▨	
□		▨		■			▨	▨	
	▨	▨		■			▨	▨	
□	▨	▨		■	▨	▨	▨		□
	▨	▨			▨	▨	▨		□

Plant Chart

	Page Number	Grown As
Lavender	427	P
Lemon Balm	428	P
Lemongrass	429	P
Lovage	430	P
Mallow	430	P or B
Sweet Marjoram	431	A
Apple Mint	431	P
Curly Mint	432	P
Peppermint	432	P
Pineapple Mint	433	P
Spearmint	433	P
Black Mustard	434	A
Nasturtium	434	A
Oregano	435	P
Parsley	436	A
Pennyroyal	437	P
Corn Poppy	438	A
Ramp	438	P
Sweet Rocket	439	B or A
Rosemary	439	P or A
Cumberland Rosemary	440	P
Rue	441	P
Sage	442	P
Pineapple-scented Sage	442	A
Winter Savory	443	P
Shepherd's Purse	443	A
Tansy	444	P
French Tarragon	445	P
Winter Tarragon	445	A
Thyme	446	P
Lemon Thyme	447	P
Lemon Verbena	447	A
Sweet Woodruff	448	P

pH 5.5–6.5	pH 6.5–7.5	Full Sun	Light Shade	Culinary	Tea/Tisane	Scent/Ornament	Leaves/Stems	Seeds	Flowers
■	■	■	■	■	■	■	■	■	■
	■	■		■			■		■
■	■	■	■	■	■		■		
■		■		■	■		■		
■		■	■	■			■	■	
■		■		■		■	■	■	■
	■	■	■	■	■	■	■		
■	■	■	■	■	■	■	■		
■		■	■	■			■		
■		■	■	■	■	■	■		
■		■	■	■			■		
■	■	■	■	■	■	■	■		
■		■		■				■	
■		■	■	■		■	■		
	■	■		■		■	■	■	
■		■	■	■		■	■		
	■	■		■	■	■	■		
	■	■		■			■	■	■
■		■	■	■			■		
■	■		■	■			■		■
	■	■		■	■	■	■		■
	■	■		■		■	■		■
	■	■		■			■		■
	■	■		■	■	■	■		■
	■	■			■	■	■		■
	■	■		■			■		■
■		■		■			■	■	
■		■		■			■		■
	■	■		■			■		
■	■	■		■	■		■		
	■	■		■			■		■
	■	■		■			■		■
	■	■		■	■	■	■		
■			■			■	■		

Roots & Tubers

Royal Chantenay Carrot

Daucus carota var. sativus
Biennial grown as annual
Half-hardy
p. 315

Full sun
50–70 days to maturity

Danvers Carrot

Daucus carota var. sativus
Biennial grown as annual
Half-hardy
p. 315

Full sun
50–70 days to maturity

Short 'N' Sweet
Carrot

Daucus carota var.
sativus
Biennial grown as
annual
Half-hardy
p. 315

Full sun
50–70 days to
maturity

Imperator Carrot

Daucus carota var.
sativus
Biennial grown as
annual
Half-hardy
p. 315

Full sun
50–70 days to
maturity

Black Salsify

Scorzonera hispanica
Perennial grown as
annual
Usually winter-hardy
p. 383

Full sun
110–130 days to
maturity

Parsnip

Pastinaca sativa
Biennial grown as
annual
Half-hardy
p. 363

Full sun
120–150 days to
maturity

Salsify

Tragopogon porrifolius
Biennial grown as
annual
Usually winter-hardy
p. 383

Full sun
110–130 days to
maturity

Root Parsley

Petroselinum crispum
var. tuberosum
Biennial grown as
annual
Half-hardy
p. 362

Full sun
80–95 days to
maturity

Icicle Spring Radish

Raphanus sativus
Cool-season annual
Half-hardy
p. 378

Full sun
27–35 days to
maturity

Daikon Winter Radish

Raphanus sativus var.
longipinnatus
Cool-season annual
Half-hardy
p. 379

Full sun
60–80 days to
maturity

Daikon Winter Radish *Raphanus sativus var. longipinnatus* Full sun
Cool-season annual 60–80 days to
Half-hardy maturity
p. 379

Snowball Turnip *Brassica rapa,* Full sun to light shade
Rapifera Group 45 days for greens, 70
Cool-season biennial days for roots
grown as annual
Usually winter-hardy
p. 403

Rutabaga

Brassica napus,
Napobrassica Group
Cool-season biennial
grown as annual
Usually winter-hardy
p. 382

Full sun
90–120 days to
maturity

Red Ball Turnip

Brassica rapa,
Rapifera Group
Cool-season biennial
grown as annual
Usually winter-hardy
p. 403

Full sun to light shade
45 days for greens, 70
days for roots

Purple Top White Globe Turnip	*Brassica rapa, Rapifera Group* *Cool-season biennial grown as annual* *Usually winter-hardy* *p. 403*	*Full sun to light shade* *45 days for greens, 70 days for roots*

Beet	*Beta vulgaris, Crassa Group* *Biennial grown as annual* *Usually winter-hardy* *p. 306*	*Full sun* *50–70 days to maturity*

Champion Spring Radish

Raphanus sativus
Cool-season annual
Half-hardy
p. 378

Full sun
27–35 days to maturity

Glowing Ball Carrot

Daucus carota var.
sativus
Biennial grown as annual
Half-hardy
p. 315

Full sun
50–70 days to maturity

Golden Beet   *Beta vulgaris, Crassa*   *Full sun*
                     Group   *50–70 days to*
                     Biennial grown as   *maturity*
                     annual
                     Usually winter-hardy
                     p. 306

Celeriac   *Apium graveolens var.*   *Full sun*
                     rapaceum   *90–120 days to*
                     Biennial grown as   *maturity*
                     annual
                     Half-hardy
                     p. 318

| **Horseradish** | *Armoracia rusticana*
Perennial grown as
annual
Usually winter-hardy
p. 341 | *Full sun*
120–150 days to
maturity |

| **Ginger** | *Zingiber officinale*
Warm-season perennial
grown as annual
Frost-tender
p. 335 | *Full sun to light shade*
150–180 days to
maturity |

| **Horseradish** | *Armoracia rusticana*
Perennial grown as
annual
Usually winter-hardy
p. 341 | *Full sun*
120–150 days to
maturity |

| **Ginger** | *Zingiber officinale*
Warm-season perennial
grown as annual
Frost-tender
p. 335 | *Full sun to light shade*
150–180 days to
maturity |

Jicama

Pachyrhizus erosus
Warm-season perennial
grown as annual
Frost-tender
p. 343

Full sun
180–210 days to
maturity

**Jerusalem
Artichoke**

Helianthus tuberosus
Perennial grown as
annual
Frost-tender
p. 342

Full sun to light shade
120–150 days to
maturity

Jicama

Pachyrhizus erosus
Warm-season perennial
grown as annual
Frost-tender
p. 343

Full sun
180–210 days to
maturity

Jerusalem
Artichoke

Helianthus tuberosus
Perennial grown as
annual
Frost-tender
p. 342

Full sun to light shade
120–150 days to
maturity

Sweet Potato

Ipomoea batatas
Warm-season perennial
grown as annual
Frost-tender
p. 394

Full sun
150–175 days to
maturity

Potato

Solanum tuberosum
Cool-season perennial
grown as annual
Half-hardy
p. 373

Full sun
90–120 days to
maturity

Sweet Potato *Ipomoea batatas* *Full sun*
Warm-season perennial *150–175 days to*
grown as annual *maturity*
Frost-tender
p. 394

White Potato *Solanum tuberosum* *Full sun*
Cool-season perennial *90–120 days to*
grown as annual *maturity*
Half-hardy
p. 373

Katahdin Potato

Solanum tuberosum
Cool-season perennial
grown as annual
Half-hardy
p. 373

Full sun
90–120 days to
maturity

Blue Potato

Solanum tuberosum
Cool-season perennial
grown as annual
Half-hardy
p. 373

Full sun
90–120 days to
maturity

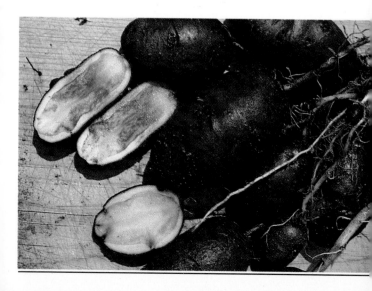

Russet Potato *Solanum tuberosum* *Full sun*
Cool-season perennial *90–120 days to*
grown as annual *maturity*
Half-hardy
p. 373

Red LaSoda Potato *Solanum tuberosum* *Full sun*
Cool-season perennial *90–120 days to*
grown as annual *maturity*
Half-hardy
p. 373

Red Torpedo Onion

Allium cepa, Cepa Group
Perennial grown as annual
Half-hardy
p. 359

Full sun
75–100 days to maturity

Stockton Red Onion

Allium cepa, Cepa Group
Perennial grown as annual
Half-hardy
p. 359

Full sun
75–100 days to maturity

Italian Red Onion   *Allium cepa, Cepa Group*   *Full sun*
Perennial grown as   *75–100 days to*
annual   *maturity*
Half-hardy
p. 359

Egyptian Onion   *Allium cepa,*   *Full sun*
Proliferum Group   *100 days to maturity*
Perennial grown as
annual
Usually winter-hardy
p. 361

Shallot

Allium cepa,
Aggregatum Group
Perennial grown as
annual
Usually winter-hardy
p. 384

Full sun
90–120 days to
maturity

Garlic

Allium sativum
Perennial grown as
annual
Usually winter-hardy
p. 334

Full sun
90 days to maturity

| Shallot | *Allium cepa,* *Aggregatum Group* *Perennial grown as* *annual* *Usually winter-hardy* p. 384 | *Full sun* *90–120 days to* *maturity* |

| Garlic | *Allium sativum* *Perennial grown as* *annual* *Usually winter-hardy* p. 334 | *Full sun* *90 days to maturity* |

Yellow Bermuda Onion

Allium cepa, Cepa Group
Perennial grown as annual
Half-hardy
p. 359

Full sun
75–100 days to maturity

White Onion

Allium cepa, Cepa Group
Perennial grown as annual
Half-hardy
p. 359

Full sun
75–100 days to maturity

Yellow Spanish Onion	*Allium cepa, Cepa Group* *Perennial grown as annual* *Half-hardy* *p. 359*	*Full sun* *75–100 days to maturity*

Onion	*Allium cepa, Cepa Group* *Perennial grown as annual* *Half-hardy* *p. 359*	*Full sun* *75–100 days to maturity*

Leek   *Allium ampeloprasum,*   *Full sun*
            Porrum Group   *80–110 days to*
            Perennial grown as   *maturity*
            annual
            Half-hardy
            p. 346

Bunching Onion   *Allium fistulosum*   *Full sun*
                      Perennial grown as   *60–70 days to*
                      annual   *maturity*
                      Half-hardy
                      p. 360

Leek

*Allium ampeloprasum,
Porrum Group
Perennial grown as
annual
Half-hardy
p. 346*

*Full sun
80–110 days to
maturity*

Bunching Onion

*Allium fistulosum
Perennial grown as
annual
Half-hardy
p. 360*

*Full sun
60–70 days to
maturity*

Jumbo Virginia Peanut

Arachis hypogaea
Warm-season annual
Frost-tender
p. 368

Full sun
120–150 days to
maturity

Skirret

Sium sisarum
Perennial grown as
annual
Usually winter-hardy
p. 385

Full sun
120–150 days to
maturity

Peanut

Arachis hypogaea
Warm-season annual
Frost-tender
p. 368

Full sun
120–150 days to
maturity

Groundnut

Apios americana
Perennial grown as
annual
Usually winter-hardy
p. 340

Full sun to light shade
120–150 days to
maturity

Berries, Corn

& Others

Alpine Strawberry *Fragaria vesca* *Full sun to light shade*
Perennial *8–14 months to*
Usually winter-hardy *maturity*
p. 393

Prickly Pear Cactus *Opuntia vulgaris* *Full sun*
Perennial *2 years to harvest*
Half-hardy
p. 313

| **Strawberry** | *Fragaria × ananassa*
Biennial or perennial
Usually winter-hardy
p. 392 | *Full sun to light shade*
8–14 months to
maturity |

| **Prickly Pear Cactus** | *Opuntia vulgaris*
Perennial
Half-hardy
p. 313 | *Full sun*
2 years to harvest |

Asparagus *Asparagus officinalis* *Full sun*
Cool-season perennial *2 years to harvest*
Usually winter-hardy
p. 293

Quinoa *Chenopodium quinoa* *Full sun*
Warm-season annual *90–120 days to*
Half-hardy *maturity*
p. 377

| Artichoke | *Cynara scolymus*
Perennial grown as
annual
Half-hardy
p. 292 | *Full sun*
150–180 days to
maturity |

| Rape | *Brassica napus,*
Pabularia Group
Cool-season annual or
biennial
Usually winter-hardy
p. 380 | *Full sun*
60–70 days to
maturity |

Sunflower	*Helianthus annuus* *Warm-season annual* *Half-hardy* *p. 393*	*Full sun* *100–120 days to* *maturity*

Strawberry **Popcorn**	*Zea mays var. praecox* *Warm-season annual* *Frost-tender* *p. 324*	*Full sun* *95–110 days to* *maturity*

Sunflower   *Helianthus annuus*   *Full sun*
                      Warm-season annual   *100–120 days to*
                      Half-hardy   *maturity*
                      p. 393

Rainbow   *Zea mays var.*   *Full sun*
Ornamental Corn   *indurata*   *120 days to maturity*
                      Warm-season annual
                      Frost-tender
                      p. 323

Skyscraper Sweet Corn

Zea mays var. rugosa
Warm-season annual
Frost-tender
p. 324

Full sun
60–90 days to maturity

Sweet Corn

Zea mays var. rugosa
Warm-season annual
Frost-tender
p. 324

Full sun
60–90 days to maturity

| **Sweet Corn** | *Zea mays var. rugosa*
Warm-season annual
Frost-tender
p. 324 | *Full sun*
60–90 days to
maturity |

| **White Popcorn** | *Zea mays var. praecox*
Warm-season annual
Frost-tender
p. 324 | *Full sun*
95–110 days to
maturity |

Tomatoes &

Peppers

Easter Egg Eggplant

Solanum melongena var. esculentum
Warm-season perennial grown as annual
Frost-tender
p. 331

Full sun
60–80 days to maturity

Dusky Hybrid Eggplant

Solanum melongena var. esculentum
Warm-season perennial grown as annual
Frost-tender
p. 331

Full sun
60–80 days to maturity

Garden Huckleberry

Solanum melanocerasum
Warm-season annual
Frost-tender
p. 342

Full sun
120–150 days to maturity

Black Beauty Eggplant

Solanum melongena var. esculentum
Warm-season perennial grown as annual
Frost-tender
p. 331

Full sun
60–80 days to maturity

| Dwarf Cape Gooseberry | *Physalis pruinosa* *Warm-season perennial grown as annual* *Frost-tender* *p. 337* | *Full sun* *70–80 days to maturity* |

| Cape Gooseberry | *Physalis peruviana* *Warm-season perennial grown as annual* *Frost-tender* *p. 337* | *Full sun* *70–80 days to maturity* |

Tomatillo   *Physalis ixocarpa*   *Full sun*
                       Warm-season annual   *90–110 days to*
                       Frost-tender   *maturity*
                       p. 396

Golden Eggplant   *Solanum melongena*   *Full sun*
                       var. esculentum   *60–80 days to*
                       Warm-season perennial   *maturity*
                       grown as annual
                       Frost-tender
                       p. 331

Golden Boy Tomato

Lycopersicon lycopersicum
Warm-season perennial grown as annual
Frost-tender
p. 397

Full sun
55–80 days to maturity

Yellow Plum Tomato

Lycopersicon lycopersicum var. pyriforme
Warm-season perennial grown as annual
Frost-tender
p. 401

Full sun
60–70 days to maturity

Yellow Cherry Tomato

Lycopersicon lycopersicum var. cerasiforme
Warm-season perennial grown as annual
Frost-tender
p. 401

Full sun
60–70 days to maturity

Yellow Pear Tomato

Lycopersicon lycopersicum var. pyriforme
Warm-season perennial grown as annual
Frost-tender
p. 401

Full sun
60–70 days to maturity

Roma VF Plum Tomato

Lycopersicon lycopersicum var. pyriforme
Warm-season perennial grown as annual
Frost-tender
p. 401

Full sun
60–70 days to maturity

Sweet 100 Tomato

Lycopersicon lycopersicum
Warm-season perennial grown as annual
Frost-tender
p. 397

Full sun
55–80 days to maturity

Square Tomato   *Lycopersicon*   *Full sun*
                       lycopersicum   *55–80 days to*
                       Warm-season perennial   *maturity*
                       grown as annual
                       Frost-tender
                       p. 397

Cherry Tomato   *Lycopersicon*   *Full sun*
                       lycopersicum var.   *60–70 days to*
                       cerasiforme   *maturity*
                       Warm-season perennial
                       grown as annual
                       Frost-tender
                       p. 401

Pixie Tomato

*Lycopersicon
lycopersicum
Warm-season perennial
grown as annual
Frost-tender
p. 397*

*Full sun
55–80 days to
maturity*

Early Pick Tomato

*Lycopersicon
lycopersicum
Warm-season perennial
grown as annual
Frost-tender
p. 397*

*Full sun
55–80 days to
maturity*

Early Girl Tomato   *Lycopersicon*   *Full sun*
lycopersicum   *55–80 days to*
Warm-season perennial   *maturity*
grown as annual
Frost-tender
p. 397

Freedom Tomato   *Lycopersicon*   *Full sun*
lycopersicum   *55–80 days to*
Warm-season perennial   *maturity*
grown as annual
Frost-tender
p. 397

Beefsteak Tomato

Lycopersicon lycopersicum
Warm-season perennial grown as annual
Frost-tender
p.397

Full sun
55–80 days to maturity

Striped Tomato

Lycopersicon lycopersicum
Warm-season perennial grown as annual
Frost-tender
p. 397

Full sun
55–80 days to maturity

Beefmaster Tomato   *Lycopersicon*   *Full sun*
                        lycopersicum   *55–80 days to*
                        Warm-season perennial   *maturity*
                        grown as annual
                        Frost-tender
                        p. 397

Burgess Stuffing   *Lycopersicon*   *Full sun*
Tomato   *lycopersicum*   *55–80 days to*
                       Warm-season perennial   *maturity*
                       grown as annual
                       Frost-tender
                       p. 397

Tree Tomato

Cyphomandra betacea
Warm-season perennial
grown as annual
Frost-tender
p. 402

Full sun
210–240 days to
maturity

Tasty Hybrid Sweet Pepper

Capsicum annuum
Warm-season perennial
grown as annual
Frost-tender
p. 370

Full sun
60–70 days to
maturity

Pimiento Sweet Pepper

Capsicum annuum
Warm-season perennial
grown as annual
Frost-tender
p. 370

Full sun
60–70 days to
maturity

California Wonder Sweet Pepper

Capsicum annuum
Warm-season perennial
grown as annual
Frost-tender
p. 370

Full sun
60–70 days to
maturity

Triton Sweet Pepper
Capsicum annuum
Warm-season perennial grown as annual
Frost-tender
p. 370
Full sun
60–70 days to maturity

Tabasco Pepper
Capsicum frutescens var. tabasco
Warm-season perennial grown as annual
Frost-tender
p. 369
Full sun
80–90 days to maturity

| Jalapeño Pepper | *Capsicum annuum*
Warm-season perennial
grown as annual
Frost-tender
p. 369 | *Full sun*
70–80 days to
maturity |

| Serrano Chili
Pepper | *Capsicum annuum*
Warm-season perennial
grown as annual
Frost-tender
p. 369 | *Full sun*
70–80 days to
maturity |

Cayenne Pepper

Capsicum annuum
Warm-season perennial
grown as annual
Frost-tender
p. 369

Full sun
70–80 days to
maturity

Tequila Sunrise
Sweet Pepper

Capsicum annuum
Warm-season perennial
grown as annual
Frost-tender
p. 370

Full sun
60–70 days to
maturity

| **Anaheim Hot Pepper** | *Capsicum annuum*
Warm-season perennial
grown as annual
Frost-tender
p. 369 | *Full sun*
70–80 days to
maturity |

| **Banana Sweet Pepper** | *Capsicum annuum*
Warm-season perennial
grown as annual
Frost-tender
p. 370 | *Full sun*
60–70 days to
maturity |

Fiesta Ornamental Pepper

Capsicum annuum
Warm-season perennial
grown as annual
Frost-tender
p. 370

Full sun to light shade
70–80 days to
maturity

Holiday Cheer Ornamental Pepper

Capsicum annuum
Warm-season perennial
grown as annual
Frost-tender
p. 370

Full sun to light shade
70–80 days to
maturity

| Aurora Ornamental Pepper | *Capsicum annuum*
Warm-season perennial
grown as annual
Frost-tender
p. 370 | *Full sun to light shade*
70–80 days to
maturity |

| Ornamental Pepper | *Capsicum annuum*
Warm-season perennial
grown as annual
Frost-tender
p. 370 | *Full sun to light shade*
70–80 days to
maturity |

Holiday Time Ornamental Pepper

Capsicum annuum
Warm-season perennial grown as annual
Frost-tender
p. 370

Full sun to light shade
70–80 days to maturity

Hungarian Wax Sweet Pepper

Capsicum annuum
Warm-season perennial grown as annual
Frost-tender
p. 370

Full sun
60–70 days to maturity

Maya Ornamental Pepper *Capsicum annuum* *Full sun to light shade*
Warm-season perennial *70–80 days to*
grown as annual *maturity*
Frost-tender
p. 370

Golden California Wonder Sweet Pepper *Capsicum annuum* *Full sun*
Warm-season perennial *60–70 days to*
grown as annual *maturity*
Frost-tender
p. 370

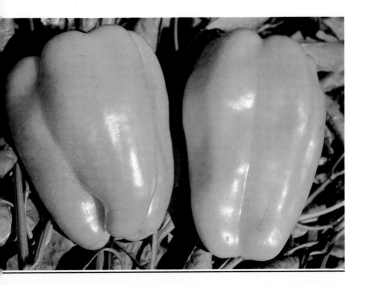

Early Prolific Sweet Pepper | *Capsicum annuum* *Warm-season perennial grown as annual* *Frost-tender* *p. 370* | *Full sun* *60–70 days to maturity*

California Wonder Sweet Pepper | *Capsicum annuum* *Warm-season perennial grown as annual* *Frost-tender* *p. 370* | *Full sun* *60–70 days to maturity*

Big Bertha Sweet Pepper

Capsicum annuum
Warm-season perennial
grown as annual
Frost-tender
p. 370

Full sun
60–70 days to
maturity

Better Belle Sweet Pepper

Capsicum annuum
Warm-season perennial
grown as annual
Frost-tender
p. 370

Full sun
60–70 days to
maturity

Hot Cherry Pepper
Capsicum annuum
Warm-season perennial
grown as annual
Frost-tender
p. 369

Full sun
70–80 days to
maturity

Clemson Spineless
Okra
Abelmoschus esculentus
Warm-season annual
Frost-tender
p. 358

Full sun
55–70 days to
maturity

Tam Jalapeño Pepper

Capsicum annuum
Warm-season perennial
grown as annual
Frost-tender
p. 369

Full sun
70–80 days to
maturity

Okra

Abelmoschus esculentus
Warm-season annual
Frost-tender
p. 358

Full sun
55–70 days to
maturity

Beans & Peas

Yard-long Bean   *Vigna unguiculata ssp.*   *Full sun*
sesquipedalis   *90–120 days to*
Warm-season annual   *maturity*
Frost-tender
p. 305

French Flageolet   *Phaseolus vulgaris*   *Full sun*
Bean   *Warm-season annual*   *50–70 days to*
Frost-tender   *maturity*
p. 297

Tendercrop Snap Bean

Phaseolus vulgaris
Warm-season annual
Frost-tender
p. 302

Full sun
50–70 days to maturity

Roma II Bush Snap Bean

Phaseolus vulgaris
Warm-season annual
Frost-tender
p. 302

Full sun
50–70 days to maturity

Blue Lake Pole Snap Bean

Phaseolus vulgaris
Warm-season annual
Frost-tender
p. 302

Full sun
50–70 days to
maturity

Azuki Bean

Vigna angularis
Warm-season annual
Frost-tender
p. 295

Full sun
120–150 days to
maturity

| Broad Bean | *Vicia faba*
Cool-season annual
Half-hardy
p. 296 | *Full sun*
75–90 days to
maturity |

| Horticultural Bean | *Phaseolus vulgaris*
Warm-season annual
Frost-tender
p. 297 | *Full sun*
55–70 days to
maturity |

Mung Bean
Vigna radiata
Warm-season annual
Frost-tender
p. 300

Full sun
90–120 days to
maturity

Pink Eye Purple
Hull Southern Pea
Vigna unguiculata
Warm-season annual
Frost-tender
p. 366

Full sun
65–90 days to
maturity

Royalty Purple Snap Bean	*Phaseolus vulgaris*	*Full sun*
	Warm-season annual	*50–70 days to*
	Frost-tender	*maturity*
	p. 302	

California Blackeye Pea	*Vigna unguiculata ssp.*	*Full sun*
	unguiculata	*65–90 days to*
	Warm-season annual	*maturity*
	Frost-tender	
	p. 366	

Winged Bean   *Psophocarpus*   *Full sun*
                   tetragonolobus   *120–150 days to*
                   Warm-season perennial   *maturity*
                   grown as annual
                   Frost-tender
                   p. 304

Scarlet Runner   *Phaseolus coccineus*   *Full sun*
Bean   *Warm-season perennial* *70–80 days to*
                      grown as annual   *maturity*
                      Frost-tender
                      p. 301

Winged Pea   *Lotus tetragonolobus*   *Full sun*
                          Cool-season annual   *60–70 days to*
                          Half-hardy   *maturity*
                          p. 367

Sugar Ann   *Pisum sativum var.*   *Full sun*
Edible-podded   *macrocarpon*   *60–70 days to*
Pea   *Cool-season annual*   *maturity*
                         Half-hardy
                         p. 364

Green Pea

Pisum sativum
Cool-season annual
Half-hardy
p. 365

Full sun
55–70 days to
maturity

Green Pea

Pisum sativum
Cool-season annual
Half-hardy
p. 365

Full sun
55–70 days to
maturity

Burpee Blue Bantam Pea

Pisum sativum
Cool-season annual
Half-hardy
p. 365

Full sun
55–70 days to maturity

Snow Pea

Pisum sativum var. macrocarpon
Cool-season annual
Half-hardy
p. 364

Full sun
60–70 days to maturity

Butterbean   *Phaseolus lunatus*   *Full sun*
Warm-season annual   *60–80 days to*
Frost-tender   *maturity*
p. 297

Soybean   *Glycine max*   *Full sun*
Warm-season annual   *60–80 days to*
Frost-tender   *maturity*
p. 303

Fordhook 242 **Lima Bean**	*Phaseolus limensis* *Warm-season annual* *Frost-tender* *p. 299*	*Full sun* *60–80 days to* *maturity*

Garbanzo Bean	*Cicer arietinum* *Warm-season annual* *Frost-tender* *p. 299*	*Full sun* *90 days to maturity*

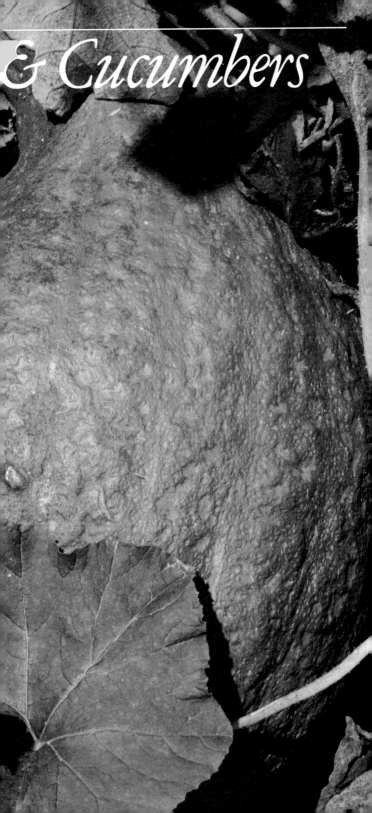

& *Cucumbers*

Crenshaw Melon   *Cucumis melo, Inodorus*   *Full sun*
Group   *110 days to maturity*
Warm-season annual
Frost-tender
p. 352

Burpee Hybrid   *Cucumis melo,*   *Full sun*
Muskmelon   *Reticulatus Group*   *65–90 days to*
Warm-season annual   *maturity*
Frost-tender
p. 353

Sweet 'N' Early Muskmelon

Cucumis melo,
Reticulatus Group
Warm-season annual
Frost-tender
p. 353

Full sun
65–90 days to
maturity

Burpee Hybrid Muskmelon

Cucumis melo,
Reticulatus Group
Warm-season annual
Frost-tender
p. 353

Full sun
65–90 days to
maturity

Casaba Melon

Cucumis melo, Inodorus
Group
Warm-season annual
Frost-tender
p. 351

Full sun
110 days to maturity

Yellow Baby
Watermelon

Citrullus lanatus
Warm-season annual
Frost-tender
p. 355

Full sun
75–95 days to
maturity

Honeydew Melon   *Cucumis melo, Inodorus*   *Full sun*
                     Group   *80–90 days to*
                     Warm-season annual   *maturity*
                     Frost-tender
                     p. 353

Chinese Preserving   *Benincasa hispida*   *Full sun*
Melon   *Warm-season annual*   *150–180 days to*
                         Frost-tender   *maturity*
                         p. 352

Sugar Bush Watermelon

Citrullus lanatus
Warm-season annual
Frost-tender
p. 355

Full sun
75–95 days to maturity

Royal Jubilee Watermelon

Citrullus lanatus
Warm-season annual
Frost-tender
p. 355

Full sun
75–95 days to maturity

| Sugar Baby Watermelon | *Citrullus lanatus*
Warm-season annual
Frost-tender
p. 355 | *Full sun*
75–95 days to
maturity |

| Sweet Favorite Watermelon | *Citrullus lanatus*
Warm-season annual
Frost-tender
p. 355 | *Full sun*
75–95 days to
maturity |

Buttercup Winter Squash

Cucurbita maxima
Warm-season annual
Frost-tender
p. 390

Full sun
90–100 days to
maturity

Scallop Summer Squash

Cucurbita pepo
Warm-season annual
Frost-tender
p. 389

Full sun
50–55 days to
maturity

| **Emerald Buttercup Winter Squash** | *Cucurbita maxima* *Warm-season annual* *Frost-tender* *p. 390* | *Full sun* *90–100 days to maturity* |

| **Chayote** | *Sechium edule* *Perennial grown as annual* *Frost-tender* *p. 320* | *Full sun* *120–150 days to maturity* |

Bottle Gourd   *Lagenaria siceraria*   *Full sun*
                    Warm-season annual   *90–100 days to*
                    Frost-tender   *maturity*
                    p. 339

Hubbard Winter   *Cucurbita maxima*   *Full sun*
Squash   *Warm-season annual*   *90–120 days to*
                      Frost-tender   *maturity*
                      p. 390

Bottle Gourd *Lagenaria siceraria* Full sun
Warm-season annual 90–100 *days to*
Frost-tender *maturity*
p. 339

Hubbard Winter *Cucurbita maxima* Full sun
Squash *Warm-season annual* 90–120 *days to*
Frost-tender *maturity*
p. 390

Kuta Vegetable Marrow Summer Squash

Curcurbita pepo
Warm-season annual
Frost-tender
p. 389

Full sun
60–70 days to maturity

White Cucumber

Cucumis sativus
Warm-season annual
Frost-tender
p. 329

Full sun
50–75 days to maturity

Bache Vegetable Marrow Summer Squash
Cucurbita pepo
Warm-season annual
Frost-tender
p. 389
Full sun
60–70 days to maturity

Banana Winter Squash
Cucurbita maxima
Warm-season annual
Frost-tender
p. 390
Full sun
90–100 days to maturity

Hercules War Club Gourd

Lagenaria longissima
Warm-season annual
Frost-tender
p. 340

Full sun
90–100 days to
maturity

Burpless Hybrid Cucumber

Cucumis sativus
Warm-season annual
Frost-tender
p. 329

Full sun
50–75 days to
maturity

Serpent Gourd

Trichosanthes anguina
Warm-season annual
Frost-tender
p. 340

Full sun
90–100 days to
maturity

Zucchini Summer Squash

Cucurbita pepo
Warm-season annual
Frost-tender
p. 389

Full sun
50–55 days to
maturity

Cucumber

Cucumis sativus
Warm-season annual
Frost-tender
p. 329

Full sun
50–75 days to
maturity

**Spacemaster Bush
Cucumber**

Cucumis sativus
Warm-season annual
Frost-tender
p. 329

Full sun
50–75 days to
maturity

| Cucumber | *Cucumis sativus*
Warm-season annual
Frost-tender
p. 329 | *Full sun*
50–75 days to
maturity |

| Liberty Pickling
Cucumber | *Cucumis sativus*
Warm-season annual
Frost-tender
p. 329 | *Full sun*
50–75 days to
maturity |

Balsam Pear

Momordica charantia
Warm-season perennial
grown as annual
Frost-tender
p. 338

Full sun
120–150 days to
maturity

Balsam Apple

Momordica balsamina
Warm-season perennial
grown as annual
Frost-tender
p. 338

Full sun
120–150 days to
maturity

| West Indian Gherkin | *Cucumis anguria*
Warm-season annual
Frost-tender
p. 335 | *Full sun*
60–70 days to
maturity |

| Balsam Apple | *Momordica balsamina*
Warm-season perennial
grown as annual
Frost-tender
p. 338 | *Full sun*
120–150 days to
maturity |

Crookneck Summer Squash

Cucurbita pepo
Warm-season annual
Frost-tender
p. 389

Full sun
50–55 days to
maturity

Burpee Golden Zucchini Summer Squash

Cucurbita pepo
Warm-season annual
Frost-tender
p. 389

Full sun
50–55 days to
maturity

| Early Prolific Straightneck Summer Squash | *Cucurbita pepo*
Warm-season annual
Frost-tender
p. 389 | *Full sun*
50–55 days to
maturity |

| Gold Rush Zucchini Summer Squash | *Cucurbita pepo*
Warm-season annual
Frost-tender
p. 389 | *Full sun*
50–55 days to
maturity |

Butternut Winter Squash

Cucurbita moschata
Warm-season annual
Frost-tender
p. 390

Full sun
75–85 days to
maturity

Acorn Winter Squash

Cucurbita pepo
Warm-season annual
Frost-tender
p. 390

Full sun
90 days to maturity

| Vegetable Spaghetti Winter Squash | *Cucurbita pepo* *Warm-season annual* *Frost-tender* *p. 390* | *Full sun* *70–80 days to maturity* |

| Jersey Golden Acorn Winter Squash | *Cucurbita pepo* *Warm-season annual* *Frost-tender* *p. 390* | *Full sun* *90 days to maturity* |

Lemon Cucumber   *Cucumis sativus*   *Full sun*
                      Warm-season annual *50–75 days to*
                      Frost-tender   *maturity*
                      p. 329

Boston Marrow   *Cucurbita maxima*   *Full sun*
Winter Squash   *Warm-season annual* *100–110 days to*
                     Frost-tender   *maturity*
                     p. 390

Turk's Turban
Winter Squash

Cucurbita maxima
Warm-season annual
Frost-tender
p. 390

Full sun
100–110 days to
maturity

Turk's Turban
Winter Squash

Cucurbita maxima
Warm-season annual
Frost-tender
p. 390

Full sun
100–110 days to
maturity

Sugar Pumpkin

Cucurbita pepo
Warm-season annual
Frost-tender
p. 375

Full sun
95–110 days to
maturity

Big Max
Mammoth
Pumpkin

Cucurbita maxima
Warm-season annual
Frost-tender
p. 376

Full sun
110–120 days to
maturity

Sugar Pumpkin

Cucurbita pepo
Warm-season annual
Frost-tender
p. 375

Full sun
95–110 days to
maturity

Howden Pumpkin

Cucurbita pepo
Warm-season annual
Frost-tender
p. 375

Full sun
95–110 days to
maturity

Cabbages

Early Jersey Wakefield Cabbage

Brassica oleracea, Capitata Group
Cool-season biennial grown as annual
Frost-tender
p. 310

Full sun to light shade
70–80 days to maturity

Savoy King Cabbage

Brassica oleracea, Capitata Group
Cool-season biennial grown as annual
Frost-tender
p. 310

Full sun to light shade
70–80 days to maturity

Emerald Cross Hybrid Cabbage

Brassica oleracea, Capitata Group
Cool-season biennial grown as annual
Frost-tender
p. 310

Full sun to light shade
70–80 days to maturity

Mammoth Red Rock Cabbage

Brassica oleracea, Capitata Group
Cool-season biennial grown as annual
Frost-tender
p. 310

Full sun to light shade
70–80 days to maturity

Dynasty Pink Ornamental Cabbage

Brassica oleracea, Acephala Group
Cool-season biennial
grown as annual
Half-hardy
p. 313

Full sun to light shade
60–80 days to
maturity

Ornamental Cabbage

Brassica oleracea, Acephala Group
Cool-season biennial
grown as annual
Half-hardy
p. 313

Full sun to light shade
60–80 days to
maturity

Ornamental   *Brassica oleracea,*   *Full sun to light shade*
Cabbage   *Acephala Group*   *60–80 days to*
                      Cool-season biennial   *maturity*
                      grown as annual
                      Half-hardy
                      p. 313

Peacock Pink   *Brassica oleracea,*   *Full sun to light shade*
Ornamental Kale   *Acephala Group*   *70–90 days to*
                      Cool-season biennial   *maturity*
                      grown as annual
                      Half-hardy
                      p. 344

Ornamental Kale	*Brassica oleracea,*	*Full sun to light shade*
	Acephala Group	*70–90 days to*
	Cool-season biennial	*maturity*
	grown as annual
	Half-hardy
	p. 344

Ornamental Kale	*Brassica oleracea,*	*Full sun to light shade*
	Acephala Group	*70–90 days to*
	Cool-season biennial	*maturity*
	grown as annual
	Half-hardy
	p. 344

Cherry Gateau Ornamental Kale

Brassica oleracea, Acephala Group
Cool-season biennial
grown as annual
Half-hardy
p. 344

Full sun to light shade
70–90 days to
maturity

Emperor White Ornamental Cabbage

Brassica oleracea, Acephala Group
Cool-season biennial
grown as annual
Half-hardy
p. 313

Full sun to light shade
60–80 days to
maturity

Kale
*Brassica oleracea,
Acephala Group
Perennial grown as
annual
Usually winter-hardy
p. 344*
*Full sun to light shade
60–70 days to
maturity*

**Dwarf Blue
Curled Vates Kale**
*Brassica oleracea,
Acephala Group
Perennial grown as
annual
Usually winter-hardy
p. 344*
*Full sun to light shade
60–70 days to
maturity*

Rape

Brassica napus,
Pabularia Group
Cool-season annual or
biennial
Usually winter-hardy
p. 380

Full sun
60–70 days to
maturity

Dwarf Blue
Curled Vates Kale

Brassica oleracea,
Acephala Group
Perennial grown as
annual
Usually winter-hardy
p. 344

Full sun to light shade
60–70 days to
maturity

Purple Sprouting Broccoli   *Brassica oleracea, Italica Group Cool-season biennial grown as annual Half-hardy p. 308*   *Full sun 80 days to maturity*

Broccoli   *Brassica oleracea, Botrytis Group Cool-season biennial grown as annual Half-hardy p. 307*   *Full sun 70–95 days to maturity*

Early Emerald Broccoli

Brassica oleracea, Botrytis Group
Cool-season biennial grown as annual
Half-hardy
p. 307

Full sun
70–95 days to maturity

Purple Head Cauliflower

Brassica oleracea, Botrytis Group
Cool-season biennial grown as annual
Half-hardy
p. 317

Full sun
50–70 days to maturity

Cauliflower

Brassica oleracea,
Botrytis Group
Cool-season biennial
grown as annual
Half-hardy
p. 317

Full sun
50–70 days to
maturity

Kohlrabi

Brassica oleracea,
Gongylodes Group
Cool-season biennial
grown as annual
Half-hardy
p. 345

Full sun
50–60 days to
maturity

Romanesco Broccoli   *Brassica oleracea, Botrytis Group*   *Full sun*
                          Cool-season biennial grown as annual   *70–95 days to maturity*
                          Half-hardy
                          p. 307

Brussels Sprouts   *Brassica oleracea, Gemmifera Group*   *Full sun*
                        Cool-season biennial grown as annual   *90–120 days to maturity*
                        Half-hardy
                        p. 309

Salad Greens

Pak-choi Chinese Cabbage

Brassica rapa, Chinensis Group
Cool-season annual or biennial
Half-hardy
p. 312

Full sun to light shade
60 days to maturity

Pe-tsai Chinese Cabbage

Brassica rapa, Pekinensis Group
Cool-season annual or biennial
Half-hardy
p. 311

Full sun
65–80 days to maturity

Collards

Brassica oleracea,
Acephala Group
Cool-season biennial
grown as annual
Usually winter-hardy
p. 322

Full sun to light shade
80–90 days to
maturity

**Great Lakes
Crisphead Lettuce**

Lactuca sativa
Cool-season annual or
biennial
Half-hardy
p. 349

Full sun to light shade
45–50 days for leaf,
90–100 days for head

**Buttercrunch
Butterhead Lettuce**

*Lactuca sativa
Cool-season annual or
biennial
Half-hardy
p. 347*

*Full sun to light shade
45–50 days for leaf,
90–100 days for head*

Cos Lettuce

*Lactuca sativa
Cool-season annual or
biennial
Half-hardy
p. 348*

*Full sun to light shade
45–50 days for leaf,
90–100 days for head*

Dark Green Boston Butterhead Lettuce

Lactuca sativa
Cool-season annual or biennial
Half-hardy
p. 347

Full sun to light shade
45–50 days for leaf,
90–100 days for head

Pain de Sucre Leaf Chicory

Cichorium intybus
Perennial
Usually winter-hardy
p. 321

Full sun to light shade
70–110 days to
maturity

**Paris White
Cos Lettuce**

*Lactuca sativa
Cool-season annual or
biennial
Half-hardy
p. 348*

*Full sun to light shade
45–50 days for leaf,
90–100 days for head*

**Bibb Butterhead
Lettuce**

*Lactuca sativa
Cool-season annual or
biennial
Half-hardy
p. 347*

*Full sun to light shade
45–50 days for leaf,
90–100 days for head*

**Winter Density
Cos Lettuce**

*Lactuca sativa
Cool-season annual or
biennial
Half-hardy
p. 348*

*Full sun to light shade
45–50 days for leaf,
90–100 days for head*

**Tom Thumb
Butterhead Lettuce**

*Lactuca sativa
Cool-season annual or
biennial
Half-hardy
p. 347*

*Full sun to light shade
45–50 days for leaf,
90–100 days for head*

**Green Ice
Leaf Lettuce**

*Lactuca sativa
Cool-season annual or
biennial
Half-hardy
p. 349*

*Full sun to light shade
45–50 days for leaf,
90–100 days for head*

**Salad Bowl
Leaf Lettuce**

*Lactuca sativa
Cool-season annual or
biennial
Half-hardy
p. 349*

*Full sun to light shade
45–50 days for leaf,
90–100 days for head*

Black Seeded Simpson Leaf Lettuce	*Lactuca sativa* *Cool-season annual or biennial* *Half-hardy* *p. 349*	*Full sun to light shade* *45–50 days for leaf,* *90–100 days for head*

Escarole	*Cichorium endiva* *Cool-season perennial* *Usually winter-hardy* *p. 332*	*Full sun to light shade* *80–90 days to* *maturity*

**Red Salad Bowl
Leaf Lettuce**

*Lactuca sativa
Cool-season annual or
biennial
Half-hardy
p. 349*

*Full sun to light shade
45–50 days for leaf,
90–100 days for head*

**Pallo Rossa
Radicchio**

*Cichorium intybus
Perennial grown as
annual
Usually winter-hardy
p. 378*

*Full sun to light shade
365–390 days to
maturity*

| Red Sails Leaf Lettuce | *Lactuca sativa* *Cool-season annual or biennial* *Half-hardy* *p. 349* | *Full sun to light shade* *45–50 days for leaf,* *90–100 days for head* |

| Rouge Di Verona Radicchio | *Cichorium intybus* *Perennial grown as annual* *Usually winter-hardy* *p. 378* | *Full sun to light shade* *365–390 days to maturity* |

Red Orach   *Atriplex hortensis var.*   *Full sun*
rubra   *60–90 days to*
Warm-season annual   *maturity*
Winter-hardy
p. 361

America Spinach   *Spinacia oleracea*   *Full sun to light shade*
Cool-season annual   *45–55 days to*
Half-hardy   *maturity*
p. 386

| Giant Japanese Red Mustard Greens | Brassica juncea
Cool-season annual
Half-hardy
p. 356 | Full sun to light shade
40–50 days to maturity |

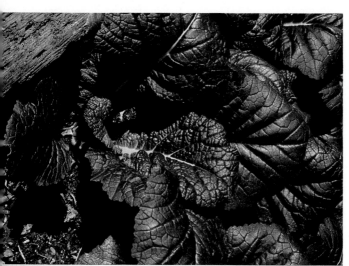

| Melody Spinach | Spinacia oleracea
Cool-season annual
Half-hardy
p. 386 | Full sun to light shade
45–55 days to maturity |

Bloomsdale Longstanding Spinach

Spinacia oleracea
Cool-season annual
Half-hardy
p. 386

Full sun to light shade
45–55 days to
maturity

Oak Leaf Lettuce

Lactuca sativa
Cool-season annual or
biennial
Half-hardy
p. 349

Full sun to light shade
45–50 days for leaf,
90–100 days for head

Malabar Spinach   *Basella alba*   *Full sun to light shade*
                        Warm-season perennial   *90–120 days to*
                        grown as annual   *maturity*
                        Frost-tender
                        p. 387

Garden Sorrel   *Rumex acetosa*   *Full sun to light shade*
                        Perennial grown as   *90 days to maturity*
                        annual
                        Usually winter-hardy
                        p. 386

**Common
Corn-Salad**

*Valerianella locusta
Cool-season annual
Usually winter-hardy
p. 327*

*Full sun to light shade
45–60 days to
maturity*

Italian Leaf Chicory

*Cichorium intybus
Perennial
Usually winter-hardy
p. 321*

*Full sun to light shade
70–110 days to
maturity*

Tendergreen
Mustard

Brassica rapa,
Perviridis Group
Cool-season annual or
biennial
Half-hardy
p. 357

Full sun
30–45 days to
maturity

Fordhook Fancy
Mustard Greens

Brassica juncea
Cool-season annual
Half-hardy
p. 356

Full sun to light shade
40–50 days to
maturity

Curly Endive

Cichorium endiva
Cool-season perennial
Usually winter-hardy
p. 332

Full sun to light shade
90–100 days to
maturity

Mustard Greens

Brassica juncea
Cool-season annual
Half-hardy
p. 356

Full sun to light shade
40–50 days to
maturity

Dandelion   *Taraxacum officinale*   *Full sun*
                         Perennial grown as   *90–100 days to*
                         annual   *maturity*
                         Usually winter-hardy
                         p. 331

Arugula   *Eruca vesicaria sativa*   *Full sun to light shade*
                         Cool-season annual   *45–60 days to*
                         Half-hardy   *maturity*
                         p. 293

Upland Cress
Barbarea verna
Cool-season biennial
Usually winter-hardy
p. 328

Full sun to light shade
45–60 days to
maturity

Curled Cress
Lepidium sativum var.
crispum
Cool-season annual
Usually winter-hardy
p. 328

Full sun to light shade
10–12 days for sprouts,
45–60 days for greens

Watercress   *Nasturtium officinale*   *Light shade*
                        Perennial grown as   *60 days to maturity*
                        annual
                        Usually winter-hardy
                        in water
                        p. 329

Miner's Lettuce   *Montia perfoliata*   *Full sun to light shade*
                        Cool-season annual   *45–60 days to*
                        Frost-tender   *maturity*
                        p. 350

Good-King-Henry *Chenopodium* *Full sun*
bonus-henricus *70–90 days to*
Perennial grown as *maturity*
annual
Usually winter-hardy
p. 336

Lamb's-Quarters *Chenopodium album* *Full sun*
Annual *60–70 days to*
Frost-tender *maturity*
p. 346

Stinging Nettle

Urtica dioica
Perennial grown as
annual
Usually winter-hardy
p. 357

Light shade
60–90 days to
maturity

Red Orach

Atriplex hortensis var.
rubra
Warm-season annual
Winter-hardy
p. 361

Full sun
60–90 days to
maturity

Purple Perilla   *Perilla frutescens*   *Full sun to light shade*
                        Warm-season annual   *60–90 days to*
                        Half-hardy   *maturity*
                        p. 371

New Zealand   *Tetragonia*   *Full sun to light shade*
Spinach   *tetragonioides*   *60–90 days to*
                        Perennial grown as   *maturity*
                        annual
                        Half-hardy
                        p. 388

Green Perilla   *Perilla frutescens*   *Full sun to light shade*
                         Warm-season annual   *60–90 days to*
                         Half-hardy   *maturity*
                         p. 371

New Zealand   *Tetragonia*   *Full sun to light shade*
Spinach   *tetragonioides*   *60–90 days to*
                        Perennial grown as   *maturity*
                        annual
                        Half-hardy
                        p. 388

Chinese Yam

Dioscorea batatas
Warm-season perennial
grown as annual
Frost-tender
p. 404

Full sun
210–240 days to
maturity

Winged Yam

Dioscorea alata
Warm-season perennial
grown as annual
Frost-tender
p. 404

Full sun
210–240 days to
maturity

Purslane   *Portulaca oleracea*   *Full sun*
Warm-season annual   *45–60 days to*
Frost-tender   *maturity*
p. 376

Malabar Spinach   *Basella alba*   *Full sun to light shade*
Warm-season perennial   *90–120 days to*
grown as annual   *maturity*
Frost-tender
p. 387

Pokeweed

Phytolacca americana
Perennial grown as
annual
Half-hardy
p. 372

Full sun to light shade
45–60 days to
maturity

Celtuce

Lactuca sativa
var. asparagina
Cool-season annual
Half-hardy
p. 319

Full sun to light shade
90 days to maturity

| Amaranth | *Amaranthus tricolor*
Warm-season annual
Frost-tender
p. 292 | *Full sun*
45–60 days to
maturity |

| Pak-choi
Chinese Cabbage | *Brassica rapa,*
Chinensis Group
Cool-season annual or
biennial
Half-hardy
p. 312 | *Full sun to light shade*
60 days to maturity |

Florence Fennel   *Foeniculum vulgare*
var. azoricum
Cool-season perennial
grown as annual
Half-hardy
p. 333

Full sun
90–110 days to
maturity

Cardoon   *Cynara cardunculus*
Perennial grown as
annual
Half-hardy
p. 314

Full sun
150–180 days to
maturity

Great Burdock   *Arctium lappa*   *Full sun to light shade*
                           Biennial   *150–180 days to*
                           Usually winter-hardy   *maturity*
                           p. 309

Celery   *Apium graveolens var.*   *Full sun to light shade*
                           dulce   *90–110 days to*
                           Cool-season biennial   *maturity*
                           grown as annual
                           Half-hardy
                           p. 318

Swiss Chard   *Beta vulgaris, Cicla Group*
Biennial or perennial grown as annual
Usually winter-hardy
p. 396

Full sun to light shade
55–65 days to maturity

Rhubarb   *Rheum rhabarbarum*
Perennial
Usually winter-hardy
p. 381

Full sun to light shade
2 years to harvest

Ruby Swiss Chard	*Beta vulgaris, Cicla Group*	*Full sun to light shade*
	Biennial or perennial grown as annual	*55–65 days to maturity*
	Usually winter-hardy	
	p. 396	

Rhubarb	*Rheum rhabarbarum*	*Full sun to light shade*
	Perennial	*2 years to harvest*
	Usually winter-hardy	
	p. 381	

Herbs

Sweet Woodruff *Galium odoratum* *Light to full shade*
Plant height: to 12 in. *Moist to average soil*
Hardy perennial
p. 448

Roman Chamomile *Chamaemelum nobile* *Full sun*
Plant height: to 12 in. *Dry soil*
Half-hardy perennial
grown as annual
p. 418

Sweet Rocket
Hesperis matronalis
Plant height: 3–4 ft.
Biennial grown as
annual
p. 439

Light shade
Moist soil

Sweet False
Chamomile
Matricaria recutita
Plant height: to 2 ft.
Hardy annual
p. 419

Full sun
Average soil

Caraway   *Carum carvi*   *Full sun*
                   Plant height: 3½–4 ft.   *Average to dry soil*
                   Hardy biennial
                   p. 416

Dill   *Anethum graveolens*   *Full sun*
                   Plant height: to 3 ft.   *Average soil*
                   Half-hardy annual
                   p. 425

Coriander | *Coriandrum sativum* | *Full sun*
Plant height: to 2½ ft. | *Dry soil*
Hardy annual
p. 423

Rue | *Ruta graveolens* | *Full sun*
Plant height: to 2 ft. | *Average to dry soil*
Hardy perennial
p. 441

Sweet Fennel
*Foeniculum vulgare
var. dulce
Plant height: 4–6 ft.
Half-hardy perennial
or biennial
p. 425*

*Full sun
Average to dry soil*

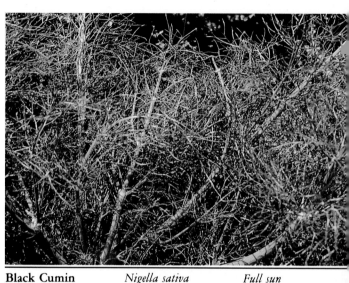

Black Cumin
*Nigella sativa
Plant height: to 18 in.
Annual
p. 424*

*Full sun
Average soil*

Dill *Anethum graveolens* *Full sun*
Plant height: to 3 ft. *Average soil*
Half-hardy annual
p. 425

Anise *Pimpinella anisum* *Full sun*
Plant height: to 2 ft. *Average to dry soil*
Annual
p. 409

Rue
Ruta graveolens
Plant height: to 2 ft.
Hardy perennial
p. 441

Full sun
Average to dry soil

Chervil
Anthriscus cerefolium
Plant height: to 12 in.
Hardy annual
p. 419

Full sun to light shade
Moist to average soil

Tansy   *Tanacetum vulgare*   *Full sun*
                       Plant height: 3–4 ft.   *Average soil*
                       Hardy perennial
                       p. 444

Sweet Cicely   *Myrrhis odorata*   *Light shade*
                       Plant height: 2–3 ft.   *Moist to average soil*
                       Hardy perennial
                       p. 421

Lovage

Levisticum officinale
Plant height: 4–6 ft.
Hardy perennial
p. 430

Full sun to light shade
Moist to average soil

Coriander

Coriandrum sativum
Plant height: to 2½ ft.
Hardy annual
p. 423

Full sun
Dry soil

eaf Celery   *Apium graveolens var.*   Full sun to light shade
                              secalinum   Moist to average soil
                              Plant height: to 12 in.
                              Half-hardy biennial
                              grown as cool-weather
                              annual
                              p. 417

Flat-leaf Parsley   *Petroselinum crispum*   Full sun to light shade
                              Plant height: 6–10 in.   Moist to average soil
                              Perennial grown as
                              annual
                              p. 436

**Curly-leaf
Parsley**

Petroselinum crispum
Plant height: 6–10 in.
Perennial grown as
annual
p. 436

Full sun to light shad
Moist to average soil

Alexanders

Smyrnium olusatrum
Plant height: to 3 ft.
Biennial
p. 408

Full sun
Moist soil

Curly Mint *Mentha spicata var. crispii* *Full sun to light shade*
Plant height: to 2 ft. *Moist to average soil*
Hardy perennial
p. 432

Angelica *Angelica archangelica* *Full sun to light shade*
Plant height: 5–6 ft. *Moist soil*
Hardy biennial
p. 408

Scented Geranium *Pelargonium 'Attar of
Roses'*
Plant height: 1½–2 ft.
*Half-hardy perennial
grown as annual*
p. 426

Full sun
Average to dry soil

Borage *Borago officinalis*
Plant height: 1½–3 ft.
Half-hardy annual
p. 414

Full sun
Average soil

Scented Geranium *Pelargonium 'Old* *Full sun*
Spice' *Average to dry soil*
Plant height: 1½–2 ft.
Half-hardy perennial
grown as annual
p. 426

Pineapple-scented *Salvia elegans* *Full sun*
Sage *Plant height: 4–5 ft.* *Average to dry soil*
Half-hardy perennial
grown as annual
p. 442

Bergamot   *Monarda didyma*   *Full sun to light shad*
Plant height: 2–3 ft.   *Moist soil*
Hardy perennial
p. 413

Nasturtium   *Tropaeolum majus*   *Full sun to light shad*
Plant height: to 6 ft.   *Moist to average soil*
Tender annual
p. 434

Añyu   *Tropaeolum tuberosum*   *Full sun to light shade*
                              Plant height: 6–8 ft.   *Average soil*
                              Tender perennial
                              grown as annual
                              p. 410

Nasturtium   *Tropaeolum majus*   *Full sun to light shade*
                              Plant height: to 6 ft.   *Moist to average soil*
                              Tender annual
                              p. 434

Pennyroyal

Mentha pulegium
Plant height: to 12 in.
Hardy perennial
p. 437

Full sun
Moist to average soil

Salad Burnet

Poterium sanguisorba
Plant height: to 12 in.
Hardy perennial
p. 414

Full sun to light shade
Average to dry soil

Caper   *Capparis spinosa*   *Full sun*
             Plant height: 2–3 ft.   *Average to dry soil*
             Tender perennial
             grown as annual
             p. 416

Black Mustard   *Brassica nigra*   *Full sun*
                      Plant height: 4–6 ft.   *Average soil*
                      Hardy annual
                      p. 434

Calendula   *Calendula officinalis*   *Full sun to light shade*
              Plant height: 1–2 ft.   *Average soil*
              Hardy annual
              p. 415

Costmary   *Chrysanthemum*   *Full sun*
              balsamita   *Average soil*
              Plant height: 2–3 ft.
              Hardy perennial
              p. 424

Winter Tarragon   *Tagetes lucida*   *Full sun*
                       Plant height: 1–2 ft.   *Average soil*
                       Half-hardy perennial
                       grown as annual
                       p. 445

Sage   *Salvia officinalis*   *Full sun*
                       Plant height: 1–2 ft.   *Moist soil*
                       Hardy perennial
                       p. 442

Purple Sage   *Salvia officinalis*   *Full sun*
                    'Purpurascens'   *Moist soil*
                    Plant height: 1–2 ft.
                    Hardy perennial
                    p. 442

Golden Sage   *Salvia officinalis*   *Full sun*
                    'Bicolor'   *Moist soil*
                    Plant height: 1–2 ft.
                    Hardy perennial
                    p. 442

Tricolor Sage   *Salvia officinalis*   *Full sun*
                         Plant height: 1–2 ft.   *Moist soil*
                         Hardy perennial
                         p. 442

Pineapple Mint   *Mentha suaveolens*   *Full sun to light shade*
                         'Variegata'   *Average soil*
                         Plant height: to 2 ft.
                         Hardy perennial
                         p. 433

Apple Mint　　　　　*Mentha suaveolens*　　　　*Full sun to light shade*
　　　　　　　　　　　Plant height: to 2 ft.　　*Average soil*
　　　　　　　　　　　Hardy perennial
　　　　　　　　　　　p. 431

Spearmint　　　　　*Mentha spicata*　　　　　*Full sun to light shade*
　　　　　　　　　　　Plant height: 1–2 ft.　　*Moist to average soil*
　　　　　　　　　　　Hardy perennial
　　　　　　　　　　　p. 433

Lemon Balm

Melissa officinalis
Plant height: 2–2½ ft.
Half-hardy perennial
p. 428

Full sun to light shade
Moist soil

Peppermint

Mentha × piperita
Plant height: 1–2 ft.
Hardy perennial
p. 432

Full sun to light shade
Moist soil

Anise Basil *Ocimum basilicum* *Full sun*
Plant height: 3–4 ft. *Average soil*
Tender annual
p. 410

Catnip *Nepeta cataria* *Full sun to light shade*
Plant height: 2–3 ft. *Average soil*
Hardy perennial
p. 417

Dark Opal
Purple Basil

Ocimum basilicum
Plant height:
12–18 in.
Tender annual
p. 410

Full sun
Average soil

Anise Hyssop

Agastache foeniculum
Plant height: 3–4 ft.
Half-hardy perennial
grown as annual
p. 409

Full sun to light shade
Average soil

Holy Basil
Ocimum canum
Plant height: to 2 ft.
Tender annual
p. 412

Full sun
Average to dry soil

Lemon Basil
Ocimum basilicum
Plant height: to 18 in.
Tender annual
p. 410

Full sun
Average soil

Lemon Verbena   *Aloysia triphylla*   *Full sun*
                    Plant height: 3–5 ft.   *Average to dry soil*
                    Half-hardy perennial
                    grown as annual
                    p. 447

Fine-leaf Tall Basil   *Ocimum basilicum*   *Full sun*
                           Plant height: to 3 ft.   *Average soil*
                           Tender annual
                           p. 410

Sweet Bay   *Magnolia virginiana*   *Full sun*
                             Plant height: 1–2 ft.   *Average soil*
                             Tender perennial
                             p. 412

Fine-leaf Bush Basil   *Ocimum basilicum*   *Full sun*
                             minimum   *Average soil*
                             Plant height:
                             12–18 in.
                             Tender annual
                             p. 410

Bay

Laurus nobilis
Plant height: shrub or
tree to 30 ft.
Half-hardy perennial
p. 412

Full sun
Average soil

Sweet Basil

Ocimum basilicum
Plant height: 3–4 ft.
Tender annual
p. 410

Full sun
Average soil

Oregano

Origanum vulgare
Plant height: to 6 in.
Half-hardy perennial
p. 435

Full sun
Average to dry soil

Greek Oregano

Origanum
heracleoticum
Plant height: to 6 in.
Half-hardy perennial
p. 435

Full sun
Average to dry soil

Italian Oregano   *Origanum onites*   *Full sun*
                       Plant height: to 12 in. *Average to dry soil*
                       Tender perennial
                       grown as annual
                       p. 435

Sweet Marjoram   *Origanum majorana*   *Full sun*
                      Plant height: *Average to dry soil*
                      12–18 in.
                      Half-hardy perennial
                      grown as annual
                      p. 431

Thyme *Thymus vulgaris* *Full sun*
Plant height: 6–12 in. *Average to dry soil*
Hardy perennial
p. 446

Golden Thyme *Thymus × citriodorus* *Full sun*
'Aureus' *Average to dry soil*
Plant height: to 8 in.
Half-hardy perennial
p. 447

| **Lemon Thyme** | *Thymus × citriodorus*
Plant height: to 8 in.
Half-hardy perennial
p. 447 | *Full sun*
Average soil |

| **French Thyme** | *Thymus vulgaris*
Plant height: 6–12 in.
Hardy perennial
p. 446 | *Full sun*
Average to dry soil |

Rosemary   *Rosmarinus officinalis*   *Full sun*
                        Plant height: 2–4 ft.   *Average to dry soil*
                        Half-hardy perennial
                        grown as annual
                        p. 439

Winter Savory   *Satureja montana*   *Full sun*
                        Plant height: 6–10 in.   *Average to dry soil*
                        Hardy perennial
                        p. 443

Creeping Rosemary   *Rosmarinus officinalis*   *Full sun*
                          'Prostratus'   *Average to dry soil*
                          Plant height: 6–12 in.
                          Half-hardy perennial
                          grown as annual
                          p. 439

French Tarragon   *Artemisia dracunculus*   *Full sun*
                          var. sativa   *Average soil*
                          Plant height: 1–2 ft.
                          Half-hardy perennial
                          p. 445

Cumberland Rosemary

Conradina verticillata
Plant height: to 12 in.
Hardy perennial
p. 440

Full sun
Average to dry soil

Shepherd's Purse

Capsella bursa-pastoris
Plant height: to 18 in.
Cool-season annual
p. 443

Full sun
Average soil

Hyssop

Hyssopus officinalis
Plant height: to 2 ft.
Hardy perennial
p. 427

Full sun
Average to dry soil

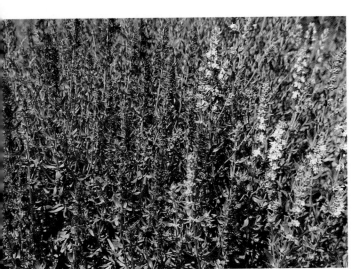

English Lavender

Lavandula
angustifolia
Plant height: 2–2½ ft.
Hardy or half-hardy
perennial
p. 427

Full sun
Average to dry soil

Clove Pink
Dianthus caryophyllus
Plant height: to 18 in.
Half-hardy perennial
p. 422

Full sun
Average soil

Corn Poppy
Papaver rhoeas
Plant height:
1½–2½ ft.
Hardy annual
p. 438

Full sun
Average to dry soil

Wild Bergamot   *Monarda fistulosa*   *Full sun to light shade*
                     Plant height: 2–3 ft.   *Average to dry soil*
                     Hardy perennial
                     p. 414

Mallow   *Malva sylvestris*   *Full sun*
                     Plant height: 3–4 ft.   *Moist to average soil*
                     Perennial or biennial
                     p. 430

Chive *Allium schoenoprasum* *Full sun*
Plant height: 8–12 in. *Average soil*
Hardy perennial
p. 420

Lemongrass *Cymbopogon citratus* *Full sun*
Plant height: 4–6 ft. *Moist soil*
Tender perennial
p. 429

Garlic Chive
Allium tuberosum
Plant height: to 12 in.
Hardy perennial
p. 421

Full sun
Average soil

Ramp
Allium tricoccum
Plant height: to 12 in.
Hardy perennial
p. 438

Full sun to light shade
Moist to average soil

Vegetables

There is no better reward for the tasks of planting, weeding, and watering a vegetable garden than the first bite of a juicy tomato, fresh off the vine and still warm from the sun—or a sweet, tender young ear of corn, picked at perfection and cooked minutes later. Included here is information on how to grow a bounty of traditional favorites, as well as a lot of not-so-common vegetables to try for a change.

Vegetable Groups

The individual writeups that follow are arranged alphabetically by the generally accepted common name. All of the large groups, such as beans and squashes, have been kept intact, so you will find lima beans under "beans" and zucchini under "squashes." Vegetables in these groups are all closely related.

Many vegetables that we think of as very different are in fact close relatives. The easiest way to understand them as groups is to know some of the major botanical genera—*Brassica, Cucumis, Cucurbita, Phaseolus,* and *Solanum*—and the families they belong to. Members of the same genus tend to share common characteristics, such as leaf shape and texture, or cultural requirements, so a shortcut to learning how to recognize and grow many vegetables is to know a genus and a few of its most common members. (For more information about classification, scientific names, and families of vegetables, refer to the Basic Botany essay.)

Brassica, a large genus of plants in the mustard family (Cruciferae), includes broccoli, Brussels sprouts, cauliflower, collards, kale, kohlrabi, mustard greens, rutabaga, turnips, and several other crops. Their nippy taste should tell you that arugula, watercress, and radishes are also members of the mustard family, although they belong to different genera. Many of these vegetables have been cultivated for more than 2000 years.

Cucumis, another ancient genus, includes the ever-popular cucumber and most of the melons in this book. (Watermelons belong to the genus *Citrullus.*) Squashes and pumpkins belong to *Cucurbita,* a genus of semitropical and tropical plants; and *Cucumis, Citrullus,* and *Cucurbita* all belong to the cucumber family, Cucurbitaceae. With watermelons and pumpkins recorded at over 100 pounds, it is no surprise that this family is famous for producing the largest fruits in the world.

Most of the beans we grow are members of the genus *Phaseolus,* although there are four other genera that make up the entire bean collection described in this book. All beans and peas are in the pea family (Leguminosae), and many have been traced to ancient civilizations. Kidney beans were cultivated in Central America as far back as 5000 B.C.; pea seeds found among the tombs of the pharaohs were presumably intended as nourishment in the afterlife.

Potatoes and eggplants (genus *Solanum*) are actually related to peppers, tobacco, tomatoes, and tomatillos. They are all members of the enormous nightshade family (Solanaceae), as are many poisonous wild plants.

Planning the Garden

Enjoy browsing through the writeups as you start to plan your garden. Save a couple of rows for experimenting with new kinds or varieties of vegetables, and try setting aside one area for a special purpose, like salad or soup crops. If space is a problem, plan carefully; the same plot of land can grow radicchio over the winter, spinach in the early spring, broccoli in early summer, snap beans in midsummer, and cabbage or cauliflower in late summer and fall. One trick is to plant varieties that mature sequentially. Even if you do not have land for a garden, home-grown vegetables are not beyond your reach; many varieties have been developed specifically for container growing. You may want to try companion planting; some people believe that growing herbs like chive and garlic next to their vegetables keeps damaging insects away.

Varieties

Even if you've never seen a square tomato or a yellow zucchini, a quick glance at any current seed catalogue will make it clear that new vegetables are "invented" every year, adding countless possibilities to the list of things that you might want to grow. Some of these new vegetables differ in color or shape from the old standards, while others are not visibly different but have been improved to resist diseases, taste better, mature quickly, or survive difficult growing conditions. Some vegetables that may be new to us are actually old standbys in other parts of the world that have only recently been introduced here. There are literally hundreds of varieties to choose from; in the text accounts we have included a heading under which you will find a selection of named old-time favorites and new varieties that have demonstrated their reliability. Some vegetables may have no varieties, however, and instead are sold simply by the species or common name.

Harvesting

Enjoying freshly picked vegetables is one of the treats of gardening, but with large harvests you might want to store some of the crop to have home-grown produce all year long. Beans lend themselves beautifully to home canning or freezing, corn on the cob can be blanched and frozen, and root crops and winter squashes will stay crisp and fresh in a root cellar that you can build yourself in a corner of the garden or cellar. It is also fun to leave a few vegetables unharvested and watch the results. A good example of this is asparagus spears; left alone, they develop into tall, bushy plants with finely divided, fernlike leaves, and in fall, the female plants produce little red berries that can be used to start new plants.

Amaranth
Amaranthus tricolor p. 239

Tampala; Chinese Spinach; Hinn Choy. An ancient and widely distributed annual with many selections, some grown for grain, some for their edible leaves and flower buds, others for ornament. The commonly cultivated amaranth has large, tender leaves that are broad and felty, usually green, sometimes splotched with brownish purple. The plant grows 3–6 ft. (0.9–1.8 m) high, but is usually pruned back to encourage branching and to delay flowering. One of the best heat-resistant greens for cooking, amaranth grows well throughout the U.S.

How to Grow
This warmth-loving annual is not frost-hardy. Direct-seed in warm, fertile, well-drained soil in full sun. Plant 3–6 in. (7.5–15 cm) apart. Amaranth is difficult to transplant except when the seedlings are quite small. In cool areas it will develop faster under a cloche or plastic tunnel.

Harvest
Some gardeners prune large plants for their tender leaves and tips. Others prefer to time plantings 2 weeks apart, and pull up the tender young plants to eat.

Artichoke
Cynara scolymus p. 121

Artichokes, or chokes, are the immature flower buds of a large, dark silvery-green perennial plant that belongs to the daisy family (Compositae). The plant has arching, elaborately cut basal leaves and grows to 5 ft. (1.5 m) high.

How to Grow
Artichokes require a long growing season and do best in Calif., but fare quite well across the South and Southwest. In the North they can be raised only in a greenhouse or from offsets (root divisions) started indoors during midwinter. Plants started from seeds give variable results; seed-grown chokes tend to be small and fibrous. It is better to buy offsets from specialists, planting one per 3-gal. (12-l) container indoors. After the last frost,

harden off the young plants and transplant to a sunny site where roots will not be disturbed. Space plants 4 ft. (120 cm) apart. Plants prefer fertile, sandy loam soil. Water frequently during dry spells. Provide straw mulch except in the West, where snails and slugs are a problem.

Harvest
Artichokes planted in spring mature from fall through midwinter. Harvest chokes with a sharp knife or pruning shears. Cut stems 3–4 in. (7.5–10.0 cm) below the bud.

Varieties
Green Globe Improved is the best variety to grow from seeds. Or select offsets from Calif., which are taken from cultivars developed cooperatively by the University of California and commercial growers.

Arugula
Eruca vesicaria ssp. *sativa p. 229*

Rocket; Roquette; Rucola; Rugula. Arugula is a sturdy, cold-tolerant leaf vegetable. A member of the mustard family (Cruciferae), it has deeply toothed leaves and looks a bit like slender, short-topped turnip greens. Its strong aroma and flavor are reminiscent of peanuts.

How to Grow
Plant seeds thickly in rows or wide bands in early spring and again in late summer. Fall sowings are possible in the South, but temperatures below 25° F (−4° C) will usually freeze all but the protected center leaf growth. Avoid summer plantings; short summer nights force the plant to flower and go to seed before sufficient vegetative growth has taken place.

Harvest
Shear off whole plants 2–3 in. (5.0–7.5 cm) above soil level, leaving the central leaf buds for renewal. You can also snap off only the outer leaves. Mix the larger leaves with milder greens for cooking or for salads.

Varieties
Usually sold by species name or as Roquette. An Italian strain is called Ruchetta.

Asparagus
Asparagus officinalis p. 120

Perhaps no other garden vegetable is so
eagerly awaited in spring as tender spears of
asparagus. Seldom given away like zucchini,
asparagus is slow to develop and takes up a
considerable amount of space in the garden.
This hardy perennial, a member of the lily
family (Liliaceae), is adapted to all parts of
the U.S. except the Deep South and warm
West, where winters are too mild. In spring,
root mats, or crowns, below ground send up
the edible young stalks. The scales at the top
and along the length of these stalks are leaf
buds that eventually produce feathery foliage
on any unharvested spears; by midsummer,
asparagus plants are tall and fernlike.

How to Grow
It is nearly impossible to grow asparagus in
hot, humid regions. It grows wild in great
abundance in some parts of the irrigated
West. The most popular way to grow
asparagus is from crowns—2-year-old
seedlings with a mat of fleshy roots. You can
also start seeds indoors or in a protected
corner of the garden, then transplant the
seedlings to a permanent bed.
Leave the plants alone for the first growing
season in the permanent bed, and take only
light cuttings the second season. This
pampering helps build up a mat of heavy
roots that can support numerous thick spears
during spring growth. Late spring is a good
time to plant asparagus in most of the
country. In the mid-South, fall or winter is
preferable.
Prepare an asparagus bed as if it were to
last forever—it may actually last 15–20 years.
Work generous amounts of organic matter
and phosphate sources deeply into the soil,
along with sharp sand if the soil is heavy
and slow-draining. Add enough material to
raise the bed 4–6 in. (10–15 cm) above the
surrounding soil. Poor drainage and water
standing around the crowns can inhibit
production and, in extreme cases, kill plants.
Beds should be no more than 3–4 ft. (90–
120 cm) wide. After amending the soil,
excavate a trench about 6 in. (15 cm) deep
down the center of the bed. If your soil is
dense clay, start out with a shallower ditch,
perhaps 3 in. (7.5 cm) deep. Set crowns or
seedlings in the ditch; water thoroughly and
cover with about 1 in. (2.5 cm) of the
excavated soil. As the tiny spears grow, add

more of the soil to the ditch until it is completely filled. In the mid-South, if you plant asparagus in the fall, top-dress the bed a few weeks before fall frost with about 1 in. (2.5 cm) of pasteurized manure and water it in. This is better than a fall feeding of soluble nitrogen, which could make the plants susceptible to winter damage. If you prefer blanched spears, mound organic mulch over asparagus beds.

Harvest
Cut asparagus spears when they are 5–7 in. (12.5–17.5 cm) high; a sharpened dandelion digger is good for this. Hold it at a low angle and push it no more than 1 in. (2.5 cm) beneath the surface of the soil to cut the spears. Be careful not to damage the mat of roots when cutting.

Varieties
Mary Washington is a well-known variety; Viking KB3 is disease-resistant.

BEANS

Snap beans, limas, garbanzos—these and many others constitute a wide variety of leguminous garden crops. Some may be eaten like snap beans, pod and all, and others are shelled for their seeds, which may be used fresh or dried.

Azuki Bean
Vigna angularis p. 158

Annuals native to Asia and related to southern peas, azuki beans grow on large bushes with short tendrils. In late summer, many pods set, averaging 4–5 in. (10.0–12.5 cm) long. The pods can be shelled at the plump green stage, but are usually allowed to dry on the vine and then shelled for dry beans, which taste slightly sweet. They can also be eaten as sprouts. Some varieties have brown seeds, others red.

How to Grow
Azuki beans need a growing season with at least 120 warm days. Plant seeds 1 in. (2.5 cm) deep and 3–6 in. (7.5–15.0 cm) apart in rows 3–4 ft. (90–120 cm) apart. The

vines also grow well when planted among stalks of late sweet corn; after the corn has been harvested, the vines twine up the stalks.

Harvest
In areas with a short growing season or late summer rains, cut the plants when the pods begin to dry and split. Stack vines loosely and cover them with slitted plastic to protect from rain but allow ventilation. Strip off and shell the pods when dry. Store the seeds with dried hot peppers to discourage weevils.

Varieties
Express, as its name suggests, is an early-maturing variety.

Broad Bean
Vicia faba p. 159

Fava Bean. Broad beans grow on erect plants to 5 ft. (1.5 m) high or more with thick, succulent stems. Pods may be as much as 6–12 in. (15–30 cm) long and have a white-woolly lining in which the edible seeds are embedded. Half-hardy annuals, these bean plants need about 70 days of cool, relatively frost-free growing weather to produce large bushes loaded with well-filled pods. Areas with a short spring are hard on broad beans, since summer heat arrives when the vines are only half-grown.

How to Grow
In most of the U.S., plant seeds in early spring. In Calif., plant them after fall rains have started. Plant about 1 in. (2.5 cm) deep, 8–10 in. (20–25 cm) apart, in rows 3–4 ft. (90–120 cm) apart. Provide brush for support as soon as seeds sprout so that the bushes do not flop or blow over as they grow. Mulch seedlings with pine needles or straw to reduce frost damage.

Harvest
When beans are half-grown, you can eat the entire pod, cooked like snap beans. Shell older pods and mix the seeds with cut-up pods. Some people are allergic to the mature seeds of broad beans; if you have never eaten them before, start with only a few seeds.

Varieties
Broad beans are often sold simply under the descriptive names "large-seeded" or "small-seeded." Many named varieties can be ordered from British seed companies. Aquadulce and Ipro are 2 early-maturing types.

Butterbean
Phaseolus lunatus p. 166

Sieva; Civet; or Seewee Bean. Butterbeans have long been eaten in the South, where, along with peas, okra, and sweet potatoes, they are staple hot-weather vegetables. Butterbeans are similar to lima beans but smaller and slightly more heat-resistant. There are climbing and bush varieties. Some produce seeds that have brown and maroon blotches when dry. Except when very small, these blotched seeds turn dark when cooked. In the past, most butterbeans were primarily white-seeded, and thus nondescript when cooked. There are now kinds that have green immature seeds.

How to Grow and Harvest
Plant and harvest butterbeans like limas. Provide tall, sturdy supports for pole varieties; a good arrangement is an A-frame arbor. Plant seeds 3 in. (7.5 cm) apart in rows 5 ft. (1.5 m) apart and straddle the rows with the arbor. This allows you access at harvest time to the pods hanging inside the structure.

Varieties
Bush: Jackson Wonder (speckled seeds), Henderson's Bush, Thorogreen, Dixie Butterpea, Bridgeton. Pole: Florida Speckled (speckled seeds), Sieva, Small White.

Dry and Horticultural Beans
Phaseolus vulgaris pp. 156, 159

Many varieties of beans have been developed specifically for green or dry shelled seeds. Although the young pods can be eaten as snap beans before fiber and strings develop, this use is incidental.
Dry beans are thought to be the ancestors of snap beans. The varieties differ greatly in habit, seed colors (ranging from white to yellow, red, pink, brown, speckled, and

black), and, to a lesser extent, flavor when cooked. Among the best known of the dry beans are kidney, pinto, navy, and black turtle beans. These commercial dry beans are seldom grown in home gardens because they can be bought cheaply in grocery stores with little or no difference in taste. An exception is the French flageolet bean, a delicate white-seeded variety often grown and dried by home gardeners.

Horticultural beans are considered a separate class. They were bred to be shelled when their large seeds reach full size but are still green and tender. The pods of many horticultural varieties are splashed with crimson or maroon when they are ready to be shelled, and the seeds are strongly bicolored. Though old-fashioned, horticultural beans are still quite popular in the Northeast and Midwest, where they are eaten green or dried for winter use.

How to Grow

Grow as you would snap beans. For seeds to start dry beans, you may have to use edible beans from the grocery store. Germination may be poor, so plant more than usual.

Harvest

Watch beans grown for dry seeds carefully, since a hot, dry spell can cause pods to split and spill seeds on the ground. To reduce seed loss, pull the plants and stack them in a well-ventilated area on a catch-cloth. With horticultural beans, you may have to let a few pods become overripe to have the majority mature enough for easy shelling. Pick and save overripe pods for dry beans.

Varieties

A few seed catalogues offer disease-resistant varieties of modern dry beans; these are preferable to grocery-store seeds. Named varieties include Black Turtle, California Pink, Great Northern, Navy or Navy Pea, Pinto, Pinquito, Red Kidney, Red Mexican, Soldier, Swedish Brown, White Half-Runner, White Kidney. Flageolet beans are available through gourmet vegetable seed catalogues. Horticultural beans include Dwarf, Taylor's, French (pole), Jacob's Cattle (bush), Vermont Bush Cranberry, Vermont Cranberry (pole).

Garbanzo Bean
Cicer arietinum p. 167

Chick Pea. Originally from se. Asia, garbanzo beans are a staple from the Mediterranean countries to India and are rich in protein and starch. These annual plants grow into bushes 1–2 ft. (30–60 cm) high and look more like vetch than peas or beans. They have compound leaves composed of 9–15 leaflets, and short, swollen pods about 1 in. (2.5 cm) long, each containing 1 or 2 wrinkled seeds. Plants do not yield much for the space occupied, but they make a good summer soil-builder for sections of the garden lying fallow.

How to Grow
Sow seeds in late spring, preferably in sandy or sandy loam soil. Space plants 6 in. (15 cm) apart. To produce enough beans to make the crop worth the effort, grow at least 24–36 plants. Hot weather does not bother garbanzo beans, but they prefer the dry heat of the West and Southwest.

Harvest
When several pods have dried, harvest the entire plant or, if you have only a few plants, gather individual pods. Dry plants in the sun on a catch-cloth so the dried seeds are caught as pods split.

Lima Bean
Phaseolus limensis p. 167

The differences between lima beans and butterbeans have been melting away as crosses are made. Lima varieties are available in both climbing and bush forms. The plants are larger and more robust than those of butterbeans and bear large pods with fat greenish seeds. Limas, less heat-resistant than butterbeans, set pods within a narrower range of temperature and humidity. But the larger, thick-walled pods are easier to shell, and the mealy green seeds are delicious fresh or dried.
In general, pole limas and butterbeans yield more per square foot and for a longer period than bush types, but the vines need support and take up considerable space.

How to Grow
Direct-seed in warm soil after danger of

spring frost is past. Plant seeds 2–3 in. (5.0–7.5 cm) apart, 1 in. (2.5 cm) deep in clay soil and 1½ in. (4 cm) deep in sandy soil. Thin seedlings to 6 in. (15 cm) apart. In hard clay soil that crusts, there is a slight advantage to planting seeds on edge— standing them upright rather than lying them flat. It is better to lay seeds in a furrow and cover with ½–1 in. (1.3–2.5 cm) of sand. Lima beans transplant poorly. Even if seeds are started in peat pots and set in the garden when still small, the plants usually mature later than those that were direct-seeded. Feed lightly with a 1-2-2 nitrogen-phosphorus-potassium ratio fertilizer; too much nitrogen is counterproductive. Wind can twist and damage seedlings that are allowed to sprawl, so provide supports for climbers as soon as seeds emerge.
Bean beetles can strip vines of leaves and are especially bad on climbing varieties. To destroy eggs left behind that might otherwise infest next season's crop, burn the vines immediately after the last picking, and rake up and burn shed leaves.

Harvest
Bean vines can be broken easily by rough picking or yanking. Always hold the spray of pods with one hand while stripping them off with the other. Keep picking pods until late in the season, when you can then allow a few to dry on the vine for dried beans. Seal dried beans in a jar with a few hot dried peppers to repel weevils and other seed-eating insects.

Varieties
Bush: Fordhook 242, Geneva, Burpee's Improved Bush. Pole: King of the Garden, Large Speckled, Prizetaker.

Mung Bean
Vigna radiata p. 160

Black Gram; Urd. This slender-podded relative of southern peas is grown mostly for dried seeds used in sprouting or for grinding into bean meal. Hairy and of open, spreading growth, these annual plants are 3 ft. (90 cm) high, with lax stems and conspicuous yellow pealike flowers. They tolerate high heat and humidity and fare best in gardens with a long, warm growing season.

How to Grow
Grow mung beans like southern peas.

Harvest
You can pick the green pods and use them as snap beans; mix them with green seeds shelled from fully grown pods. Otherwise, leave pods on plants to dry. To accomplish this in short-season climates, you may have to pull the vines at the end of the season to stop growth. Dry the vines in the field for a few days, moving them to a ventilated shelter to complete drying. If vines show signs of mold, turn the pile frequently and set up a fan to speed the drying. Seeds will become moldy if not kept bone dry after shelling; seal them in a jar with the desiccant pouches that come in foil packages of coffee.

Varieties
A few specialists in Oriental vegetable seeds sell the improved mung varieties that are grown in India, se. Asia, and s. China, but most gardeners have to settle for the bulk mung bean seeds generally used for sprouts.

Scarlet Runner Bean
Phaseolus coccineus p. 162

Case Knife Bean. Runner beans look much like pole snap beans, but their foliage is darker green and denser, and they have showy scarlet flowers. The pods are dark green, straight, and oval in cross section; older pods have a striated surface. These plants are perennial and may overwinter as heavy, deep taproots in areas with mild winters; nonetheless, most gardeners treat them as annuals. This bean is better known in the U.S. as an ornamental than as a vegetable. Yet the young pods are every bit as good as conventional snap beans—perhaps even more flavorful.

How to Grow
Direct-seed in warm soil after danger of frost is past. Full sun and good air drainage are necessary. In cool climates, plant seeds against a wall or fence facing west or south to intensify the solar heat and ward off wind. Plant seeds 1 in. (2.5 cm) apart in clusters of 3–4 seeds spaced 2–3 ft. (60–90 cm) apart. Run the vines of climbing types up teepees, trellises, or arbors at least 6 ft. (1.8 m) high.

Harvest
Strings and parchment may develop in pod walls as beans approach maturity, so harvest when pods are 3–4 in. (7.5–10.0 cm) long.

Varieties
The species includes varieties with either scarlet or white blossoms; the scarlet is more ornamental. Its exotic-looking seeds are vivid purple with black markings. A few seed companies, mostly European, offer dwarf or bush forms. Scarlet Runner is a red-flowered variety; Emergo, Thomas, White Dutch Runner, and Case Knife have white flowers.

Snap Bean
Phaseolus vulgaris pp. 157, 158, 161

Only 50 years ago, most green bean varieties had fibrous strings along the pod seam and a parchmentlike lining in the pods. Gardeners harvested these "string beans" at immature stages, or removed the strings and boiled the beans thoroughly to soften the fiber in the pod walls. In recent years, more or less stringless varieties have appeared, and today only heirloom varieties have strings and fiber.

Modern snap beans come in a wide range of varieties. Pods may be green, yellow (wax beans), or purple; oval, round, or broad and flat; and 5–12 in. (12.5–30.0 cm) long at maturity. Pole snap beans mature somewhat later than bush varieties but almost always yield pods for a longer period. Modern varieties of bush beans, however, are nearly as productive as pole types.

How to Grow
Fresh bean seeds germinate at a rate of 75–90 percent, but certain varieties with long, slender white seeds are notoriously poor germinators. Plant seeds after the frost-free date but soon enough to give you a good crop before the dog days of summer. Not even robust pole snap beans will continue to bear seeds in the midsummer heat of the lower South and Southwest. Where summers are exceedingly short and soil remains too cool to permit proper germination, start seeds indoors in peat pots and transplant seedlings to the garden.

For bush snap beans, plant seeds 2 in. (5 cm) apart in rows 2 ft. (60 cm) apart or in bands 6–12 in. (15–30 cm) wide. Thin seedlings to 3–4 in. (7.5–10.0 cm) between plants. For pole beans, plant 2–3 seeds by each pole or string and thin to the strongest plant. Give the young runners a little help at first by twining them clockwise around supports.

Harvest
Pick your beans as soon as pods are large enough to eat. Don't let them wait; allowing pods to age on the plant will reduce yield. To pick, hold the fruiting stem with one hand and strip off pods with the other. To avoid spreading diseases, harvest when the foliage is dry.

Varieties
Before choosing varieties, consult your local Cooperative Extension Service office to see which bean diseases are prevalent in your area; then select resistant types. You sacrifice little or nothing in flavor or production when you plant resistant kinds. Varieties that resist common bean mosaic virus and tolerate bean rust disease are available. Read catalogues and seed packages carefully. Listed here are a few popular modern varieties. Standard bush, green pods: Venture, Blue Lake Bush 274, Jumbo, Romano Bush, Tendercrop, Roma II, Greensleeves, Burpee's Tenderpod, Earliserve, Topcrop, Bluecrop, Rainier, Provider. European bush, slender pods: Triumph de Farcy, Vernandon, Daisy, Delinel, Plano, Chelinex. Bush, colored pods: Royal Burgundy, Royalty Purple Pod, Keygold, Roc D'Or, Goldcrop (AAS), Slenderwax. Pole, green pods: Blue Lake, Kentucky Wonder Resistant, Selma Star, Romano, Northeaster, Dade, Alabama Pole No. 1, Venture. Pole, wax or striped pods: Selma Zebra, Meraviglia de Venizia, Burpee Golden.

Soybean
Glycine max p. 166

Soybeans are probably native to e. Asia, where they have been grown for at least 4500 years. These frost-tender annuals are rather tall, erect bushes with rounded, furry leaves and numerous short, hairy pods that cling closely to the stems. Home-garden varieties, selected for earlier maturity, shorter plants, larger seeds, and longer pods with a higher seed count, are superior to the adapted grain (dry bean) varieties. Dry seeds are black or yellow; most black-seeded varieties are adapted to tropical conditions. Rich in fat and protein, soybean seeds must be cooked thoroughly, even in the immature green stage, to make them fully digestible. Soybeans also make a fine warm-weather green manure crop for soil improvement.

How to Grow
Plant seeds in warm soil in full sun after the spring frost-free date. Space seeds 2 in. (5 cm) apart in double rows or wide bands. Go easy on manure or nitrogen fertilizer, and inoculate the soil with the proper nitrogen-fixing bacteria to ensure good growth. Although soybeans are heat-resistant, they don't set pods if summers are dry as well as hot. Varieties are now available for most areas, except where there are fewer than 120 relatively warm, frost-free days.

Harvest
Pods are ready for harvest when fully grown and beginning to turn yellow. Boil pods in salted water for 20 minutes; cook for only 5–10 minutes if the beans are going to be further cooked with meats or other vegetables. Squeeze the boiled pods to pop the beans out. Soak dried beans for several hours and cook for 4 hours to make them digestible.

Varieties
Early: Maple Arrow, Fiskeby V, Frostbeater.
Midseason: Prize, Yellow, Green.

Winged Bean
Psophocarpus tetragonolobus p. 162

Goa Bean; Four-angled Bean; Princess Pea. Tender perennials from the Old World tropics, these plants are taller and more massive than snap beans and have similar but darker green foliage and loose sprays of reddish-brown or white blossoms. Flowers are followed by curious pods to 9 in. (22.5 cm) long, each with 4 fluted wings along its length. The skin is waxy and the flesh semitranslucent in young pods. Winged beans have attracted much interest in recent years because the edible pods are high in protein, and the leaf tips, flowers, underground tubers, and seeds shelled from overripe pods can all be eaten as well.

How to Grow

Winged beans are adapted only to areas with a long, warm fall season where the first frost comes no earlier than Thanksgiving. No matter how early you plant seeds, winged beans will not fruit until early fall; after that, there must be a long frost-free period to ensure a worthwhile harvest. Plant seeds 1 in. (2.5 cm) deep in groups of 2 or 3 around the poles of a tall, sturdy teepee or other support for the vines to climb.

Harvest

Pull the pods at the half-grown stage, when they are 4–5 in. (10.0–12.5 cm) long. Pods can be steamed. Roast ripe or dry seeds to make them digestible. In the Deep South and warm West, the tuberous roots grow quite large and can be peeled, sliced, or grated, and eaten raw or cooked.

Yard-long Bean
Vigna unguiculata ssp. *sesquipedalis p. 156*

Asparagus Bean; Long Horn Bean. This bean looks like a long-podded climbing southern pea, with robust vines twining like pole beans and growing 6–8 ft. (1.8–2.4 m) high. The "yard-long" claim is valid under optimal conditions, but in most North American gardens mature pods average only 1½–2 ft. (45–60 cm) long.

How to Grow

These beans prefer long, warm summers, and they withstand extremes of heat and humidity. They will grow as far north as the lower Great Lakes, but in such areas pods set sparsely and size up late, just before frost. Plant as you would southern peas. Provide supports 6–8 ft. (1.8–2.4 m) high. Some seeds imported from Asia may carry a virus that causes young plants to become mottled and stunted. Pull out any infected plants before the virus spreads.

Harvest

Begin pulling pods to eat as snap beans when they are 12 in. (30 cm) long. For shelling beans, pull older pods when the pod walls show a tinge of yellow, at which stage they zip open fairly easily. At the season's end, pull and dry all mature pods for dry storage and freeze any remaining snappers.

Beet
Beta vulgaris pp. 95, 97

Crassa Group. Grown as annuals, garden beets belong to a group of biennial plants selected from an ancient European species. This group also includes sugar beets, grown for sugar extraction, and mangel-wurzels, grown for livestock feed. Garden beets are cultivated principally for their roots, which come in many shapes and colors: long and cylindrical, oblong, top-shaped, and nearly round; dark purple-red, dark red, yellow, and white. The leaves of garden beets are also edible, and varieties have been developed to suit both food purposes.

How to Grow
Beets are only moderately frost-resistant and do not grow well in hot, dry weather. Early plantings sometimes bolt to seed prematurely. Therefore, do not plant beets until 2–3 weeks before the average spring frost-free date. Before planting, wash seeds in water with a mild detergent, then rinse well and dry. For maximum yield, direct-seed beets 2–4 in. (5–10 cm) apart in wide bands and grow in full sun, except when planted in late summer in warm climates. Cover direct-seeded beets with ¼–½ in. (6–13 mm) of sand or sifted compost. They will germinate in 2–3 weeks. You can also transplant beets at early stages, but handle them lightly. Thin excess seedlings only when they are large enough to eat as greens. In warm areas, you can sow a second beet crop in late summer. Provide shade to assist germination and ensure the survival of early seedlings.

Harvest
Pull roots and all, commencing when seedlings can be thinned and used for greens or baby beets. In cool climates, spring-seeded beets can stay in the ground through summer without losing much quality. In warm climates, the roots will deteriorate in hot soil. Old, large roots may be fibrous. Stringiness and white zoning in younger beets usually means poor seed breeding. To harvest all-leaf beets, shear off the entire plant about 3 in. (7.5 cm) above the soil line or snap off older leaves. If stems are stringy, strip off leaf blades and discard the stems.

Varieties

For many years Detroit Dark Red was the standard garden beet. Hybrids such as Pacemaker II and Sweetheart offer extra-sweet flavor. The hybrid Red Ace is not quite as sweet but has smoother roots that will keep in the garden for long periods. A good dual-purpose beet that keeps well during winter is Lutz Green Leaf. For color novelties, try Burpee's Golden and the sweet, vitamin-rich white beet Albina Veraduna. Perpetual Spinach is an all-leaf variety.

BROCCOLI

Like cauliflower, cabbages, kale, and other cole crops, broccoli was derived from a species of wild cabbage, *Brassica oleracea*. Through cultivation, this species has become so complex that scientists have divided it into several botanical groups; the 2 kinds of broccoli featured here belong to different ones. Common broccoli (*B. oleracea*, Botrytis Group) was developed to have a dense, central flowering head on a thick stem. Sprouting broccoli (*B. oleracea*, Italica Group) is a wild-looking form that has loose, leafy stems and edible flower shoots but no central head.

Broccoli
Brassica oleracea pp. 206, 207, 209

Botrytis Group. This popular vegetable, a biennial grown as an annual, has grayish-green leaves and fleshy edible stems that support large, tight, central heads of densely clustered flower buds. Heads may be green, blue-green, or purple-green. The plants are taller and usually broader than the closely related cauliflower.

How to Grow

Broccoli needs a long, cool growing season. Plants are not as frost-hardy as cabbage. Set out well-hardened transplants after danger of spring hard frost is past, or in late summer for fall or winter harvest. Space 12–18 in. (30–45 cm) apart.

Harvest

Cut the central stem 2–3 in. (5.0–7.5 cm)
below where it branches and forms buds.
Peel the lower part of the stem where skin is
tough. Separate the head where it branches
and soak it for 30 minutes to float out any
worms. Quality is best before yellow flowers
show in the buds. Some varieties form side
shoots after the central head has been
harvested.

Varieties

Premium Crop (AAS) is a widely adapted
hybrid. Another hybrid, Green Duke,
withstands the rigors of spring planting in
southern gardens. Green Comet is an old
standby. Romanesco, an Italian variety, has
decorative, light green heads in which the
clusters form a spiral pattern. Purple broccoli
varieties also exist.

Sprouting Broccoli
Brassica oleracea p. 206

Italica Group. Italian Broccoli; Asparagus
Broccoli. This vegetable resembles common
broccoli in its early stages of growth but
forms no central head. Numerous slender
flowering shoots arise from the central stem.
Both green and purple varieties exist. Some
gardeners prefer sprouting broccoli to the
heading type because it has a longer
harvesting period.

How to Grow

Grow as you would common broccoli.

Harvest

When plants are in the bud stage, cut the
individual sprouts just above where the skin
becomes tough. Sprouts are eaten with a few
small terminal leaves on them. Eating quality
deteriorates considerably as the buds open
into flowers.

Varieties

Seeds are hard to find; read descriptions
carefully to be sure you are getting true
sprouting broccoli. De Cicco is a named
variety.

Brussels Sprouts
Brassica oleracea p. 209

Gemmifera Group. These plants have an upright central stem; along the stem, dozens of little "sprouts" resembling miniature cabbages are packed tightly between the bases of the leaf petioles. If left on the plant the sprouts eventually mature into flowering shoots.

How to Grow
At one time, Brussels sprouts were seldom seen outside protected coastal gardens, where they were usually harvested in fall and winter. Today there are fast-growing, more widely adapted hybrids, but spring crops are still chancy. Brussels sprouts are not as frost-hardy as cabbage at any stage of growth. Start with large, vigorous, hardened seedlings, set them out early, and protect them from moderate to hard frosts. Plant 2½–3 ft. (75–90 cm) apart.

Harvest
Pluck or snip off the firm sprouts, working up from the base of the plant. Aphids or plant lice can ruin a sprout crop; if they appear, start a preventive spraying program. Insecticidal soap is effective and nontoxic to humans.

Varieties
Three well-established hybrids are Captain Marvel (early), Prince Marvel (midseason), and Jade Cross E, a heavy-producing late cultivar.

Great Burdock
Arctium lappa p. 241

Gobo. This biennial European plant has large, rough leaves and grows to impressive sizes. It is harvested primarily for its long, light brown root and is much cultivated as a vegetable in the Orient. Larger than rhubarb, burdock takes up a lot of garden space and may become established as a weed.

How to Grow
Grow burdock in deep sandy or sandy loam soil so that roots become long enough to make the project worthwhile. Leave a wide walkway around the bed to accommodate

the sprawling plants. Plant in spring in the North, or in early fall where winters are mild. Direct-seed in clumps 1–2 ft. (30–60 cm) apart. Thin to 2–3 seedlings per clump. When plants are mature, cut off the burlike seeds to prevent spreading.

Harvest
Dig roots before soil freezes or, in mild winter zones, before top growth resumes in spring. Dig up at least the top 12 in. (30 cm) of the roots, or bottoms will regrow. Roots dry out quickly, so cook and eat promptly. Add to soups, stews, or stir-fried vegetables.

CABBAGES

Cabbages belong to the mustard family (Cruciferae) and are related to broccoli, cauliflower, and other vegetable crops in the genus *Brassica*. Most familiar are the head cabbages (*B. oleracea,* Capitata Group), which include smooth green or red kinds and crinkly-leaved Savoys. Chinese cabbages are of 2 sorts: Heading types (*B. rapa,* Pekinensis Group), known collectively as Pe-tsai, have either cylindrical or barrel-shaped heads; nonheading types, or Pak-choi (*B. rapa,* Chinensis Group), have loosely clustered leaves on succulent stems but form no tight, central head. Ornamental cabbages (*B. oleracea,* Acephala Group) are grown mainly for decorative use and add color to the garden.

Cabbage
Brassica oleracea pp. 198, 199

Capitata Group. Cabbages may have round, conical, or flattened heads; the color may be green, blue-green, or reddish purple; and the leaf texture smooth or waffled, as in Savoy cabbages. Head sizes at maturity range from mini-cabbages that weigh 1 lb. (.45 kg) to Alaska-grown kraut varieties that weigh 60 lbs. (27.2 kg) or more. Cabbage plants have such short stem joints (internodes) that on some varieties the heads are virtually coreless. The broad outer leaves lie flat on the ground, and the "wrapper" leaves ascend and clasp to form heads, which may be loose or dense, depending on the variety.

How to Grow
Cabbages prefer cool weather and will withstand light frosts. Start spring crops early outdoors from well-hardened transplants. For fall or winter crops, direct-seed in late summer. Fast-maturing varieties are recommended for spring planting. Expert home gardeners often plant 2 or 3 varieties that mature in sequence to prolong the harvest. Be careful not to set in too many cabbage plants; heads go out of prime eating condition rather fast. Later-maturing types are preferred for fall crops, which, except for a few more insect problems, grow better than spring cabbage. Space plants 1 ft. (30 cm) apart for midget varieties and up to 4 ft. (120 cm) apart for large, late kraut varieties.

Harvest
Pick spring cabbage before hot weather causes heads to split, and fall cabbage before very cold weather freezes the heads. In some varieties small side heads form after the central head is cut.

Varieties
Early: Golden Acre (not a hybrid) tolerates cabbage yellow disease; the hybrid Darkri is well rated for flavor. Midseason: King Cole, Greenback, Roundup; the hybrid Blue Ribbon tolerates 3 diseases and resists yellows. Late: Deep blue-green varieties include Blue Boy, Rio Verde, and Grand Slam. Savoy: Savoy King (AAS). Red cabbages: Most are midseason to late; Preko is an early red hybrid.

Chinese Cabbage (heading)
Brassica rapa p. 212

Pekinensis Group. Pe-tsai; Celery Cabbage; Napa Cabbage. Varieties come in different shapes: Heads may be long, slender, and cylindrical, with dark green tip leaves, as in Michihli types; or short and barrel-shaped, with yellowish-green or yellow leaves, as in Napa types. The leaf petioles are broad and succulent. Chinese cabbage is cooked, stir fried, or added to salads.

How to Grow

The early onset of warm weather occasionally causes spring-planted Chinese Cabbage to deteriorate before heads reach full size. Avoid very early spring planting, because plants may bolt before heading. Direct-seeding in late summer or fall produces larger heads of high quality. Space plants 1–1½ ft. (30–45 cm) apart. Heads can be protected against frost but will be killed by hard freezes. All Chinese cabbages are difficult to transplant, because they tend to "check" in growth from the slightest cultural or environmental stress. Use peat pots if starting indoors. If flea beetles and root maggots are troublesome, try using spun-bonded row covers to protect the crop and bring it along faster.

Harvest

Harvest the entire plant. Trimmed heads will store for 2–3 weeks if refrigerated in a plastic bag.

Varieties

Among the newer varieties are the early Spring A-1, the tall Jade Pagoda hybrid, and Tropical Delight, a heat-resistant Napa cabbage. Michihli is an old standard.

Chinese Cabbage (nonheading)
Brassica rapa pp. 212, 239

Chinensis Group. Pak-choi; Bok Choy; Celery Mustard; Chinese Mustard. Nonheading Chinese cabbage resembles Swiss chard. This beautiful vegetable is ideal for small gardens and gives good value for the space it occupies. The deep green leaves have a powdery bloom and broad, white petioles that are shingled at the base. The inner leaves cluster but do not form a head.

How to Grow

Pak-choi is a cool-weather vegetable. Direct-seed in early spring and again in late summer. Pak-choi is difficult to transplant except when seedlings are quite small.

Harvest

Take the entire plant or snap off outer leaves.

Varieties
Joi Choi is a hybrid pak-choi. Lei Choi is slow-bolting.

Ornamental Cabbage
Brassica oleracea pp. 200, 201, 203

Acephala Group. Ornamental cabbage, grown principally for colorful edgings and for massing in flower beds, comes in white, cream, purple, pink, green, and lavender bicolor variations. Its upward-facing habit makes the plant look like a stack of nested bowls. The outer leaves of mature plants are tough, but the center leaves make colorful coleslaw and can be boiled. You can also use leaves to line salad plates, or remove the center leaves from young heads to make fancy "bowls" for various fillings.

How to Grow
Flowering cabbage is not nearly as tender as heading cabbage. Start from young plants to get an idea of the colors to expect. Grow as you would garden cabbage but aim for the fall growing season, if possible. The plants are more spectacular when they develop during the cool days of fall. Light frosts don't hurt the plants and intensify flavor. Water plants deeply during dry spells and spray occasionally for cabbage worms.

Harvest
Cut heads just before heavy frost. If you want to eat the cabbage, discard outer leaves.

Varieties
The best garden centers offer a number of varieties. Seed catalogues offer mostly color mixtures.

Cactus
Opuntia spp. *pp. 118, 119*

Opuntia is a very large New World genus that includes several edible species; those known as flat cacti are variously called prickly pear, tuna, Barbary fig, and Indian fig. The many species range in size from low, sprawling kinds to treelike forms 20 ft. (6 m) high. Some are grown for their colorful fruits, called prickly pears; others, for their edible pads, called nopales or nopalitos. Most varieties have spines and prickly bristles (glochids) that must be singed off before the pads can be prepared for eating.

How to Grow
Flat cacti grow easily in warm, dry areas of the West and Southwest and almost as well across the South if given extra-good drainage. Some species are hardy farther north. Where winter temperatures drop to near 0° F (−18° C), the top pads may freeze, but the lower, bark-covered stems usually survive. The low-growing, dark green *O. humifusa* is the only truly winter-hardy species.
Prepare raised beds with sand and organic matter. Space plants about 4 ft. (1.2 m) apart. Propagate cacti by rooting individual pads or pieces of the plant. Let the cut surfaces dry for about 2 weeks, then sink the pad or piece edgewise into sand or sandy soil to a depth of 2–3 in. (5.0–7.5 cm). When small, the plants will grow in tubs of sandy soil, but they rapidly outgrow them.

Harvest
Prickly pears usually turn dark when ripe, and are sweet and juicy when ready. If frost threatens, pick fruits a bit early and ripen indoors. Pads can be singed, then sliced and steamed at any stage of growth. Wear gloves to handle pads or prickly pears and use tongs while singeing or brushing to remove the prickles. Although small and innocent-looking, glochids can penetrate the skin and cause considerable discomfort.

Varieties
Burbank's Spineless Cactus is a well-known cultivar free of spines and glochids.

Cardoon
Cynara cardunculus p. 240

A perennial, cardoon grows 6–8 ft. (1.8–2.4 m) high. It resembles the related artichoke, but the gray-green leaves are shingled and overlap at the base. The wide, fleshy, edible stems form loose stalks or heads like celery. Cardoon plants retain their vase shape until late in the season, when they shoot up a branching central stem on which several buds form that look like small artichokes. These develop into purple thistlelike flowers.

How to Grow
Grow cardoon from offsets, or from seeds, which may be hard to find. Start indoors in early spring and transplant to fertile soil after frost danger is past. Space plants 5 ft. (1.5 m) apart. Where winters are mild, direct-seed in late summer for fall or winter harvest.

Harvest
Slide a sharp knife under the plant to sever the root. Chop off the leaves about where the green blades begin. The stalk or head of clasped leaves is comparable in size to a head of celery. Remove all vestiges of leaves; they tend to be bitter. Tie the loose head with string to keep it together, and steam like other vegetables.

Varieties
Large Smooth is the most popular variety.

Carrot
Daucus carota var. *sativus* pp. 88, 89, 96

Biennials grown as annuals, carrots originated in the Mediterranean area, or possibly Persia. Modern carrots have evolved from large, rough roots once used for feeding livestock and for sugar extraction. Most commercial carrots are long, slender, and tapered, but varieties exist in a wide range of shapes, sizes, and days to maturity.

How to Grow
Home gardeners usually grow thick, medium-length cylindrical varieties or, in heavy soils, short, broad-shouldered, wedge-shaped types. Carrots grow best in a 2 x 8-in. (5 x 20-cm) or 2 x 10-in. (5 x 25-cm) frame filled with equal parts of sand, peat moss, and sifted compost, limed and fertilized. Early in the season, cover the frame with clear plastic and tack it down to collect heat. When weeds begin to sprout, remove the plastic and rake the soil to kill them. Direct-seed carrots 1–2 weeks before the frost-free date; plant in rows, sowing thinly. Replace plastic until seeds sprout, then remove. Straight, separate rows, spaced 12 in. (30 cm) apart, will help you tell carrot seedlings from weedlings, and simplify

cultivation. Seedlings can tolerate light frosts.

Cover the frame with plastic screening to keep out insects. Stretch the screening over sturdy wire hoops that will keep the cover 16 in. (40.5 cm) above the soil surface, giving tops room to grow. Tuck the screen at the corners to exclude small root maggot flies. If you grow carrots in the open garden in the n. or n.-cen. U.S., time plantings to avoid root-maggot infestation. Consult your County Extension Office.

Seed germination can be improved by sowing seeds thinly in a V-shaped furrow pressed into the soil with the edge of a board. Cover seeds with ⅛–¼ in. (3.2–6.0 mm) of sand or sifted compost. Peg down a cover of old burlap, presoaked in water containing a little detergent. Mist once or twice daily. When the first carrot seedlings emerge, remove the burlap (during evening hours); continue to mist the seedlings for a few days.

Thin carrots as soon as seedlings are large enough to grasp. Be ruthless. Crowding, even at young stages, can stunt and distort roots. Thin again when the roots are finger-size. Let the remaining carrots stand about 4 in. (10 cm) apart. Fertilize once or twice during the season; don't use manure or rough compost, which can make the roots fork and grow rough and hairy.

Harvest

Carrots will keep in the ground for several weeks, but they must not be allowed to go dry or they may split when watered. Mature carrots can tolerate moderate freezes if protected with straw mulch. In the North, spring-sown carrots often carry right through to fall with little loss of quality, but in warm climates the flavor deteriorates in hot weather, so time plantings to have crops in spring and fall. In severe winter areas, pull carrot roots before the ground freezes solid and sandwich them between layers of straw or dry leaves. Cover the pile with plastic and peg it down. You can reach in and pull out carrots as needed.

Varieties

Refinements to look for are smooth roots that are easy to wash and need no peeling; uniform interior color—no light core or whitish zoning; and smooth, light-colored shoulders that do not require trimming off.

Here are some of the more popular kinds: Cylindrical, stump-rooted: Nantes, Toudo hybrid, Rondino, Nandor. High vitamin A content: A-Plus hybrid, Juwarot. Baby carrots: Baby Fingers, Little Finger, Lady Finger. (Standard carrots picked at small sizes lack flavor and sweetness.) Round: Kundulus, Pariser Markt. Wedge-shaped: Chantenay, Forto hybrid, Tamba. Long, slim: Gold Pak (AAS).

Cauliflower
Brassica oleracea pp. 207, 208

Botrytis Group. Cauliflower grows on short, cabbagelike plants that form large, flat central clusters of flower buds called curds. The inner leaves on some varieties curve upward and inward to cover and blanch the curd. On other varieties, the outer leaves must be tied together with a rubber band to shade the curd from sun. Unblanched curds may turn an unattractive brownish green. Purple varieties, however, need no blanching.

How to Grow
Cauliflower needs a long, cool growing season and is hypersensitive to having its growth checked. Seedlings that are overly hardened, carelessly transplanted, stressed by weather, or planted too deep may "button"—form small heads on stunted plants. Purchase plants or start seeds indoors 8–10 weeks before the frost-free date. After hardening off, transplant seedlings to the garden. Space them 12–18 in. (30–45 cm) apart, more if soil is very fertile. Light frost will not hurt the seedlings.

Harvest
When the flower buds are small and the head is smooth, cut just beneath the head. Older curds grow rough and bumpy and begin to deteriorate.

Varieties
Snow Crown, an AAS hybrid, is widely adapted. White Contessa has the additional heat resistance needed for southern gardens. Alert hybrid is very early and self-blanching.

Celeriac
Apium graveolens var. *rapaceum p. 97*

Celery Root; Knob Celery; Turnip-rooted
Celery. Although it somewhat resembles the
related celery, this plant is grown for its
edible root, a knobby, turniplike structure
3–4 in. (7.5–10.0 cm) in diameter. The
plants are of open growth habit, with
celerylike leaves on relatively slender stems
growing from the root. Celeriac root tastes
somewhat like celery, but stronger.

How to Grow
Celeriac seeds are fine and slow to sprout.
Seedlings grow slowly and are susceptible to
damping-off. Chances are, you won't be able
to find started plants. In the North, start
seeds indoors very early. In warm climates,
start seeds outdoors under lath shade in
late summer to grow large seedlings
for transplanting when the weather turns
cool. Space seeds 6–12 in. (15–30 cm)
apart.
Celeriac needs lots of water and adequate
plant nutrients to produce large roots.
Prepare raised beds with manure or compost
and incorporate phosphate and calcium
sources. Arrange for drip/trickle irrigation or
circle the bed with an irrigation furrow.
Mulch with straw or bank up around plants
to protect roots for late harvest.

Harvest
Grow enough plants to take your first meal
from small roots, 2–3 in. (5.0–7.5 cm)
in diameter, thinned from the bed. Pull the
entire plant. A few of the small central stems
and leaves may be tender enough to throw
in with the peeled roots a few minutes
before they are fully cooked.

Varieties
Try Blanco, a good modern variety, or the
French variety De Reuil.

Celery
Apium graveolens var. *dulce p. 241*

Growing in the garden, celery is a bushy,
mounded plant; the head or stalk you see on
produce counters is only the center part,
with all the tough outer stems trimmed off.
Varieties come in 3 colors: golden, green,
and a rare reddish-green selection.

How to Grow

No other vegetable demands as much attention, but celery fresh from the garden is indescribably good. A biennial grown as an annual, celery has to grow fast without stress or interruption to develop large, succulent plants during the short cool spring or fall season.

Purchase seedling plants if possible. Growing your own from seeds is difficult unless you have a greenhouse. If the plants are exposed to temperatures of 40–45 °F (4.5–7.0 °C) for 7–10 days, they will go to seed. To avoid this, grow plants in the warm indoors and do not transplant until about the average frost-free date. In the North and in cool highland and coastal gardens, spring is sufficiently long and cool for good stalks to develop before summer heat riddles the plants. But in warm-summer climates, delay planting until late summer and start seeds in a nursery bed protected by lath shade or muslin. Transplant when cool weather comes.

Set seedlings 9–12 in. (22.5–30.0 cm) apart. Keep the celery bed moist but not soaking wet, and fortify frequently with plant nutrients.

When fall frost threatens, stand 1 x 12-in. (2.5 × 30.0-cm) boards on each side of the celery row and bank soil up to hold them in place. Scatter straw over the tops of the plants. Protecting the plants this way not only allows them to keep for 3–4 weeks, but also blanches them to a beautiful golden-yellow.

Harvest

Take one head at a time. Begin eating the thinnings when they are half-grown. If you need less than a full head, you can snap off a few of the tender stems, as long as you don't destroy the center leaf buds.

Varieties

Green: Tall Utah 52-70, Summit (fusarium-tolerant), Green Giant, Tendercrisp. Golden: Golden Plume, Monarch Golden.

Celtuce
Lactuca sativa p. 238

Stem Lettuce; Asparagus Lettuce; Chinese Lettuce. The coined name "celtuce" suggests a cross between celery and lettuce, but this

vegetable is actually a variety of lettuce cultivated for its thick, edible stem and romaine-like leaves. The stem, 6–8 in. (15–20 cm) long and about 1½ in. (4 cm) in diameter, can be cooked like broccoli and tastes like a cross between a mild summer squash and an artichoke. The leaves can be used for salad.

How to Grow
Celtuce grows best in cool seasons. Plant and cultivate it like leaf lettuce. Space plants 8–10 in. (20–25 cm) apart.

Harvest
Use young outer leaves as greens. A few weeks later the stalks will be ready to harvest; peeled, they can be eaten raw or cooked.

Chayote
Sechium edule p. 177

Mirliton; Vegetable Pear. A member of the cucumber family (Cucurbitaceae), chayote is a semi-hardy perennial vine that bears waxy-green, pear-shaped fruits, some spiny, some ridged. Native to tropical America, it needs a long growing season and considerable warmth for fruits to mature. Vines may grow to 15 ft. (4.5 m) long in the mid-South, and to 30 ft. (9 m) in the Southwest.

How to Grow
Fruits don't begin to set until the garden receives at least 12 hours of sunlight and the plants are large enough to support them. These requirements suit chayote best to the Deep South, where it will live over winter with a light mulch. It can be grown as an annual across the mid-South but has a rather short fruiting season before the vines are killed by frost.
Except in nearly frost-free areas, start chayote by potting up 2–3 fruits in 1-gallon (3-l) containers in midspring. Multiple plants ensure good pollination but are not strictly necessary. Lay the fruit on its side and press it halfway into the soil. Cover the pot with plastic wrap and set it in a warm spot, 75–80 °F (24.0–26.5 °C). Water occasionally. The single seed, hidden in the puckered end of the fruit, will strike roots and send out a shoot. When that happens, remove the

plastic and set the pot in full sun in a warm
corner. Once danger of frost is past, tap the
plants out of their pots and set them in
manured garden soil. Leave 4 ft. (1.2 m)
between plants. The sunny side of a building
or fence is a good spot. Provide tall, strong
trellises, or run the vines up into an open
tree. Between rains, soak plants deeply each
week, using manure tea or soluble fertilizer.
Discontinue feeding when first blooms
appear.

Harvest
Pick fruits as soon as they stop growing
larger. Save a few for next year's planting.
Store in a ventilated plastic bag in the
refrigerator at about 40°F (4.5°C) with a
few paper towels in the bag to soak up
moisture; fruits usually keep for 60–90 days.
If stored warm, they will begin to sprout in
a month or two.
Chayote fruits can be peeled, sliced, and
cooked like summer squash but are relatively
bland and need seasoning. Fruits can also be
scooped out and stuffed like peppers. In mild
climates where chayote lives over winter, the
tuberous roots grow quite large and are
eaten candied, boiled, or roasted.

Varieties
Many selections of chayote are grown in
Mexico and Central America—white,
apple-green, or brownish, smooth or spiny.
Gardeners in the U.S., however, must settle
for whatever grows from the chayote fruits
they purchase at the grocery.

Leaf Chicory
Cichorium intybus pp. 215, 226

Resembling cos or romaine lettuce in its
growth habit, leaf chicory forms upright
heads of large, loosely wrapped, dark green
leaves with a slighty bitter tang. Another
form known as Italian chicory has deeply
notched leaves and long stems. Leaf chicory
is more widely grown in Europe than in the
U.S.; a variety is cultivated for the creamy
white buds known as Belgian endive, or
Witloof chicory. Still another variety
(Magdeburg) is grown for its roots, which
are roasted and ground as a coffee additive.

How to Grow

Chicory is a hardy perennial. Plant seeds 6–12 in. (15–30 cm) apart in the garden in midspring in the North and late summer in the Deep South. If you let leaf chicory live over winter, it will shoot up tall stems of attractive light blue flowers in the summer.

Harvest

Spring-planted leaf chicory is ready to eat just before hard frost in the fall, at which time it has only a slightly bitter tang. Chicory planted in late summer is ready to eat by late winter or early spring.

Varieties

Sugarhat; Catalogna is an Italian variety.

Collards
Brassica oleracea p. 213

Acephala Group. Collards resemble nonheading cabbage and have broad, blue-green, smooth leaves. Lower leaves descend with age, while the upper or crown leaves are often cupped. Though similar to the very closely related kale, collards taste slightly different and are preferred across the South.

How to Grow

Collards prefer cool weather and will withstand several degrees of frost; plants also endure dry weather and heat better than cabbage. Direct-seed collards in early spring in the North, and in late summer in warm climates. Seedlings transplant easily if you need only a few plants or if a quicker start is desired. Collards grow quite large and should be thinned to stand 2 ft. (60 cm) apart.

Harvest

Small, tender leaves are best for cooking, but when you harvest them don't cut out the terminal growth or you will set back leaf production. Cool weather sweetens the taste in fall. To sweeten summer-harvested leaves, refrigerate them for 3–4 days.

Varieties

Hicrop hybrid collards have the edge on older, open-pollinated varieties; Vates is a very uniform, standard variety.

CORN

Native to the New World, corn has been a valuable food crop at least since the Incas cultivated it. Modern corn is actually a tall annual grass, and all kinds, including the 3 featured here—ornamental corn, popcorn, and sweet corn—are simply varieties of a single species, *Zea mays*.

Ornamental Corn
Zea mays var. *indurata* p. 123

Flint Corn; Indian Corn; Calico Corn. Ornamental corn comes in a marvelous array of colors, sizes, and shapes. The dried kernels can be ground for corn meal, and young ears can be harvested at milk stage and boiled or barbecued. Most gardeners, however, grow Indian corn solely for ornament; the ears are shucked back to expose the colorful kernels and the husks tied into bunches.

How to Grow
Plant ornamental corn 2–3 weeks after you or your neighbors plant sweet corn, or the two types may cross. Plant like sweet corn but leave plenty of room for the large, late-maturing plants. In the South, gardeners build "hills"—low mounds of soil—3 ft. (90 cm) apart, and plant 6 seeds per hill. Later the plants are thinned to 3 per hill so that they stand roughly 12 in. (30 cm) apart.

Harvest
Ornamental corn doesn't snap easily off the stalk. Rather than yank the ears and risk breaking the stalks, snip them off with pruning shears. If harvesting for edible use, test for tenderness with your thumbnail; corn is ready if a little juice squirts out when you pierce a kernel. Pick before kernels turn tough and doughy. If harvested for ornament, shuck back the ears and place them in a plastic bag with mothballs for 2–3 days to kill weevils and seed-eating larvae. Then sun-dry the ears to dissipate the chemical smell.

Varieties
Grow from shelled kernels or order from catalogues. Indian Fingers has slender ears only 3–4 in. (7.5–10.0 cm) long.

Popcorn
Zea mays var. *praecox pp. 122, 125*

High-quality bulk popcorn seed is so readily
available and inexpensive in grocery stores
that you may choose not to plant it;
popcorn does take up a lot of garden space
and requires a long season to reach maturity.
Nevertheless, excellent popcorn hybrids with
white or golden kernels are available, as well
as ornamental selections, including one with
ruby-colored kernels. Hybrids pop more
reliably and expand to greater volumes than
the old open-pollinated popping corns.

How to Grow
See ornamental corn. Plant 6–9 in.
(15.0–22.5 cm) apart or in hills 2–3 ft.
(60–90 cm) apart. If sweet corn has been
planted within a quarter-mile radius, delay
planting popcorn for 2–3 weeks to avoid
cross-pollination, which can ruin the flavor
of sweet corn.

Harvest
Dry ears on the stalk. Ears will shed water
better if you break stalks down as soon as
the husks start to dry. If cold wet weather
threatens, snap off the ears, shuck them back,
and dry them on a screen rack in a warm,
well-ventilated room. Dust the ears with a
sprinkling of pyrethrum to discourage
seed-eating insects.

Varieties
Yellow: Creme-Puff Hybrid. Early yellow:
Tom Thumb. White: Popwhite, White
Cloud hybrid, Burpee's Peppy Hybrid.
Ornamental: Cutie Pops, Symphonie,
Strawberry.

Sweet Corn
Zea mays var. *rugosa pp. 124, 125*

Freshly harvested sweet corn is so noticeably
superior to its store-bought counterpart
that it well deserves its popularity in home
gardens. Nothing tastes like an ear of corn
cooked as soon as it is picked. Sweet corn
with yellow kernels is the favorite, but across
the South, white varieties are preferred. Some
of the newer hybrids have bicolor—white
and yellow—kernels, and these are becoming
increasingly common. Ears range in size
from slender and 6 in. (15 cm) long with

8 rows of kernels to heavy and 9 in. (22.5 cm) long or more, with 16–18 rows of kernels. Generally, the later the variety, the larger the ear. The most desirable varieties have large ears and deep, tender kernels.

Relative sweetness is another variable. Standard sweet corn is quite flavorful when cooked soon after harvest. But there are now ultra- and super-sweet hybrids, as well as bicolor hybrids with one super-sweet parent, that are bred for enhanced sugar. The sugar in these sweeter varieties does not convert to starch as rapidly as in standard varieties. Recently developed super-sweet hybrids can remain in the field for a few days when ripe without losing peak quality.

In the North, where the growing season is short, early and extra-early hybrids are preferred. Elsewhere these varieties can be planted in late summer and harvested just before fall frost. Growers rely on midseason (main-crop) or late hybrids for heavy yields of corn for freezing, canning, or fresh use.

How to Grow

Sweet corn is a frost-tender annual, but some gardeners gamble and plant seeds 2–3 weeks prior to the average frost-free date. Vigorous hybrids can come back from a light frost, but prolonged, cold wet weather can rot seeds, especially those of the super-sweet hybrids.

Sweet corn must have full sun. Early crops do better in fast-draining sand or loam, while later, larger varieties like the nutrient and water reserves of heavier loam or clay soils.

Starting corn indoors and transplanting is expensive and is recommended only in the far North. Instead, where seasons are short, apply a clear plastic mulch as soon as the soil has warmed and plant corn seeds through slits cut in it.

Direct-seed corn 2 in. apart in rows 2–3 ft. (60–90 cm) apart. Cover seeds with 1 in. (2.5 cm) of soil. In hot, dry climates, plant seeds 1½–2 in. (4–5 cm) deep in furrows that have been previously flooded. Plant sweet corn in a block of several short rows. Thin seedlings to stand 6–12 in. (15–30 cm) apart, depending on plant size, soil fertility, and your ability to keep the corn watered.

Extremely dry or hot weather can affect pollination, as can prolonged rain and high winds. Poor kernel formation can also be caused by nutritional deficiencies.

Sweet corn needs a moderate amount of fertilizer. Early varieties usually need only one preplant application of complete fertilizer plus a mulch of compost. Later varieties draw more heavily on the soil and need a supplementary feeding when 12–18 in. (30–45 cm) tall. Use a 10-10-10 or similar ratio fertilizer. In the South, 13-13-13, plus important micronutrients, is a popular formula.

Harvest

When the silks look brown, pull back a strip of corn shuck on one ear to expose a few kernels. Test for tenderness with your thumbnail. Sweet corn is in its prime at "milk" stage—when milky juice squirts out of the pierced kernel. In the "dough" stage it is a little overripe—still usable for creamed corn and barbecuing, but a bit chewy for boiling. Pull down and twist the ears to snap them off the stalk.

You can control corn earworms and tomato fruitworms somewhat by spraying mineral oil on the silks a day or two after you see a dusting of pollen on them.

Varieties

The choice is immense. Among the factors to consider are days to maturity (early, midseason, or late); kernel color (yellow, white, or bicolor); ear size (small, medium, large); relative sweetness (standard, very sweet, super-sweet, or ultra-sweet).

Super-sweet and ultra-sweet varieties should be grown in isolation so that they won't cross with standard types. Here are just a few of the more popular hybrids. Early standard: Aztec, Early Sunglow, Party Time, Polar Vee, Seneca Star. Midseason standard: Candystick, Honey & Cream, Seneca Chief (AAS). Midseason very sweet: Crusader. Midseason super-sweet: Butterfruit Bicolor. Midseason ultra-sweet: How Sweet It Is (AAS). Late standard: Silver Queen. Late very sweet: Great Taste, Kandy Korn E.H. Late super-sweet: Burpee's Sugar Sweet, Florida Staysweet.

Common Corn Salad
Valerianella locusta p. 226

Mache; Lamb's Lettuce; Feldsalat. Corn salad is a homely, weedy-looking vegetable that forms small rosettes of smooth, spoon-shaped leaves. In Europe it is a forage crop for sheep and a pest in wheat and corn fields, but is nonetheless coveted by fine chefs, who prize these early spring greens.

How to Grow
Corn salad is quite hardy and in most climates will overwinter, withstanding temperatures of about 5°F (−15°C). Straw mulch may be needed where very cold weather occurs without snow cover. Plant seeds thickly from late summer through fall and again in early spring. Cover with ¼ in. (6 mm) sand. Grow in full sun. Feed and water occasionally to maintain good foliage color.

Harvest
Begin pulling corn salad when leaves are large enough to eat. When flowerheads shoot up, harvest all the plants; those left to flower deteriorate quickly. Store corn salad in a plastic bag in the refrigerator but don't wash until just before use; it should keep for 2–3 weeks. Before eating, separate the wadded-up leaves and rinse thoroughly to remove sand.

Varieties
The French variety A Grosse Graine is available, as is the early Cavallo. Broad Leaved is a standard variety.

CRESS

It should come as no surprise that the pungent salad plants commonly known as cress are all members of the mustard family (Cruciferae). Watercress (*Nasturtium officinale*), native to Europe but naturalized in North American streams, is probably the most familiar. Upland cress (*Barbarea verna*) and the peppery sprouts of curled cress (*Lepidium sativum* var. *crispum*) are both easy to grow and good substitutes for watercress.

Curled Cress
Lepidium sativum var. *crispum p. 230*

Garden Cress; Peppergrass. A quick-growing, piquant vegetable, curled cress is usually added in small amounts to salads or cold stuffings, or used as a garnish. It makes a fine substitute for watercress in spring and fall. The medium-green leaves are deeply cut and lacy-looking.

How to Grow
Plant seeds thickly in full sun in early spring. Feed and water occasionally to promote quick, tender growth. The plants develop so rapidly that they should be seeded in short rows every 2 weeks to keep fresh leaves coming. Stop planting during summer. Begin sowing seeds again in late summer under light shade. Water fall crops frequently. Curled cress usually survives until temperatures drop to 20°F (−6.5°C). To raise crops of edible sprouts indoors, sow seeds on damp blotters; seedlings will appear in 4–5 days.

Harvest
Curled cress is ready for harvest when 6–12 in. (15–30 cm) high. You can take the entire plant, but if you have only a few, try shearing plants back halfway; strong ones will regrow.

Varieties
Most seeds sold as curled cress produce pretty plants with rather plain leaves; some European sources offer improved, fancy-leaf varieties.

Upland Cress
Barbarea verna p. 230

Early Winter Cress; American Cress; Belle Isle Cress; Scurvy Grass. Originally from Europe, this cool-weather biennial has naturalized widely and may escape to become a troublesome weed. Plants grow quickly into dandelionlike rosettes of dark green, deeply lobed leaves. Upland cress is used in salads, or to add a nippy taste to mixed greens for cooking.

How to Grow
Direct-seed in late summer for fall and early spring harvest. Plants are small and can stand

3–6 in. (7.5–15.0 cm) apart. Provide afternoon shade in hot climates. Where winters are very cold and snow cover sparse, sow seeds in very early spring. Upland cress is also a good winter greenhouse crop.

Harvest
Pull entire plants.

Watercress
Nasturtium officinale p. 231

In cool, flowing brooks, watercress plants form mats of floating stems and leaves, anchored to the shore by roots. Although this hardy perennial prefers an aquatic environment, home gardeners will find it simple to grow as a terrestrial plant.

How to Grow
Watercress grows almost as well in moist soil under light shade as in flowing water. Start from seeds or from cuttings of fresh watercress sprigs rooted in water; either way is easy and fast. Soak seeds for 12–24 hours before planting. Watercress is winter-hardy in fast-flowing streams but can freeze in containers or in the garden, so keep soil constantly moist and lightly shaded. Maintain soil pH close to 7.0 and fertility at moderate to high levels. Thin plants to stand 12 in. (30 cm) apart. Plants do well in a shallow, 5–7-gal. (1–2-l) container with drainage holes, such as a plastic basin. Set the container in a large saucer and water plants from the bottom, but do not let water stand in the saucer.

Harvest
Watercress will endure frequent but not severe cutting back. Snip off tips beyond where they set anchor roots.

Cucumber
Cucumis sativus pp. 180, 182, 184, 185, 192

Cucumbers grow on sprawling, medium-length vines with rough, dark green, 3-pointed leaves. Seeds are available for 3 classes: short, blocky varieties developed primarily for pickling; long, cylindrical "slicers" for fresh use; and very long, ridged "Oriental" or "burpless" cucumbers with

tapered stem ends. In recent years breeders have improved this garden crop immensely, introducing varieties resistant to several diseases and with reduced bitterness; breeders have also recently developed cucumber plants with short, compact vines that cover an area no more than 4 ft. (120 cm) wide. All-female (gynoecious) varieties now exist for greater fruit yield, as do self-fertile (parthenocarpic) varieties that set fruit without pollination, producing seedless cucumbers.

How to Grow
Plant cucumber seeds in warm soil 7–10 days after the average frost-free date. Cucumbers are frost-tender and need full sun and good air circulation. From the central states northward, use black plastic mulch to help speed maturity. To maximize production, plant in raised beds (except on deep sand) with plenty of manure worked into the soil. Plants should be at least 12 in. (30 cm) apart. In areas with 5 or more warm growing months a second crop can be planted after midsummer and picked before frost.
Gardeners who grow many vines let them sprawl and run, but others prefer to train vines up cages or slanted trellises. Supports simplify picking and reduce wear and tear on vines.
Gynoecious hybrids must be planted with a few seeds of a standard variety to provide male flowers so that pollination can occur. Parthenocarpic varieties, on the other hand, must be isolated from other cucumber types to avoid pollination, since the object is to produce seedless fruits.

Harvest
Pick cucumbers before they reach full size, when they begin to fade or turn yellow. Overly mature fruits have tough seeds and are marginally palatable.

Varieties
Ask your County Cooperative Extension Service office for a list of cucumber varieties recommended for your area. Look for those with multiple disease resistance. Gynoecious varieties are designated GY.
Short, blocky picklers: Wisconsin SMR 58, Pioneer GY, Lucky Strike GY, Liberty (AAS). Long, straight slicers: Dublin GY (early), Raider GY, Victory GY (AAS), Poinsett, Early Triumph, Slicemaster GY. Nonbitter slicers: Sweet Slice, Burpless,

Peppi, Marketmore 80, Amira, Park's
Burpless Bush, Euro-American Hybrid.
Parthenocarpic garden types: Sweet Success
(AAS), County Fair. Bush types (all slicers
except as noted): Bush Crop, Spacemaster,
Patio Pick, Bush Whopper, Bush Champion,
Bush Pickle (pickler). Novelties: Lemon
(lemon shaped), China, Vert de Massy (for
cornichons), Armenian.

Dandelion
Taraxacum officinale p. 229

Cultivated dandelion plants form large
clumps of long, dark green, brittle leaves
that invite plucking for the cookpot; not
all the wild bitterness has been bred out.
Cultivated dandelions resemble the common
lawn pest, but are more massive.

How to Grow
Grow this perennial as a hardy annual. Start
seeds indoors in peat pots in early spring, or
late summer in warm climates. Transplant to
rich, moist soil in full sun. Leave 4–6 in.
(10–15 cm) between plants.

Harvest
Harvest spring-sown dandelions in late
spring. Do not let plants flower and go to
seed, or they will become weedy pests.
Harvest the fall crop through midwinter;
take roots and all to eliminate any chance of
regrowth and flowering. Half-grown plants
sweetened by cold weather are the best. You
can improve the flavor of greens cut in warm
weather by storing them in a refrigerator for
a few days. A plastic bag will reduce wilting
from water loss.

Varieties
Cultivated dandelions are ordinarily sold by
the species name only, or by a descriptive
name such as "thick-leaved."

Eggplant
Solanum melongena var. *esculentum pp. 128,
129, 131*

Aubergine; Brinjal; Melongene. This ancient
Asian food plant has gained popularity in
the U.S. thanks to the introduction of
early-maturing varieties that set fruit over a

wider range of temperatures. Modern eggplant varieties develop upright bushes with large, furry leaves and stiff, hard stems. Most plants grow 1½–2 ft. (45–60 cm) high, but some varieties adapted to the South can top 3–4 ft. (90–120 cm). Many shapes and sizes of fruit are available, from large, plump, and ovoid to long and slender. Domestic varieties are purple, purple-black, or white; Asian varieties include yellow, green, and purplish red.

How to Grow

To germinate well, eggplant seeds need warm soil—75–80° F (24.0–26.5° C)—and are usually started indoors 8–10 weeks prior to the frost-free date. Seedlings need strong sunlight or fluorescent light in late winter, and they should not be set in the garden until 2–3 weeks after the average frost-free date; cold soil can shock them. Transplant in the evening to ease the transition. Set plants about 2½ ft. (75 cm) apart and cover the seedlings with bottomless 1-gal. (3-l) plastic jugs to ward off wind and cold. Remove jugs after 2–3 weeks.

In most areas, eggplants benefit from black plastic mulch, but in the lower South and warm West, soil temperatures can rise too high under it. Verticillium wilt is a serious and widespread soil-borne disease. Some gardeners grow eggplant in containers to avoid it.

Harvest

Eggplant is ready to harvest when fruits are half-grown and skin is still shiny. Mature fruits have dull skin; the seeds turn dark and the flesh may be bitter. Use pruning shears or heavy kitchen scissors to snip off the tough stems. Wear cotton gloves if the stems, leaves, or caps of fruits are spiny.

Varieties

Oval fruits: Dusky, Beauty Hybrid, Florida Market (for the South), Early Beauty. Long fruits: Ichiban, Agora.

Curly Endive; Escarole
Cichorium endiva pp. 219, 228

Endive and escarole are basically the same vegetable, but endive has cut and curled leaves, whereas escarole has smooth, broad leaves. Restaurants frequently use endive to line salad bowls or mix with lettuce in tossed salads. The leaves are chewier and more substantial than those of lettuce.

How to Grow
Spring-planted endive or escarole does well only where summers are quite cool. It should not be planted extra early; prolonged cold weather can trigger seedlings to bolt and flower prematurely. If subjected to hot weather before they are large enough to harvest, endive and escarole may acquire a bitter taste. For successful crops in the North, plant in midsummer; in the Deep South and warm West, plant in early fall. Space plants 12 in. (30 cm) apart. In warm soil the plants get a good start and grow rapidly, maturing during cool fall or winter weather. Fall endive is a welcome change from lettuce.
Blanching, a process that takes 2–3 weeks, turns the naturally dark green plants an attractive creamy white and reduces bitterness. If you have only a few plants, cover them with inverted bushel baskets. Use a temporary plywood A-frame to cover a row of several plants. Wait until plants are dry to cover them, since moisture collected in the heads may cause them to rot.

Harvest
Take the entire plant. The inner leaves are best for salads; the outer leaves, together with plants left unblanched, can be cooked with other fall greens. This perennial often attempts to come back after it has been cut, but the quality is not as good. Experienced gardeners replant every year.

Varieties
Curly endive: Grossr-Pomant Seule, Salad King, Green Curled. Escarole: Nufema (early), Batavian Full Heart.

Florence Fennel
Foeniculum vulgare var. *azoricum p. 240*

Finocchio. Florence fennel looks much like the herb sweet fennel, but it has a swollen leaf base (commonly called a bulb) comprised of wide-ribbed, tightly clasped solid stems. The finely divided, needlelike foliage resembles dill but is apple-green instead of bluish green, and has the aroma

and flavor of anise. The bulbs are edible raw
or cooked and the foliage may be used as a
garnish.

How to Grow
Bulbs develop best in cool weather; grow
like a cool-season annual. In the North start
seeds early in peat pots indoors; after
hardening off, transplant seedlings to the
garden 2–3 weeks before the frost-free date.
Space plants 6–12 in. (15–30 cm) apart.
Although Florence fennel is half-hardy, late
spring freezes can kill unprotected seedlings.
In mild areas, late summer is a good time
for starting seeds. Under favorable conditions
the bulbs usually size up before winter. Some
gardeners pull loose soil up around the bulbs
to blanch them.

Harvest
Pull the entire plant. Trim off stems ½–1 in.
(13–25 mm) from the bulb. The larger stems
can be chopped and cooked with the bulb.
Use the foliage for garnishing.

Varieties
An early variety is Romano Precoce.

Garlic
Allium sativum pp. 108, 109

Members of the onion family, garlic plants
have large, flattened leaves somewhat like
those of bearded iris. At the base they
produce segmented bulbs covered with a
papery white skin; the bulbs can be broken
into several cloves, which are used for
seasoning. Elephant, or giant, garlic is a
different species (*Allium scorodoprasum*) with
larger, milder cloves.

How to Grow
Garlic does not set fertile seeds but is
reproduced from cloves. Divide bulbs into
cloves and plant 2–3 in. (5.0–7.5 cm) deep
and 3 in. (7.5 cm) apart in well-drained soil
in full sun. Midspring is the best time for
planting except in the South and warm
West, where late summer planting works
well. Most bulbs will survive in the ground
over winter except in extremely cold areas.
The following summer, cease watering when
foliage turns yellow and break tops over at
the base to hasten drying.

Harvest
After 2–3 weeks, when broken plant tops are
brown and dry, gently lift the bulbs and
sun-dry them for a few days. The plants can
then be plaited into garlic chains or the tops
removed and the bulbs stored in a dark area.
Small cloves may grow into unsegmented
"rounds"; these can be replanted to develop
into larger bulbs with the typical count of
7–10 cloves.

Varieties
Silverskin is the common variety; others are
available in Calif., the center of commercial
production. You can also buy potted,
sprouted cloves the size of small scallions.

West Indian Gherkin
Cucumis anguria p. 187

Gooseberry Gourd; Bur Gourd. West Indian
is the true old-time gherkin, but it has been
largely displaced by juvenile cucumber
impostors. The long vines have deeply
3-lobed leaves that distinguish the plants
from cucumbers or melons. The fruits, borne
on long stems, are 2 in. (5 cm) long and
covered with soft spines.

How to Grow
Gherkins can be grown as far north as s.
Mich. if black plastic mulch is used. Fruits
begin to set about 30 days after early
cucumbers. Grow like any rambling vine
crop, but allow plenty of room; a wire trellis
makes harvesting easier.

Harvest
Fruits are ready to harvest when 1½–2 in.
(4–5 cm) long. When tinged with yellow,
gherkins are too seedy. Peel and eat like
cucumbers, or pickle them.

Ginger
Zingiber officinale pp. 98, 99

Ginger is a tall, dark green, lilylike plant
that grows from a spreading mat of edible
tuberous roots (rhizomes). A fairly common
perennial in mild-winter areas, ginger can
become a pest in moist, fertile soil. Farther
north it is usually grown in containers.

How to Grow
Sprout pieces of ginger root in a shallow, 5–10-gal. (20–40-l) container of potting soil or sand; transplant them to the garden when a strong root system has formed, leaving 12 in. (30 cm) between plants. Grow ginger in light shade except in northern gardens, where it benefits from reflected light and heat. Water fairly often. In the North, move containers to a cool storage area indoors before frost. Let plant tops dry; when they turn yellow, trim off. Water monthly, just enough to keep roots from drying out. In spring, move containers to a sunny, protected spot to start top growth.

Harvest
Grow more than one plant so you can have starter roots for the next year. Dig the roots with a spading fork just before frost. To harvest from containers, grabble for roots with your hands or dump out the root ball. Store at room temperature. Rhizomes may be sliced or grated for fresh use in stir-fry recipes, or crystallized; dried and ground, the roots yield the familiar spice.

Good-King-Henry
Chenopodium bonus-henricus p. 232

Goosefoot; Mercury; Fat-hen; Wild Spinach. An aggressive, spreading plant to 3 ft. (90 cm) high, this perennial potherb has a deep rootstock that sends up many stems with spinachlike, arrow-shaped leaves. The tender young leaves and branch tips are often cooked with other potherbs.

How to Grow
Good-King-Henry grows best in rich, fairly moist soil. After frost danger is past, direct-seed in furrows, pressing seeds into the soil with the edge of a board. Plant 2–3 seeds every 6–12 in. (15–30 cm). When seedlings are large enough to eat, thin by pulling entire plants, leaving the remainder 1½–2 ft. (45–60 cm) apart. Feed with high-nitrogen fertilizer 3 times yearly.

Harvest
Prune or pinch off branch tips for the cookpot. Well-nourished plants will rebranch with each shearing, but don't let seeds form or you will risk a weed problem.

Cape Gooseberry
Physalis peruviana p. 130

Ground Cherry; Husk Tomato. Originally from the New World and introduced throughout the tropics, this species is seldom seen in the U.S. except in Pennsylvania Dutch country and parts of the Midwest. The sprawling vines grow to 2 ft. (60 cm) high, spreading 3–4 ft. (90–120 cm) wide. Fruits, ½–¾ in. (13–19 mm) in diameter, are enclosed in loose, papery husks blushed with purple. When ripe the fruits look like yellow cherry tomatoes. They are much smaller and sweeter than tomatillos and can be eaten raw or used in preserves.

How to Grow
Start seeds indoors and grow like tomatoes. Plant in sandy loam soil; if soil is clayey, plant in raised beds. Space plants 12 in. (30 cm) apart. Use black plastic mulch; in the Deep South, paint the plastic white to reduce heat absorption. Do not work manure into the soil or feed heavily, or the vines will grow too lush and set fruits sparingly. Don't overplant; a mulched plant can yield up to 3 lbs. (1.35 kg) of fruit.

Harvest
Fruits drop when ripe or nearly so; they are sweetest when fully ripe. Plastic or packed straw mulch keeps fallen fruits clean.

Dwarf Cape Gooseberry
Physalis pruinosa p. 130

Strawberry Tomato; Ground Cherry. Most seed companies offer this species rather than *P. peruviana* because the plants are smaller and more manageable—18–20 in. (45–50 cm) high and 2–3 ft. (60–90 cm) wide. Fruits are much like those of *P. peruviana* in size and flavor, but the husks are distinctive; they fit tightly, curling back to reveal the ripe fruits.

How to Grow
Grow like tomatoes, but space plants 12 in. (30 cm) apart. About 70 days of warm, frost-free weather are required for first fruits to mature. If whiteflies are a problem, spray undersides of leaves with insecticidal soap.

Harvest
Fruits drop when ripe. They can be prepared
like vegetables or eaten as a fruit; the taste is
reminiscent of apples.

GOURDS

Unlike their edible close relatives—melons,
pumpkins, squashes, and cucumbers—
ornamental gourds are grown chiefly for
show. All belong to the cucumber family
(Cucurbitaceae) and have similar cultivation
requirements. Some have oddly shaped or
grotesque fruits that may be dried, while
others are extremely decorative and are
grown to cover porches or fences. All are
tendril-bearing vines that will sprawl unless a
support is provided.

Balsam Apple
Momordica balsamita pp. 186, 187

A food crop in the Orient, the balsam apple
is grown only for ornament in this country.
It differs from the balsam pear in having
deeply lobed, sharply toothed leaves; the
fruit, only 3 in. (7.5 cm) long, tapers toward
both ends. The "apple" in the name does
not refer to the gourd's shape but to the
brilliant red arils (tissue) inside, revealed
when the mature orange skin splits.

How to Grow and Harvest
Cultivate and harvest like balsam pear.

Balsam Pear
Momordica charantia p. 186

Bitter Cucumber; Bitter Melon; La-Kwa.
Frost-tender plants grown as warm-weather
annuals, balsam pears are lush, high-climbing
tropical perennial vines. The foliage is large,
deeply lobed, and dark green, and the flowers
are yellow. Where summers are long and
warm, the vines produce attractive,
oblongish, warty fruits with waxy, light
green to greenish-white skin. At maturity the
fruits develop an orange blush; the rind dries
and splits to reveal the bright scarlet arils
(tissue) surrounding the brown or white
seeds. The fruits are eaten in the Orient, but

are chiefly cultivated as ornamentals in
the U.S.

How to Grow
Start seeds indoors in pots 6–8 weeks prior
to the spring frost-free date, except in the
South and warm West, where direct-seeding
works well. Transplant seedlings to the
garden when soil is warm and all danger of
frost is past. Set plants 2 ft. (60 cm) apart.
In the North, run the vines up a fence or
wall facing west or south. Provide a tall,
sturdy arbor, trellis, or wire support.

Harvest
For a decorative display, leave a few balsam
pears on the vine to mature and split open.
If you want to try eating balsam pears,
harvest fruits when half-mature and no more
than 6 in. (15 cm) long; they taste only
slightly bitter then, but older fruit can be
formidably bitter and chewy.

Varieties
Two edible forms are grown in the Orient,
one with long fruit, the other with short.
The long-fruited type is more popular in
the U.S.

Bottle Gourd
Lagenaria siceraria pp. 178, 179

White-flowered Gourd; Calabash. This gourd
is the fruit of a musky-scented vine native to
the Old World tropics; a quick-growing
perennial, it can reach 30 ft. (9.0 m). The
vine has a sticky-hairy stem and branched
tendrils. Leaves are green and broadly oval or
kidney-shaped; flowers are white and showy.
The variable fruit, 3–36 in. (7.5–90.0 cm)
long, may be round or flattish, crooknecked,
and shaped like a bottle, dipper, club, or
dumbbell. Although young fruits can be
eaten, bottle gourds are principally grown for
ornament.

How to Grow
After frost danger is past, plant seeds in
groups of 3 at the base of a tall trellis or
other support. Gourd seeds are large and
have a high germination rate. Feed once or
twice during growing season and water
during dry spells.

Harvest

If you wish to eat the fruits, pick them when they are less than a week old and have tender skins. Scrape off skin with a paring knife and cut off ½ in. (13 mm) from both ends. Cook like summer squash. To dry, harvest gourds just before frost. Leave 2–3 in. (5.0–7.5 cm) of stem on the fruit, and handle carefully to avoid bruising. Dry gourds in a warm, well-ventilated room.

Hercules' War Club Gourd
Lagenaria longissima p. 182

This gourd, probably simply a form of *L. siceraria,* is a popular vegetable in the Orient, particularly in China, where it is called "upo." Growing on vigorous plants, the light green fruits are long and thin, narrowing toward the stem. They may be as much as 3 ft. (90 cm) long but are best eaten when only 6 in. (15 cm) long. Fruits taste like a tender, creamy summer squash.

How to Grow and Harvest
See balsam pear.

Serpent Gourd
Trichosanthes anguina p. 183

Snake Gourd; Club Gourd. A tall-growing annual vine with angled, hairy stems and branched tendrils, this plant has white flowers and broadly angled or lobed leaves. The fruit is 1–5 ft. (0.3–1.5 m) long, greenish white, and cucumberlike; slender and tapering, it varies in shape and may be curved, coiled, or club-shaped. Used as food in India, where it is native, the serpent gourd is grown in the U.S. as a curiosity.

How to Grow and Harvest
See bottle gourd. Serpent gourds may be cooked but are not used for drying.

Groundnut
Apios americana p. 115

American Potato Bean; Wild Bean. This food crop was valued by Native Americans and by frontiersmen, who likened the

leguminous plant to beans because of its pods, and the small, starchy, edible tubers, borne in strings, to potatoes. The plants do look like sparsely leaved pole beans, and they bear short clusters of fragrant brownish flowers. In the wild, the species grows as a perennial from Tex. north to Minn. and to the East Coast. The plant prefers sandy, fertile soil in open woods or thickets.

How to Grow
Order seeds or plants from wildflower specialists. Grow as an annual from tubers or from seeds harvested from the pods. Plant in fertile, sandy soil and treat the plants as you would pole beans. Success should come from interplanting among sweet corn, because groundnuts prefer light shade.

Harvest
Dig tubers in the fall and dry thoroughly. Be careful to keep the strings of little tubers more or less intact to minimize loss and reduce volunteers.

Horseradish
Armoracia rusticana pp. 98, 99

This winter-hardy perennial herb, native to se. Europe, is so aggressive and persistent that it has escaped from gardens and has naturalized in some areas. Horseradish plants are 2–2½ ft. (60–75 cm) high at maturity and have large, coarse leaves resembling the common weed curly dock. The edible root is stout and deep.

How to Grow
Horseradish grows well in a 30-gal. (100-l) plastic garbage pail with the bottom cut out. Sink the pail 12 in. (30 cm) deep into the ground for stability and fill the container with potting soil to within 2 in. (5 cm) of the top. Plant it with a root cutting in the spring.

Harvest
In midsummer, remove the potting soil to a depth of 18 in. (45 cm); rub off any side roots from the main root. Replace the potting soil. Harvest the root in late autumn; the summer rubdown will have

prevented branching, and you should have a long, smooth central root. Cut off any side roots and bury them in a bed of moist sand, mulched against freezing. Most will have rooted by the following spring. Harvest horseradish every year to keep the plant from invading your garden. Old roots are stringy and make inferior horseradish dressing.

Varieties
Maliner Kren is the true Bohemian variety.

Garden Huckleberry
Solanum melanocerasum p. 129

This tender annual grows 2½–3 ft. (75–90 cm) tall and has large leaves on robust, spreading plants. Great numbers of small white flowers are followed by clusters of shiny black berries ½–⅝ in. (13–16 mm) in diameter. This species is distinct from *S. nigrum,* the deadly nightshade, which should be avoided.

How to Grow
Plant as you would tomatoes, preferably using plastic mulch, which makes it easier to collect ripe fruits that drop. Pick up all fruits, because they can be the source of troublesome volunteers.

Harvest
Pick only ripe fruits, but do not eat them raw. Cook for use in pies or preserves, or mix them with dark-colored vegetables. The black juice will stain.

Jerusalem Artichoke
Helianthus tuberosus pp. 100, 101

Sunchoke; Girasole. A native hardy perennial grown for its edible tubers, the Jerusalem artichoke is a relative of the sunflower; it is not related to the globe artichoke. (The name is a corruption of the Italian name, girasole.) This species is robust, durable, and widely adapted. The tubers have a texture like early potatoes but taste slightly sweeter, and can be eaten raw or cooked like potatoes. They contain inulin, a carbohydrate that diabetics can assimilate. Plants reach 6 ft. (1.8 m) high in sunny, dry locations and grow much taller in fertile soil and semishade. Clumps spread rapidly and can become a weedy pest. The dark-centered yellow flowers are filled with small seeds, which are attractive to birds. Too rough-looking to be used as a landscape plant, Jerusalem artichoke is usually relegated to a far corner of the garden.

How to Grow
Grow from tubers that can be ordered by mail or purchased from health food stores or gourmet produce shops. Plant the tubers 2 in. (5 cm) deep and 2 ft. (60 cm) apart, in early spring or late summer. The plants are not fussy about soil but they have a better yield when fertilized with manure and watered during dry spells.

Harvest
In the fall, dig the tubers carefully, sifting the soil to prevent unwanted escapes. Dry tubers thoroughly and store in a cool, dry place.

Varieties
The few named varieties are usually available only to commercial growers.

Jicama
Pachyrhizus erosus pp. 100, 101

Xiquima; Sakalu; Yam Bean. Jicama is a familiar root vegetable on the West Coast and throughout the Southwest where Mexican food is popular; it is also grown in parts of the Orient. The climbing vines grow 15 ft. (4.5 m) high and bear poisonous seeds in pods 6–8 in. (15–20 cm) long. The edible root is lobed, tapered, and brownish white, with snow-white flesh. The roots usually weigh 8–16 oz. (227–454 g); they contain about 10 percent starch and 1 percent protein. In the U.S., we seldom see the beautiful sprays of mauve, butterflylike blossoms of jicama because the vines are usually killed by frost before they bloom.

How to Grow
Except in nearly frost-free areas, the roots will not reach a worthwhile size. Direct-seed in sandy soil in a warm, dry area. Leave 12 in. (30 cm) between plants. Prune off

the blossom sprays to divert energy into root formation.

Harvest
Young roots taste better than large, fibrous old tubers that have survived several winters. Harvest 8–10 months after planting seeds. Each plant produces 1 tuber. Peel, slice thin, or grate for salads, or mix the tuber with fruits and marinate in orange juice. Jicama can also be added to other vegetables and cooked.

Kale
Brassica oleracea pp. 204, 205

Acephala Group. Kale is like a nonheading cabbage and differs slightly from collards in appearance and taste. Most kale varieties have erect, green to deep blue-green leaves with fringed or wavy edges and long petioles.

How to Grow
Kale prefers cool weather and will withstand several degrees of frost. Plant kale seeds in the garden in early spring and again in late summer. If you need only a few plants or if a quicker start is desired, transplant seedlings. Since plants grow quite large, thin them to 2 ft. (60 cm) apart.

Harvest
Kale is harvested like collards. Small, tender leaves are better for cooking, but don't cut out the terminal growth or you will set back leaf production. Cool fall weather sweetens the taste; refrigerate summer-harvested leaves for 3–4 days to get the same result.

Varieties
Dwarf Blue Curled Scotch kale is a compact, dark blue-green variety with fancy frilled leaves. Winterbor Hybrid is extra hardy.

Ornamental Kale
Brassica oleracea pp. 201, 202, 203

Acephala Group. Ornamental, or flowering, kale is a colorful plant with frilly leaves and an open growth habit. The leaves are richly colored and variegated with purple, cream,

pink, white, or rose. It is edible but not bred for tenderness.

How to Grow
Though often sold as a spring bedding plant, flowering kale prefers cool weather and does best in fall gardens, or in winter gardens where the temperature remains above about 20° F (−6.5° C). Sow seeds in the garden and protect seedlings from cabbage worms and aphids. If grown in spring, start indoors 8–10 weeks before the frost-free date and set out as soon as soil can be worked. Harden off transplants thoroughly. Space plants 12–18 in. (30–45 cm) apart.

Harvest
Only the small leaves are tender. Snap these off and cook them like cabbage.

Varieties
Peacock Pink, Cherry Gateau, Frizzy Red, Frizzy White, Red on Green, White on Green.

Kohlrabi
Brassica oleracea p. 208

Gongylodes Group. Turnip Cabbage; Stem Turnip. A close relative of cabbage, kohlrabi grows from an erect stem that forms a turniplike swelling just above ground level. The edible swollen stem is often called a bulb. Kohlrabi leaves, arising from the bulb on long petioles, have a color and texture comparable to cabbage. There are green- or purple-skinned varieties, both of which have greenish-white flesh. Ready to eat only a few weeks after direct-seeding, kohlrabi is a vegetable that deserves to be more popular.

How to Grow
Plant seeds in early spring and again in late summer. Summer plantings are possible in cool climates. Thin plants to stand 3–4 in. (7.5–10.0 cm) apart in rows at least 2 ft. (60 cm) apart. Keep soil moist and fertile to maintain the rapid growth the plants need to form tender bulbs free of strings and pith.

Harvest
Pull up the entire plant. Trim off the leaves

and stout taproot. Bulbs may be eaten raw or peeled, diced, and cooked with the tender young leaves.

Varieties
Rapid is a good early variety; Grand Duke is a midseason green hybrid; Purple Danube is an improvement over the old Purple Vienna.

Lamb's Quarters
Chenopodium album p. 232

Most gardeners know that this tall, aggressive annual is edible, but they weed it out of their food gardens anyway. It can, however, add variety to other summer greens. The large, productive plants have smooth, whitish-green terminal leaves.

How to Grow
You may have to collect starter seeds from plants in vacant lots. Plant only a few seeds. Start them early indoors in peat pots and transplant to the garden after danger of frost is past. Set seedlings 1½–2 ft. (45–60 cm) apart in fertile soil in full sun. Water often and feed with manure tea or water-soluble fertilizer. Shear off the tiny clusters of beadlike blossoms that form on the stem tips to keep seeds from setting.

Harvest
Clip or pinch off the terminal growth from the branch tips, tender stems, and leaves. The flower buds and immature seeds are also good to eat.

Leek
Allium ampeloprasum pp. 112, 113

Porrum Group. Leeks are very popular in England but less so in America. Resembling large scallions with flattened leaves, leeks are milder than onions and are grown chiefly for their long, thick, tender white stems.

How to Grow
Leeks take a long time to produce large stems. Where winters are severe, start seeds indoors in late winter and transplant pencil-size seedlings to the garden as soon as soil can be worked. Plant seedlings in a furrow 6–10 in. (15–25 cm) deep, split down

the length of a raised bed. Where winters are mild, direct-seed in the garden in late summer under lath shade. Thin plants to 4–6 in. (10–15 cm) apart when they are large enough to handle. As the leeks grow, push soil up around stems to blanch them white. Keep soil moist and fertile to encourage growth. If temperatures threaten to fall below 10° F (−12° C), mulch with pine needles or straw.

Harvest
Dig up spring-sown leeks in late fall before the ground freezes. Dig up fall-sown leeks in spring or early summer of the following year, before soil becomes hot.

Varieties
Argenta, Unique, Nebraska (cold-hardy), King Richard (early), Broad London, Titan.

LETTUCE

Crisp, tender lettuce is the most desirable of all salad plants. The most commonly cultivated kinds of lettuce are derived from the species *Lactuca sativa,* an annual originally from Eurasia and a member of the daisy family (Compositae). These varieties generally fall into 4 classes, based on their overall shape and growth habit— butterhead, cos or romaine, crisphead, and leaf. Much of the How to Grow information that appears under butterhead lettuce applies to the 3 other classes as well; methods specific to each class are described under their separate headings. Miner's lettuce is a different species (*Montia perfoliata*), but is also used as a salad green or potherb.

Butterhead Lettuce
Lactuca sativa pp. 214, 215, 216, 217

Butterhead lettuce has a small, loosely folded head surrounded by a rosette of ground-hugging leaves. Some varieties are dark green, others light colored or purple-red. At maturity, the heads have creamy interiors.

How to Grow
Don't grow too much lettuce; it deteriorates quickly after reaching maturity and can't be

frozen or canned, so plant only a few feet of a row at a time. Lettuce is a cold-tolerant, cool-weather annual that bolts to seed in warm weather when the nights grow short. Some "slow-bolting" varieties will last up to 2 weeks longer before going to seed. Still, no lettuce is suitable for summer or late spring planting at northern latitudes because of bolting; farther south the seeds will not germinate in soil warmer than 75°F (24°C).

Soil for growing lettuce should be well drained and fertile to force fast growth. Thin plants early and severely to about 12 in. (30 cm) apart because crowding can delay development. Early spring sowings will benefit from raised beds, which warm up faster. Top beds of heavy clay with a layer of sand ½–1 in. (1.3–2.5 cm) deep to absorb solar energy and promote fast growth during cool spring weather.

Butterhead lettuce is only slightly more difficult to grow than leaf lettuce. Plant seeds in early spring and again in late summer through fall. The best time is early fall, when plants will have just enough time to mature before the onset of very cold weather. To ensure heading before hot weather comes, start seedlings indoors and transplant them to the garden, but protect from heavy freezes.

Harvest
Begin harvesting lettuce as soon as thinnings are large enough to eat. Take the entire plant or snap off outer leaves.

Varieties
Cindy, Bibb, Buttercrunch (AAS), Dark Green Boston, Summer Boston, Kagran, Winter Density, Four Seasons (red).

Cos or Romaine Lettuce
Lactuca sativa pp. 214, 216, 217

Cos or romaine lettuce has an upright, cylindrical or torpedo-shaped head that is firmly wrapped at maturity. It is medium to light green with a creamy interior.

How to Grow and Harvest
Cos or romaine lettuce takes longer to mature than leaf and butterhead; plant it in late summer or fall, when it has plenty of time to form large heads. Start and harden

off spring plantings indoors; transplant them 2–3 weeks before the frost-free date to ensure heading; plant 8–12 in. (20–30 cm) apart. Harvest like butterhead lettuce.

Varieties
Parris Island, Valmaine, Ballon.

Crisphead Lettuce
Lactuca sativa p. 213

Sometimes erroneously called "iceberg," a named variety within this class, crisphead lettuce includes not only the commercially grown type familiar in supermarkets, but also a few midget varieties for small gardens.

How to Grow
Crisphead lettuce is the latest to mature and is thus impractical as a spring crop in areas where hot weather arrives less than 60 days after the last hard frost. It's best to plant seeds in the garden in early fall. Thin plants to stand 8–12 in. (20–30 cm) apart. You can also start seeds indoors and set out sizable seedlings 2–3 weeks before the frost-free date, protecting them against hard frosts. Seeds planted in late summer will germinate better if you shade the soil to keep it cool and reduce evaporation. Head lettuce may develop pink or brown interior streaks if the soil isn't kept uniformly moist.

Harvest
Begin harvesting when heads are half-grown. Cut the entire plant, and trim off most of the outer leaves.

Varieties
Ithaca, Great Lakes, Premier Great Lakes, Minetto (miniature), Red Grenoble, Valdor (cold-resistant), Tom Thumb (miniature).

Leaf Lettuce
Lactuca sativa pp. 218, 219, 220, 221, 224

The most popular in North American home gardens is leaf lettuce, a nonheading plant with plain, rumpled, oaklike or frilly leaves ranging in color from apple-green through reddish bronze.

How to Grow
Leaf lettuce is the easiest to grow and most reliable. Plant seeds in early spring and again after the hottest days of summer are over. In cool climates, you can make 2 or 3 spring plantings, timed 2 weeks apart. Little is gained by starting seeds indoors.

Harvest
Combine thinning and harvesting until plants stand far enough apart to reach full size. Pull entire plants or snap off outer leaves. Leaf lettuce, especially the bronze varieties, may go bitter in hot weather. Refrigerate it for 2–4 days to reduce bitterness.

Varieties
Black Seeded Simpson, Grand Rapids, Green Ice, Green Wave, Royal Oak Leaf, Red Sails (AAS), Salad Bowl (AAS), Red Salad Bowl, Slo Bolt, Matchless.

Miner's Lettuce
Montia perfoliata p. 231

Winter Purslane; Cuban Spinach. Miner's lettuce was a godsend to prospectors starved for greens during the 1849 gold rush. It carpets meadows during the spring rainy season and lasts for weeks longer in shaded glens. The small plants have oval to lance-shaped basal leaves on long petioles and distinctive, disk-shaped stem leaves that appear to be threaded along the slender stems; they make beautiful edible garnishes and can be used as salad or as potherbs.

How to Grow
Miner's lettuce may naturalize in flower beds receiving light shade from deciduous trees. Although it likes cool weather, it will withstand only light frost. In cooler climates, plant seeds 2–3 in. (5.0–7.5 cm) apart in early spring and allow plants to set seeds and naturalize; in the South, plant in fall. Late summer plantings for fall harvest may be killed by frost before they can set seeds. Keep soil rich in organic matter and uniformly moist. A mulch of sifted compost will prolong production.

Harvest
Pull up the entire plant. If you want the

crop to renew itself, leave a few plants to
set seeds.

MELONS

Included here are the fruits of 3 genera of
the cucumber family (Cucurbitaceae). All
are tendril-bearing vine crops that have large,
fleshy fruit, usually with a rind. *Cucumis melo*
is a warm-temperate annual with trailing or
climbing, soft, hairy vines. This complex
species is divided into several botanical
groups, 2 of which are commonly cultivated.
The Reticulatus Group, or netted melons,
includes Persian melons and muskmelons.
(Although muskmelons are often called
cantaloupes, the true cantaloupe belongs to
the Cantalupensis Group. Once grown in the
Colonies, it is now seldom seen in the U.S.)
The Inodorus Group, or winter melons,
includes casabas, crenshaws, and honeydews.
Citrullus lanatus, the familiar watermelon, is
a tender annual that grows from prostrate
vines with branched tendrils. *Benincasa
hispida,* the Chinese preserving melon, is a
pumpkinlike vine that bears large fruit with
a thin but tough skin.

Casaba Melon
Cucumis melo p. 172

Inodorus Group. Casabas are large melons,
tapering toward the stem and weighing
4–8 lbs (1.8–3.6 kg). The rind is yellow with
ridges or ribs, and the flesh greenish. Like
other melons in the Inodorus Group—
pink-fleshed crenshaws and honeydews—the
casaba is a long-season, late-maturing fruit of
very high quality, best when dead ripe but
not soggy.

How to Grow and Harvest
Grow and harvest like muskmelon; where
summers are 5 months or shorter, use clear
plastic mulch, which traps more heat than
black plastic and causes the vines to grow
densely and shade out weeds. Plant in a
sunny corner or by a heat-reflecting wall.

Varieties
Casabas, crenshaws, and honeydews were
once restricted to the dry West and
Southwest because they were subject to
mildew disease and rotted after summer
rains; now, humidity-tolerant hybrids are
available. Mail-order seed companies in Calif.
offer the best selection of casaba melons.

Chinese Preserving Melon
Benincasa hispida p. 173

This frost-tender, wide-spreading annual, a
native of se. Asia, has yellow flowers and
rank-smelling foliage. Fruits are oblong to
cylindrical and grow to 16 in. (40.5 cm)
long. The rind is waxy-white and covered
with fine, silky hair. Occasionally grown in
the U.S. as a curiosity, this melon is used in
China for making sweet preserves.

How to Grow
Plant the large, pumpkinlike seeds 12 in.
(30 cm) apart on raised mounds of well-
drained soil and feed heavily with manure or
manure tea until fruits have set. Grow in
full sun and give vines room to ramble over
the ground or up a strong trellis or arbor.
This plant is best adapted to climates with a
growing season of 8–11 months and
abundant rainfall or irrigation.

Harvest
Fruit matures late summer to fall. Pick the
melons at small sizes and cook like summer
squash. Larger melons can be used for
stuffing.

Varieties
A Taiwanese variety produces fruit up to
3 ft. (90 cm) long.

Crenshaw Melon
Cucumis melo p. 170

Inodorus Group. Crenshaws are large and
oval, with smooth, dark green rinds that
turn yellowish green when ripe. Older
varieties may have greenish flesh; newer
hybrids are salmon-pink inside.

How to Grow and Harvest
Cultivate and harvest like casaba.

Varieties
Burpee Early Hybrid; Honeyshaw.

Honeydew Melon
Cucumis melo p. 173

Inodorus Group. Honeydew melons are
silvery white, smooth, and round, and
usually have green or white flesh. Newer
varieties may have orange or pink-tinted
flesh. Average size is 2–4 lbs. (0.9–1.8 kg).

How to Grow and Harvest
Cultivate and harvest like casaba.

Varieties
Hybrids that tolerate humid climates are
now widely adapted. Popular varieties
include Venus Hybrid, Kazakh, Tam Dew,
Honeygrow, and Bush Star Hybrid.

Muskmelon
Cucumis melo pp. 170, 171

Reticulatus Group. All the many varieties
listed in catalogues and seed displays as
muskmelons, melons, or cantaloupes belong
to this group. Fruits range in size from
1–4 lbs. (0.45–1.8 kg) and may be round,
oval, boat-shaped, or banana-shaped. Rinds
may be nearly smooth, netted with cordlike
veins, warted, or ribbed. Older varieties may
have pronounced ribs from stem end to
blossom end, while modern kinds developed
for shipping have no trace of them. At
maturity, the rind may be whitish green,
cream, yellowish, pink-tinged, or dark green;
the flesh may be white, greenish, orange, or
pink-tinged. Persian melons are large, dark
green varieties that mature late. The seed
cavities in modern varieties are no larger
than an ice cream scoop, but are bigger than
a coffee mug in the old, large, open-
pollinated varieties. Flavors run the gamut
from barely acceptable to extremely sweet
and musky, and not entirely according to
variety; a great deal of moisture in the soil
during the 3 weeks leading up to maturity
gives melons a bland and watery taste.

How to Grow

Muskmelons need optimum drainage, so grow them on raised beds 5–6 ft. (1.5–1.8 m) wide. The top of the bed should slope down from the apex to shed heavy rains that might collect and rot fruits. Mulch beds with black plastic; in hot climates, use straw or dried lawn clippings over newspapers or cardboard. To maximize yield, install drip or trickle irrigation under the mulch. Spun-bonded row covers or large squares of aluminum foil will keep away beetles that carry a fatal bacterial wilt. Direct-seeding works best except in areas with short, cool summers. There, start seeds indoors 3–4 weeks prior to the spring frost-free date and transplant 2–3 weeks after the average date for the last frost. Thin seedlings or set transplants 12 in. (30 cm) apart. Cover seeds or transplants with bottomless plastic jugs to protect early growth from frost and to help fruits mature before pickleworm invasions. Remove caps from jugs; this creates a chimney that keeps contained air from becoming too hot, but protects plants from frost exposure.

Harvest

Pick some fruits before fully ripe and bring indoors to complete ripening. Then, if heavy rains spoil your chances of vine-ripened fruit, you will not have lost all of them. Leave 2–3 in. (5.0–7.5 cm) of stem when picking, and handle carefully. Do not wash fruits until just before use. Wiggle the stem where it joins the fruit. If it comes off easily, leaving a disk-shaped concavity, it is at "full-slip" stage and is ready to pick and eat. Persian melons turn color slightly and develop a strong melon fragrance, most noticeable at the blossom end. Their stems don't "slip" and must be clipped to leave a 2-in. (5-cm) stub. If after picking you can't detect a strong perfume, let fruit ripen indoors for a few days.

Varieties

When selecting varieties of sweet melons, look for those that resist mildew and fusarium wilt. Early: Sweet 'n' Early, Sweetheart, Scoop, Sweet Granite, Earlisweet. Midseason: Ambrosia, Burpee Hybrid, Gurney's Giant, Star Headliner, Superstar, Canada Gem. Bush or short vine types: Minnesota Midget, Short 'n' Sweet, Bush Star. European gourmet types: Charentais,

Haogen, Ogen, Jivaro. Persian melons: Try
mail-order seed companies.

Watermelon
Citrullus lanatus pp. 172, 174, 175

Popular in warm climates throughout the
world, watermelons are grown for their
sweet, juicy flesh and, in China, for edible
seeds. Watermelons range from very large
and heavy fruits to moderate-size and small
hybrids developed to fit into refrigerators.
The rind is hard and green, often striped.
The flesh may be pink, red, or even yellow,
with a faint pineapple scent. Seedless
watermelons are available but expensive. The
vines of standard varieties are long and
rambling; space-saving hybrids spread to a
diameter of only 5–6 ft. (1.5–1.8 m).

How to Grow
Early-maturing hybrids and warmth-retaining
plastic mulch enable gardeners to grow
watermelons almost everywhere except
Alaska and the cool Northwest. Direct-seed
watermelons; where the growing season is
short, start seeds indoors in large peat pots
3–4 weeks prior to the spring frost-free date.
Plant or transplant 2–3 weeks after the
frost-free date. Thin plants to stand 2–3 ft.
(60–90 cm) apart. In the North, place clear
plastic mulch over raised beds to warm the
soil; make small slits in the plastic through
which to plant seeds. Later, you may need to
cover the plastic with straw mulch to block
weed growth.

Harvest
Large melons take 100 days or more of warm
weather from seeding to harvest, but the
new early hybrids may be fully ripe in 75–80
days. Harvesting watermelons is a guessing
game, especially the first melon of the
season. Examine the curling tendrils where
the fruit stem joins the vine, and pick fruit
after the tendrils turn brown. Some
gardeners pick when the underside of the
melon starts to turn yellow; others prefer to
thump the melon and judge ripeness by
pitch, picking only bass or baritone fruits.

Varieties
Watermelon varieties are numerous. Most of

the large varieties are open-pollinated; the "icebox" types are mostly hybrids. Look for resistance to watermelon wilt and anthracnose diseases. Early icebox: fruits 5–10 lbs. (2.25–4.50 kg), occasionally more. Selections include Garden Baby, Fordhook Hybrid, Yellow Baby (AAS), and New Hampshire (AAS). Second early icebox: fruits 10–15 lbs. (4.5–6.8 kg), occasionally more. Selections include Sugar Baby, Sugar Doll, Sweet Favorite (AAS), and Bush Jubilee. Midseason to late: large fruits, 15–35 lbs. (6.8–15.9 kg) or more. Charleston Gray, Bush Charleston Gray, Dixie Queen, and Black Diamond. Seedless: Tri X 313 Hybrid, Triple Sweet Hybrid.

Mustard Greens
Brassica juncea pp. 223, 227, 228

Indian Mustard; Brown Mustard. Mustard greens look a bit like turnip greens, but the leaves are yellowish to medium green and quite broad. At maturity, the plants are large, loose, and open.

How to Grow
Direct-seed mustard thickly in early spring and again in early fall. Mustard is emphatically a cool-weather crop and will quickly bolt, flower, and set seeds if planted too late in spring. Transplanting is not practical. Begin thinning plants as soon as they are large enough to eat; mustard won't attain full size if grown closer together than 12 in. (30 cm). During the short, cool days of fall, mustard greens will grow to large sizes but still remain tender. Plants are frost-hardy but not quite as cold-resistant as collards or turnips.

Harvest
Snip off leaves 3–4 in. (7.5–10.0 cm) above the soil; new leaves will grow. The greens have a slight peppery tang and may be cooked alone or with other greens, or chopped for salads when quite small. If plants bolt, you can eat the flowering shoots and tender young pods.

Varieties
Some varieties have large, smooth leaves that are easy to wash free of sand and soil. Others have fancy curled or fringed leaves. The recently introduced Savanna hybrid matures

earlier and bolts later than most standard varieties.

Tendergreen Mustard
Brassica rapa p. 227

Perviridis Group. Spinach Mustard. Tendergreen is often planted as an alternative to the larger mustard greens. If harvested young, both the glossy green leaves and succulent petioles are edible. Tendergreen plants, smaller than those of mustard greens, are 8–12 in. (20–30 cm) high when ready to harvest.

How to Grow
Plant as you would mustard greens, in early spring and again from late summer through fall. Begin to eat the thinnings when they are half-grown. Mature plants should stand 6 in. (15 cm) apart.

Harvest
Snap off outer leaves or harvest the entire plant. Old plants have a thickened crown, which can be peeled and pickled.

Stinging Nettle
Urtica dioca p. 233

Wild nettles, long popular in Europe, are enjoying a boom in the U.S. These ungainly perennials, to 2½ ft. (75 cm) high, are irritating to handle and don't belong in the kitchen garden. However, plants can be established in light shade in an out-of-the-way corner in moist soil. The young leaves, oval to heart-shaped and deeply toothed, are used like spinach.

How to Grow
Stinging nettles are widely distributed as a weed. You can take cuttings or seeds from naturalized stands. Plant 6 in. (15 cm) apart in spring after danger of frost is past.

Harvest
Wearing gloves and long sleeves, clip tender tip growth; cook like spinach.

Okra
Abelmoschus esculentus pp. 152, 153

Gumbo; Gombo. Okra is a great hot-climate vegetable that will grow wherever southern peas succeed. Plants grow 3–8 ft. (0.9–2.4 m) high, depending on whether you plant a dwarf or tall variety. The large, lobed, slightly spiny leaves have long stems that branch from a heavy, woody central stem. Yellow blossoms blotched with brownish black grow from the leaf axils, followed quickly by the ribbed, edible pods.

How to Grow
Okra likes clay or clay loam soil, average moisture, and moderate soil fertility. Before planting seeds, wash them in dishwashing soap, rinse thoroughly, and soak overnight in tepid water; drain and dry. After danger of frost is past, plant seeds in groups of 3, with 12 in. (30 cm) between groups. If the soil is heavy clay, build up beds to keep rainwater from standing around the crowns.

Harvest
Pick okra every 2–3 days, when pods are still less than 5 in. (12.5 cm) long. Test for tenderness with your thumbnail. Cut off pods with a paring knife, but don't remove the caps. Use as soon as possible after picking and do not refrigerate; the dry air in a refrigerator causes pods to deteriorate rapidly. Some people are sensitive to okra spines; wear long sleeves when harvesting.

Varieties
Blondie (AAS), Clemson Spineless (AAS), Red River, Annie Oakley Hybrid, Park's Candelabra Branching.

ONIONS

The onions are a large and diverse group. Included here are the large white, yellow, or red bulbs with papery skins; green, edible-stemmed Egyptian onions; and bunching onions known as scallions. The tender young shoots of bulb onions, harvested before they are mature, are also used as scallions. Shallots, leeks, and garlic, although closely related to onions, are treated separately in this guide.

Onion
Allium cepa pp. 106, 107, 110, 111

Cepa Group. The underground bulb of this pungent, strong-smelling plant has been extremely popular for centuries. Onions come in numerous shapes and colors—white, yellow, brown, or purple-red. The color has little effect on a variety's flavor, which depends more on whether the variety was developed for long storage. Short-day onion varieties produce bulbs on short days during winter and early spring, while long-day varieties bulb when days are longer; day-length preference is usually indicated in catalogues and on seed packets.

How to Grow
Onions are half-hardy perennials grown like long-season annuals. There are 3 ways to grow them: from sets (small, dry onion bulbs whose growth has been interrupted), from transplanted seedlings, and by direct-seeding.
Sets sprout and regrow, sloughing off the old bulbs. All set varieties are long-day. The best results come from medium-size sets, ⅜ – ¾ in. (9.0–19 mm) in diameter. For dry bulbs, plant sets 3–4 weeks before the average frost-free date. Work up the soil and press sets into it, root disk down, about 1 in. (2.5 cm) deep and 1–2 in. (2.5–5.0 cm) apart in rows or in bands about 12 in. (30 cm) wide. Don't expose young onions to prolonged cold weather, which could force them to bolt. In the North, successive plantings for scallions can be made through late summer. In the lower South and warm West, do not plant during the hot summer months.
Onions grown from seedlings are planted in midspring. Start seedlings indoors early, or purchase them when pencil-size. If dry, soak them for 2–3 hours before planting. Poke holes in prepared soil and plant the seedlings 2–3 in. (5.0–7.5 cm) apart in bands to 12 in. (30 cm) wide. Seedlings will recover from light frosts. In mild-winter climates, you can also plant seedlings of short-day varieties in late summer or fall.
Direct-seeding is the least expensive way to grow a lot of onions. Sow seeds in furrows in prepared soil. For dry bulbs plant as early as the soil can be worked in spring. In areas with mild winters, direct-seeding also works for fall plantings. For scallions, direct-seed in closely spaced rows or wide bands.

In mild-winter areas choose short-day varieties and plant in late summer or fall; they are ready for harvest in late spring. You can also plant sets or seedlings of long-day varieties in spring, but will probably get only scallions or small bulbs for your labor. Hot weather and dry soil stop bulb development and force early maturity. In areas with hot summers and short but severe winters, plant long-day onions in spring. Fall-planted short-day varieties might live over winter, but they often bolt to seed in spring before sizable bulb can form. Farther north, plant long-day onions in spring. There you can get a good crop from direct-seeding, sets, or transplanted seedlings.

Harvest
To have scallions, thin plantings of mature onions. When the tops of dry bulbs start to turn yellow, break them over to hasten drying.
Loosen bulbs with a spading fork and let them dry in the field for a few days. Then braid the tops and hang bulbs in a chain, or trim off the tops and store bulbs in a mesh bag in a dry, dark place. Medium-size, firm onions, with many layers of dried scales but no thick neck, store best. The large, sweet, slicing varieties are not good for long storage.

Varieties
Long-day: Early Yellow Globe, Yellow Sweet Spanish, Burpee Sweet Spanish Hybrid, White Sweet Spanish, Snow White Hybrid, Southport Red Globe, Carmen Hybrid.
Short-day: Yellow Bermuda, Granex (Vidalia) Hybrid, White Bermuda, Italian Red, Torpedo, Stockton Red.

Bunching Onion
Allium fistulosum pp. 112, 113

Welsh Onion; Green Onion. Native to Asia, this little perennial onion sends up multiple shoots from a single seed and will produce summer scallions from early spring planting. Depending on the variety, small or no bulbs form, only a slight basal thickening.

How to Grow
Bunching onions are only half-hardy, so grow them as annuals in areas with severe winters. Sow seeds 2–3 in. (5.0–7.5 cm) apart

in early spring, or divide existing clumps.
Grow on well-drained, fertile soil in full sun.

Harvest
Shear off established clumps 2 in. (5 cm)
above ground level. To avoid shocking the
plant when cutting, take only half the shoots
from a clump. New shoots will form and be
ready for cutting in 4–6 weeks.

Varieties
Beltsville Bunching, Evergreen Hardy White,
Long White Summer Bunching.

Egyptian Onion
Allium cepa p. 107

Proliferum Group. You can find this durable
onion naturalized around abandoned
homesteads. Although Egyptian onions are
not as tender as scallions or as tasty as bulb
onions, a few are good for filling in the
garden when other onions are out of season,
even in midwinter. Egyptian onions do not
set seeds but are reproduced by bulbils that
form on the top of the strong central leaves.
No true bulbs are formed, only a dense
cluster of tadpole-shaped bulblets.

How to Grow
Divide clusters as they dry in late summer,
or plant the bulbils as you would onion sets.
You can multiply a clump into a row in a
year's time. These onions are hardy except at
extremely low temperatures, and can survive
a hard freeze in well-drained soil.

Harvest
Egyptian onions are best eaten when young.
As the shoots age, the taste becomes strong
and the green tops become fibrous. Bulbils
can also be eaten, but require tedious
peeling.

Orach
Atriplex hortensis pp. 222, 233

Mountain Spinach. This tall, frost-hardy
annual is widely adapted as a weed in many
parts of the world. Where naturalized, orach
grows 4–6 ft. (1.2–1.8 m) tall and 2–3 ft.

(60–90 cm) wide, but is held to a more manageable size when cultivated. Orach is more popular in Europe than in the U.S., and has long been cultivated there for medicinal and culinary uses. Here it is grown as a potherb for its tender young greens.

How to Grow
In spring as soon as the soil can be worked, direct-seed in bands 12 in. (30 cm) wide. Use preplant fertilizer, and water frequently to force fast, tender growth. Plant orach at 3–4 week intervals from early spring through late summer to have a constant supply of tender young plants for harvest. Orach tolerates alkaline soil, drought, and will endure both hot and cold weather.

Harvest
Orach greens are at their best in spring or fall. Pull up entire plants when they are young and have only 6–8 leaves. If plants grow large, pick only small, tender leaves for table use. Early harvest prevents orach from dropping seeds and becoming a weedy pest.

Varieties
Orach seeds and plants are not widely available, but specialists carry red, green, and white varieties. White orach, actually greenish white, is the most desirable for cooking. Very young leaves can be mixed with other greens for salads.

Root Parsley
Petroselinum crispum var. *tuberosum p. 91*

Turnip-rooted Parsley. Once a popular alternative to turnips, parsnips, and beets, root parsley is rarely seen today on produce stands. The plants look much like plain or flat-leaf parsley; the roots are creamy white, medium-long, and slender.

How to Grow
Grow like leaf parsley, but provide a deeply worked, sandy loam seedbed free of coarse particles. Before the ground freezes solid, but after field mice have found shelter elsewhere, mulch with straw to extend harvest season into winter. Cold intensifies the sweetness of the roots.

Harvest
In late fall, loosen soil and pull roots as

needed. In mild-winter areas roots can stay in the ground over winter, but pull them before they bolt to seed in spring.

Varieties
Hamburg Thick-Rooted.

Parsnip
Pastinaca sativa p. 90

Known to ancient Greeks and Romans, this large-rooted biennial is grown as an annual. The edible, tasty taproot may be 3½ in. (9 cm) in diameter and 10–18 in. (25–45 cm) long; from its thick, rough top arise long-stemmed, divided, dark green leaves. Reaching a height of 3 ft. (90 cm) or more, these robust plants produce only a modest amount of food for the space they occupy.

How to Grow
Grow parsnips from seeds, which are large, flat, and notoriously short-lived. A deep, moderately fertile, loamy soil free from stones and coarse pieces of compost is necessary to produce large, smooth roots without forks. In heavy soil, dig holes 2 ft. (60 cm) deep with posthole diggers, then fill them with soil amended with compost. Each hole will support 2 plants.
Direct-seed in early spring in northern and central states. In areas with mild winters, plant seeds in late summer to mature during winter. To help seeds germinate in hot soil, flood a furrow with water, let the water soak in, and repeat. Plant seeds 1 in. (2.5 cm) apart and cover with ⅛ in. (3.2 mm) sand. Lay a board over the seeded furrow. Mist every few days and replace the board. Seeds may require 3–4 weeks to sprout. Thin seedlings to 12 in. (30 cm) apart for large roots. Don't let the soil go very dry for long periods; roots may split from rapid water intake when a heavy rain comes. Parsnips require 4 months to grow, and taste better after cool weather has converted some of the root starch to sugar.

Harvest
In the North before the ground freezes hard, bank up plants with straw to keep soil soft. In the South, dig roots as needed and store a few at a time in plastic bags in the

refrigerator. The cooling will make the root sweeter.

Varieties
Hollow Crown, Harris Model, All-America.

PEAS

The plants in this section represent 3 genera in the pea family (Leguminosae). Included are cool-weather-loving green garden peas and their edible-podded relatives, snap peas and snow peas. Southern peas, including black-eyed varieties, also appear here; warm-weather staples across the South, they are actually a species of shell beans. Least familiar are winged peas, an unusual vegetable with winged, edible pods.

Edible-Podded Pea
Pisum sativum var. *macrocarpon* pp. 163, 165

Edible-podded peas encompass more than just the familiar snow pea used so much in Oriental cuisines. Snow peas have flat pods and are eaten when half-mature; vines of these varieties range 2–6 ft. (0.6–1.8 m) high. Introduced only a few years ago are the newer edible-podded snap peas, a boon to gardeners. The oval to round pods can be snapped like beans and eaten at any stage before they turn yellow. When yellow, the pods can be shelled for berries. Most snap pea varieties have strings, but these zip off quickly. The newest varieties are stringless, but pods are smaller and fewer per plant. Also recently available are snap peas with resistance to powdery mildew disease. The original AAS winner, Sugar Snap, is a high-climbing vine, to 8 ft. (2.4 m) high, with somewhat more frost resistance than shell peas.

How to Grow
Grow like green peas.

Harvest
Harvest flat-podded snow peas at the half-mature stage, when pods are 1½–3 in. (4.0–7.5 cm) long, except Oregon Sugar Pod II, which can stay on the vine until the pods start to turn yellow. Don't rush to harvest

the round-podded snap peas; the flavor
improves until the pods have reached full
size, and have begun to develop a pebbly
surface and fade in color.

Varieties
Bush snow peas: Norli, Snowflake.
Medium-tall snow peas: Oregon Sugar Pod
II, Dwarf Gray Sugar. Tall snow peas:
Mammoth Melting Sugar. Bush snap peas:
Little Sweetie, Sugar Daddy, Sugar Mel,
Sugar Ann (AAS). Tall snap peas: Sugar
Snap (AAS), Snappy.

Green Pea
Pisum sativum pp. 164, 165

Garden Pea; English Pea. Peas are not the
most space-efficient vegetable, but they are
delicious fresh and well worth planting.
These cool-weather annuals mature early, just
after spinach. Varieties with large pods are
easier to pick and shell but usually bear late
in the season and are reliable only in areas
with cool summers. Ultra-dwarf varieties bear
early and fit into small gardens, but are only
marginally productive. The best bet for a
home garden is usually one of the midseason
varieties developed for processing. These
robust, knee-high vines bear easy-to-shell
pods that are 3½ in. (7.5–9.0 cm) long with
7–9 berries each. Some varieties are resistant
to powdery mildew, fusarium wilt, pea
enation virus, and other diseases.

How to Grow
Peas are particular about soil. Sandy,
well-drained soil that warms up quickly is
ideal. Plant seeds very early, as soon as the
soil has thawed or dried out enough to be
worked—well before the frost-free date in
the North, and during fall or winter in the
Deep South and warm West. If the garden
has not been planted with peas in recent
years, treat seeds with a bacterial inoculant
that helps these legumes extract nitrogen
from the air.
In spring plant pea seeds ½–1 in.
(1.3–2.5 cm) deep in full sun. Fall peas,
which are difficult at best, can be planted
deeper in the warm soil of late summer.
Space seeds 1–2 in. (2.5–5.0 cm) apart in
rows or wide bands. Support dwarf or
middle-height varieties with brush, string,
or chicken wire run between 2-ft. (60-cm)

stakes driven 1 ft. (30 cm) into the ground.
This facilitates harvest greatly. Tall varieties
need arbors or poles to climb.
Early plantings of pea seeds shouldn't rot in
well-drained soil, especially if they are treated
with a fungicide. Seedlings are frost-resistant
and, when small, will survive a few degrees
below freezing.

Harvest
Pick peas when pods are plump enough to
shell easily. Don't wait too long; the berries
quickly become tough, especially on the
petits pois (tiny pea) varieties. Pull pods
carefully, holding the fruiting stem with one
hand. Don't overlook ripe pods among the
foliage.

Varieties
Bush: Green Arrow, Little Marvel, Wando,
Knight, Almota. Bush, petits pois: Precovil,
Frizette, Alaska. Bush, "leafless" (plants have
masses of tendrils instead of normal leaves):
Novella II. Tall: Multistar, Telephone,
Alderman.

Southern Pea
Vigna unguiculata pp. 160, 161

Cowpea. Black-eyed peas are considered a
subspecies. Southern peas are an essential
hot-weather vegetable for gardens in the
South and warm West, producing when the
weather is too hot and humid for snap beans
and arriving in time to go with okra.
Southern peas are tropical plants with seeds
more like beans than green peas. Depending
on variety, plants may be erect, bushy, and
nonvining, or rampant and sprawling with
short runners. The shiny, dark green leaves
are about the size of snap beans. Pods are
6-9 in. (15.0-22.5 cm) long and splay out
above the foliage on long, smooth stems like
fingers, usually 2 per stem. They may be
slender, plump, smooth, or lumpy,
depending on variety, and white, cream, or
purple. Southern peas can be snapped and
eaten like green beans when young or, when
mature, shelled for their green seeds.

How to Grow
Direct-seed 2 weeks after the average
frost-free date; earlier seedlings may rot. Seed
germination rate is rarely better than 50-60
percent. In full sun, plant seeds 2-4 in.

(5–10 cm) apart and 1 in. (2.5 cm) deep in beds slightly elevated for drainage. Later, thin seedlings to about 6 in. (15 cm) apart. Rows should be 2½–4 ft. (75–120 cm) apart. Runner varieties thrive when interplanted among widely spaced rows of sweet corn, where the vines can run up the cornstalks. Because southern peas are legumes, they need only moderate amounts of nitrogen fertilizer. But if soil is poor, this long-season crop will need a side dressing of 5-10-10 fertilizer when plants are 12 in. (30 cm) tall. Plants grow well when treated with a seed inoculant that supplies a beneficial bacteria.

Harvest
Pick southern peas when the pods begin to turn color, but before they dry. Use both hands, holding the stems with one while snapping off the pods with the other. At the end of the season, pull the remaining pods off the plants and dry them. Soak the dried seeds before cooking.

Varieties
Crowder peas (pods tightly packed with squarish seeds): Mississippi Silver, Colossus, Hercules. Purple hull: Mississippi Purple, Pink Eye, Arkansas #83 Hybrid. Cream peas: Big Boy, Sadandy, Zipper Cream. Black-eyed peas: California Blackeye, Magnolia Blackeye, California No. 5.

Winged Pea
Lotus tetragonolobus p. 163

This trailing annual herb is grown for its edible pods and seeds. The pods, to 3 in. (7.5 cm) long, have 4 ribs or wings from end to end, and a fibrous core, which is partly why this vegetable is not more popular. The plants are small and somewhat decorative, with stems to 16 in. (40.5 cm) long; sparse, purplish-red flowers; and leaves composed of 3 oval leaflets. They do best in areas with long, cool spring seasons.

How to Grow
On your first try, grow only a few plants. Start seeds early indoors in peat pots. Transplant outdoors 2–3 in. (5.0–7.5 cm) apart in fertile, well-drained soil at about the frost-free date, or 2 weeks earlier if you can protect them from frost. In clay soils, plant in raised beds. Plants dry up and die by

midsummer after harvest, except where
summers are quite cool.

Harvest
Begin harvesting as soon as there are enoug
pods for a meal. Steam with butter or herbe
oil and eat them like artichoke leaves,
discarding the stringy cores.

Peanut
Arachis hypogaea pp. 114, 115

Goober; Groundnut. Frost-tender annuals,
peanuts belong to the pea family and are
native to Brazil. They have gained popularit
in home gardens now that early-maturing,
large-seeded varieties have been introduced.
The cloverlike plants are neat and attractive,
growing about 1½ ft. (45 cm) high and 2 ft
(60 cm) wide. Female blossoms are yellow;
when fertilized, they turn face down and
corkscrew into the ground. Each corkscrew,
or peg, develops into 1–4 peanuts 2–6 in.
(5–15 cm) below the soil surface. Each
peanut contains 2–5 seeds within a
papery shell.

How to Grow
Grow peanuts in full sun in sandy or sandy
loam soil. Shell out seeds just before
planting. Once soil is warm enough, plant
seeds 12 in. (30 cm) apart in pairs, in rows
2–2½ ft. (60–75 cm) apart. Hilling up the
soil around the plants is usually beneficial,
but if you choose not to do this, you can
grow the plants closer together. Bush types
leave spaces between rows clear for weeding,
but runner types fill this space with foliage,
so weed while a path remains open. Cease
irrigation once pods begin to ripen.

Harvest
Dig up plants with a spading fork and
air-dry for several days. It helps to have
someone lift plants and shake them gently
while you loosen the soil underneath. Don't
expect to salvage all the peanuts; some will
fall off and, in warm climates, may take
root. You can dig up these small seedlings
carefully with a trowel and transplant them.

Varieties
Park's Whopper has large seeds; Spanish is

an early variety with small seeds; Jumbo
Virginia has short pods with large seeds;
Florigiant is adapted for the lower South.

PEPPERS

Peppers are native to tropical America and
have become staples for all kinds of uses,
from sauces and salads to condiments.
Included here are the sweet peppers and hot
peppers, as well as the ornamental peppers,
which are becoming increasingly popular.
Perennials treated as annuals, pepper plants
are shrubby and upright, growing to 30 in.
(75 cm) high; they have lance-shaped leaves
and white flowers.

Hot Pepper
Capsicum annuum pp. *142, 143, 144, 145,
152, 153*

Hot peppers range from the long, thin, red
Cayenne to large, firm, green Anaheim
peppers for stuffing, cone-shaped Jalapeños,
and fiery cherry-shaped fruits. All belong to
the same species as the sweet peppers except
for the Tabasco, a late variety of *C. frutescens.*
Faint-hearted gardeners avoid planting hot
peppers, perhaps associating them with the
image of the macho pepper-popper. But the
flavor of many summer vegetables can be
improved with discreet additions of finely
chopped fresh hot peppers; add zest to
winter dishes with dried or pickled peppers.

How to Grow
Grow as you would sweet peppers. Most
varieties are later and need more heat than
sweet peppers to produce heavily. Black
plastic mulch helps in cool areas.

Harvest
Hot peppers contain capsaicin, a skin irritant,
so wear gloves when picking or handling.

Varieties
Serrano and Thai peppers are fiercely
hot, and bird peppers (*C. annuum* var.
glabriusculum) and cherry varieties are a
close second; Jalapeño and Cayenne are
medium-hot; Anaheim peppers are mild.
Tabasco has a unique flavor when ground
and made into pepper sauce. Paprika peppers

are very mild; the seeds are ground to make
the spice.

Ornamental Pepper
Capsicum annuum pp. 146, 147, 148, 149

Varieties of these decorative plants produce
upright, slender to cone-shaped fruits that
may be yellow, orange, red, purple, or nearly
black. Many new varieties are heat-resistant
and tolerate humidity; some are quite small
and make good pot plants.

How to Grow
Start seeds indoors 8–10 weeks before the
frost-free date. Set plants in the garden
6–12 in. (15–30 cm) apart, 2–3 weeks after
the frost-free date. They prefer warm weather
and do best in enriched soil.

Harvest
Though chiefly grown for decoration, some
are edible; most, but not all, are medium-
hot, and a few are mild or sweet. Harvest
like sweet or hot peppers.

Varieties
Fiesta, Holiday Cheer, Holiday Time,
Aurora, Maya, Candlelight, Jigsaw.

Sweet Pepper
*Capsicum annuum pp. 140, 141, 142, 144, 145,
148, 149, 150, 151*

Sweet peppers exist in a wide range of sizes,
shapes, and fruit colors. Mature fruits may
weigh 1–4 oz. (28–113 g). Shapes range from
the typical bell-shaped, 3- or 4-lobed type to
irregular, oblong fruits, and even tapered,
horn-shaped, heart-shaped, or wedge-shaped
ones, or small, round fruits resembling
cherry tomatoes. Sweet peppers come in
green, yellow, or gold; most turn red at
maturity. There are now also deep purple or
chocolate-colored fruits. Pepper plants were
once rather tricky to grow; today's widely
adapted hybrids meet or exceed the
expectations of most home gardeners.

How to Grow
Start seeds indoors 8–12 weeks before the
spring frost-free date; plants should be
3–6 in. (7.5–15.0 cm) high by the time the

soil warms up. Don't rush to transplant seedlings; wait 2–3 weeks after the first frost-free date. Set plants 2½ ft. (75 cm) apart in rows 3 ft. (90 cm) apart. Cover plants with clear or milky (not opaque), bottomless plastic 1-gal. or 3-l jugs. Go easy with fertilizer; use a 1-2-2 ratio formula (such as 5-10-10).

Harvest
If you have a lot of bushes, twist and snap off the fruits; if you have just a few plants, take the time to snip off fruits with needle-nose shears.

Varieties
Place a high priority on a variety's resistance to tobacco mosaic virus, a widespread and often fatal plant disease. If you live where summers are either quite cool or long and hot, check with your County Cooperative Extension Service; certain early hybrids perform better in cool areas, and a few main-crop (midseason) varieties can set fruits in hot weather.
Seeds of the best new hybrids are expensive, and some commercial growers use old standards. Here are some of the better varieties: Large green: Lady Belle, Yolo Wonder, Big Bertha, Park's Whopper, Bell Boy, Pro Bell II, Ace (early). Large golden: Golden Bell, Golden Summer. Yellow: Gypsy (short), Banana (long). Special-purpose: Sweet Cherry (pickling), Pimiento (pickling), Cubanelle (frying and pickling).

Perilla
Perilla frutescens pp. 234, 235

Perilla is a tall, erect, half-hardy annual grown for its edible, furry, green or purple leaves. At maturity it is about 3 ft. (90 cm) high. Green perilla is a popular potherb in the Orient. Purple perilla (*P. frutescens atropurpurea*) has attractive curly, dimpled leaves with wavy, deeply cut margins; were it not so lanky, it would make a pretty foliage plant. Both kinds are resistant to heat and humidity, and mature so rapidly that they can be grown successfully in northern states. Home gardeners sometimes confuse the purple perilla with purple basil. Although both can escape cultivation, perilla may become a weed, while basil is easily eradicated.

How to Grow
In the South and warm West, direct-seed in warm soil; where growing seasons are short, start indoors and transplant after frost danger. Seeds are small and fine, so you need only press them into the soil. Grow plants i full sun, 6–12 in. (15–30 cm) apart. Hasten growth with plant food and water. Prune old plants to encourage branching.

Harvest
Take entire young plants for cooking, or tender tip leaves of mature plants.

Pokeweed
Phytolacca americana p. 238

Poke Sallet. This plant is plentiful around old barns and feedlots and is usually harvested from the wild rather than grown as a garden vegetable. Widely adapted, pokeweed is perennial in the South and warm West and grown as an annual elsewhere. Thriving in rich, well-watered soils, the sprawling, colorful plants grow 6–10 ft. (1.8–3.0 m) high and have oblong leaves with red stems and sprays of jet-black berries. The young shoots are used as a potherb. The huge, fleshy root is poisonous.

How to Grow
As early as the soil can be worked, direct-seed 6–8 in. (15–20 cm) apart in bands 12 in (30 cm) wide. Cover seeds with ½ in. (13 mm) sand or soil and grow in full sun. To have a constant supply of tender young greens, plant at intervals—every 4–6 weeks—until late summer. Give plants plenty of manure water to force tender growth.

Harvest
Pull up plants for harvest when they are only 12–18 in. (30–45 cm) high and have 6–8 large, tender leaves. Using a spade, dig deep to pry up the root, or it will snap off and sprout new top growth. Cut off and discard the poisonous root. When boiling the greens, pour off 1 or 2 batches of the cooking water to remove much of the oxalic

acid that puts a "bite" into the flavor. Do
not eat leaves from old plants; they can
make you ill.

Potato
Solanum tuberosum pp. 102, 103, 104, 105

White Potato; Irish Potato. Three major
classes of potatoes are sold in American
markets: the mealy, dry tubers developed for
baking, the moist-fleshed white potatoes for
boiling and frying, and the red-skinned "new
potatoes" for boiling. White, russet, and red
are only a few of the colors of potatoes, and
different flavors are also available. But
commercial growers are reluctant to offer
oddities such as potatoes with yellow flesh or
purple skin. At one time more than 800
potato cultivars were grown in the Andes,
their ancestral home.
Potato plants grow 12–18 in. (30–45 cm)
high and to 4 ft. (120 cm) wide. Some
varieties set flowers, which don't affect tuber
formation. Small fruits resembling little
green tomatoes may follow the flowers. Do
not eat these; they contain toxins.

How to Grow
Although the tubers will keep for several
weeks, don't grow more than a dozen or so
plants unless you have a dark, cool (40° F;
4.5° C) storage area that is protected from
freezing. About 4 months are required from
planting to harvest, so if you have a small
garden and little storage space, consider
vegetables that mature faster.
You can grow potatoes from pieces of tubers
or from true seeds. Certified seed potato
tubers are free of major potato diseases and
can be ordered in early spring or purchased
at seed and feed stores. True potato seeds are
gradually becoming popular with gardeners.
When you start from tubers, cut them into
"seed pieces." These segments contain 2 or
more eyes (buds) and a chunk of potato
tissue to nourish the sprouts while they are
taking root. Pieces should weigh 2–3 oz.
(57–85 g) each; plants grown from smaller
pieces usually get off to a slow start. Sprouts
from large pieces or small whole tubers can
revive if hit by a light frost.
Plant pieces 3–4 in. (7.5–10.0 cm) deep (half
this depth in heavy clay) and 12 in. (30 cm)
apart. Make rows 3–4 ft. (90–120 cm) apart.
Start as early as green peas, provided that

drainage is good—in sandy soil or in raised beds with compost-rich soil. In areas with cool summers and a growing season of 5 months or more, a later planting can be made in midspring. If commercial seed potatoes are unavailable, you can use seed pieces from your own summer harvest as long as you air-dry and treat them with fungicide to reduce rotting. After sprouts emerge, scatter a little straw over them, but not enough for mice to hide in. Add more straw if a heavy freeze is predicted.

If you start with true seeds, plant them indoors 8 weeks before the frost-free date. Germinate at about 70° F (21° C). Transplant the small seedlings to individual pots and, after hardening off, set them in the garden when the weather is still cool but the danger of spring frost is past. A too-early start or excessive hardening off can cause plants to begin setting tubers when they are too small to bear the burden.

Set aside an area of the garden for potatoes, since they are the only vegetable crop that needs an acid soil of pH 4.8 to 5.4. Potatoes also require calcium and magnesium, but instead of applying lime, use gypsum (calcium sulfate) and Epsom salts (for magnesium), which will not raise the pH. Incorporating 3 in. (7.5 cm) of sphagnum peat moss also helps.

Potatoes tend to set tubers near the surface; if the soil washes away, tubers exposed to sunlight turn green and are too bitter to be eaten. Avoid sun-greening by adding straw mulch under the vines as they grow. Or you can set seed pieces on a deep layer of rotting straw or hay, cover them with more of the same, and then ridge up soil 2–3 in. (5.0–7.5 cm) deep to hold down the organic matter. Mulched tubers grow large and are exceptionally smooth and easy to wash.

Harvest

Starting 2 ft. (60 cm) out from the center of the plant, carefully pry up the soil with a spading fork. Work your way in, sliding the tines under the tubers so they can be lifted without being punctured. After one pass through the potato bed, turn the soil over again to find more tubers. Don't wash or bruise the tubers. Store them so that they do not touch, in a completely dark, cool place. If they start to sprout, rub off the eyes when peeling; sprouts should not be eaten.

Varieties
Potatoes grown from tubers include the red varieties Red Pontiac, Red LaSoda, Norland Red, and Sangre; and the white varieties Kennebec, White Cobbler, Katahdin, and Russet Centennial. Those grown from seed include Homestead Hybrid and Explorer.

PUMPKINS

No Halloween or Thanksgiving would be complete without the bright orange pumpkins that signal harvest season. Featured here are 2 different species in the cucumber family (Cucurbitaceae): *Cucurbita pepo,* the familiar small to medium-size pumpkins, used for jack-o'-lanterns or pies; and the huge fruits of *Cucurbita maxima,* actually a mammoth variety of winter squash often grown for "giant pumpkin" contests.

Pumpkin
Cucurbita pepo pp. 194, 195

The orange, furrowed fruits of jack-o'-lantern or sugar pumpkins grow on sprawling, prostrate vines with prickly stems and leafstalks and large, lobed, triangular leaves. They are closely related to several kinds of squash, including acorn and zucchini. These pumpkins seldom weigh more than 2–20 lbs. (0.9–9.0 kg); some miniature kinds weigh only 1–2 lbs. (.45–.90 g). Besides those grown for decoration or for their edible flesh are "naked-seeded" varieties, which have hull-less, edible seeds.

How to Grow
See winter and summer squash. Pumpkins are frost-tender annuals. Direct-seed at about the frost-free date in fertile, well-drained soil. When this pumpkin species is grown under optimum conditions, its fruits do not exceed medium size, but plants respond with greater numbers of fruit.

Harvest
Pick pumpkins before frost, leaving a 3-in.

(7.5-cm) stem stub attached to the fruit.
Handle fruits carefully. Store in a cool,
dry place.

Varieties
Jack-o'-lantern: Spirit (AAS), Cinderella
Bush, Jack O'Lantern, Jackpot, Howden.
Small pie: Small Sugar, New England Pie,
Spookie. Miniature: Jack Be Little, Sweetie
Pie. Naked-seeded: Triple Treat, Lady
Godiva.

Mammoth Pumpkin
Cucurbita maxima p. 194

Mammoth pumpkins are closely related to
Hubbard and other winter squashes. The
very large, pinkish-orange or gray fruits are
usually pear-shaped, often bulging where
they touch the ground. They grow on
prostrate annual vines with blunt, round or
heart-shaped leaves and yellow flowers.

How to Grow and Harvest
See winter squash. Growers of prize-winning
fruits hand-pollinate plants to make them set
fruit early; when 2 fruits are set, all
subsequent blossoms are removed. Once the
fruits are safely on the way to maturity, one
is sacrificed so that the plant's energy will be
concentrated on the remaining specimen,
which will grow to 100 lbs. (45.5 kg) or
more.

Varieties
Show King, Big Max, Big Moon, Hungarian
Mammoth (gray or bluish green), Atlantic.

Purslane
Portulaca oleracea p. 237

Pusley; Verdolaga. Even the weedy wild
purslane is a good potherb or salad
ingredient, but the cultivated variety is larger
and more succulent. A trailing annual,
purslane has reddish, fleshy stems whose
joints produce roots when they come in
contact with the soil. The thick, fleshy leaves
are spoon-shaped and to 2 in. (5 cm) long;
the small flowers are bright yellow.
Cultivated purslane grows about 3 in.
(7.5 cm) tall and 12–18 in. (30–45 cm) wide.
The plants are succulent and brittle.

How to Grow

If purslane doesn't already grow in your garden, don't plant it there; instead, grow it in a large, shallow container, such as a sandbox, where it won't escape. Never put clippings into the compost heap, as they will take root. To plant, press seeds into soil surface and do not cover. Or plant pieces of existing plants; they will root. Grow in full sun. Provide occasional light feedings, and water during dry spells. Purslane prefers sandy soil. In moderately moist soil 2 or 3 successive plantings are possible.

Harvest

Purslane is good to eat only when young; flavor deteriorates once the plant starts to flower. Take whole branches until blossoms begin to appear. Do not eat the ornamental flowering species, *P. grandiflora.*

Quinoa
Chenopodium quinoa p. 120

Quinoa is a tall, erect, half-hardy annual with stiff stems and short seed heads. Its seeds can be eaten in the green stage, or dried and cooked as a cereal. Like several other members of the goosefoot family (Chenopodiaceae), its foliage is also edible. Quinoa is a staple grain at high elevations in the Andes and has been touted as a potential new food crop for the northern hemisphere. It can be grown successfully in the South and Southwest, where nights are long enough in the fall for it to set seeds, but is a marginal crop elsewhere in the U.S.

How to Grow

Seeds are hard to find; seed exchanges are a possible source. Early planting is of no benefit. Wait until midsummer and direct-seed in warm soil in rows 3 ft. (90 cm) apart. Thin seedlings to 12 in. (30 cm) apart.

Harvest

Use the young leaves, stem tips, and fruiting buds for cooking and salads. When the seed heads are about half dry, cut them off, leaving several inches of stem. Gather into bunches and hang to dry over a catch-cloth. When dry, pull off the heads and rub to free

the seeds. Cooked like rice, quinoa seeds
have a nutty, squashlike taste.

Radicchio
Cichorum intybus pp. 220, 221

Radicchio is a variety of leaf chicory that
resembles a small red cabbage. It forms a
tight head of deep red or magenta leaves
veined in white and ranges in size from that
of a large radish to that of a large grapefruit

How to Grow
Plant seeds 8–10 in. (20–25 cm) apart in
midspring in the North and in late summer
in the Deep South. Radicchio needs a long
cool season to develop. It matures in late fall
in northern climates and into the winter and
early spring in warmer areas. It may send up
very long, dark green, hairy leaves early in its
growing cycle. If left over winter, plants will
produce flowering stalks that bear attractive
light blue flowers in summer. To ensure a
crop of radicchio, cut the plant to the
ground in early fall so that the dark red
heads can form.

Harvest
See leaf chicory.

Varieties
Rossa di Treviso and Rossa de Verona are
recommended; Giulio and Augusto can be
planted in mid- to late summer for a late fall
crop except in short-season areas.

RADISHES

Included here are 2 distinct radishes—the
spring radish, which is commonly used in
salads, and the Oriental or winter radish,
which is less well known but becoming
increasingly popular.

Spring Radish
Raphanus sativus pp. 92, 96

This cool-weather annual forms small
rosettes of rough, dark green leaves and
swollen roots. The young leaves can be
mixed and cooked with turnip or mustard

greens. Spring radishes are usually eaten raw, before they become pithy or pungent with age.

There are several varieties, which come in a number of shapes and colors: round, oval, cylindrical, or tapered like an icicle. The roots may be white, red, red and white, pink and white, or a mixture of white, rose, and purple. Most spring radishes are at their best when grown quickly in fertile soil and pulled when less than ¾ in. (19 mm) in diameter.

How to Grow
Direct-seed in sandy or sandy loam soil as early in spring as the soil can be worked. On heavy, dense soil, build raised beds with good drainage; dig furrows 2 in. (5 cm) deep and fill nearly to the top with sand. Scatter the seeds and cover them with ⅛–¼ in. (3.2–6.0 mm) of sand. Thin plants to stand 12 in. (30 cm) apart.

Plant only a few feet of row at a time, making successive plantings every 2 weeks until midspring. Summer plantings will bolt to seed before they develop roots large enough to eat. Plantings made in early fall usually grow quite well.

When the seedlings have 4–6 leaves, drench them with manure tea or soluble complete fertilizer to stimulate rapid growth. Under favorable conditions, radishes will be ready to pull 3½ weeks after the seedlings emerge.

Harvest
Begin pulling radishes when they are barely large enough to eat, in order to make room for the remainder to grow with minimum competition.

Varieties
Red: Comet, Cherry Belle (AAS), Ribella, Redball, Prinz Rotin. White: White Icicle, Burpee White. Bicolored or mixed colored: French Breakfast, D'Avignon, Easter Egg.

Winter Radish
R. sativus var. *longipinnatus pp. 92, 93*

Oriental Radish; Daikon. The winter radishes are not used enough in the U.S., although many of the old standby winter varieties have been grown for decades by knowledgeable gardeners. The name comes from the custom of harvesting the roots in winter.

How to Grow

Plant seeds during late summer or later to prevent these plants from going to seed. Thin plants to 6–12 in. (15–30 cm) apart. Flowering is triggered by the short nights of summer. In the North, direct-seed in cold frames to add 30 days to the growing season. Elsewhere, direct-seed in open ground. In cold climates mulch plants with straw or pine needles. Tack mulch down with chicken wire to keep it from blowing away. The roots will continue to gain weight and become sweeter. Where winters are mild, no mulch is needed.

Harvest

Begin harvesting when roots are still small so that those remaining have room to expand to large sizes. The young greens are edible. Winter-sweetened roots are excellent when sliced and added to salads or soups.

Varieties

Old standby winter varieties with medium-size roots roughly equivalent to turnips in weight include Round Black Spanish, Long Black Spanish, Chinese White, and China Rose. In recent years interest in the much larger Oriental radishes has caused the introduction of several Japanese varieties for soups, stews, and pickling: Summer Cross, April Cross, Tama, All Season, Minowase, and Miyashige.

Rape
Brassica napus pp. 121, 205

Pabularia Group. Colza. Some selections of rape are direct-seeded from late summer through fall for pasturing livestock. Others are grown to produce birdseed or processed to make rape oil. Rape plants are too large and coarse for small gardens, but are occasionally grown for greens because they are so frost-hardy. Some gardeners grow rape to turn under as an inexpensive green manure crop. The large, rough plants have bristly, lyre- or fiddle-shaped leaves with thick, clasping petioles.

A relative of forage rape called Hanover salad (*B. napus,* Pabularia Group) has long been grown as a forage and green manure crop in parts of the South. Planted in late summer,

Hanover salad will sprout with the fall rains and survive the winter. The plants are lower growing than true rape, with narrower, curled or fringed blue or purple-blue leaves.

How to Grow
Seeds of rape and Hanover salad are inexpensive; sow them thickly and rake them into prepared soil. Seeds planted in late summer or fall produce leaves by winter.

Harvest
Snip off leaves as you would mustard greens.

Rhubarb
Rheum rhabarbarum pp. 242, 243

Pie Plant. Rhubarb is a stout perennial grown for its fleshy, pinkish to red leafstalks, which have a pleasantly acid taste and can be used to make tart, delicious pies or as a base for wine. The stalks, 1–2½ ft. (30–75 cm) high, bear large, reddish-green leaves to 18 in. (45 cm) wide. Although rhubarb leaves can be handled safely, the leaf blades are poisonous when eaten; trim off and discard all green leaf matter before using the stalks.

How to Grow
Plants are best grown from root divisions. You can grow rhubarb from seeds, but production takes about a year longer, and the stalks will be thinner and paler. Thorough soil preparation is vital. In early spring, make the bed 3 ft. (90 cm) wide by 10 ft. (3 m) long. Dig in 2–3 large bags of steam-pasteurized cattle manure to spade depth. Add lime fertilizer as indicated by soil tests. These additives will result in a raised bed. Cover the bed with black plastic or landscape cloth. Cut out small openings and insert the plants. You will need only 2–3 plants; space them 3 ft. (90 cm) apart. Water occasionally by inserting a hose in a hole and letting it trickle for a half hour or so. Grow rhubarb in full sun; in areas with warm summers, plants need afternoon shade. Use plastic mulch, or lay moistened newspapers thickly over the bed and cover them with dried lawn clippings. Control snails, slugs, and earwigs with metaldehyde plus carbaryl pellets.
These cold-hardy plants require winter dormancy and may perish where winters are

mild. In areas with severe winters, plant tops
will freeze to the ground. Mulch each winter
with a mixture of compost, phosphate, and
potash sources, 2–3 in. (5.0–7.5 cm) deep.

Harvest
Wait until the second growing season to
harvest. From spring through early summer,
carefully snap off the outer leafstalks at the
base. (Don't use a knife, which could slip
and sever the growing point.) Harvest
sparingly so that you don't shock the plant;
discontinue when you have taken about half
the new growth.

Varieties
Cherry Red, Valentine, and MacDonald are
all good varieties to start from plants and are
more uniform than seed-grown rhubarb.
Victoria is the only variety widely available
from seeds.

Rutabaga
Brassica napus p. 94

Napobrassica Group. Swede; Swedish Turnip.
Rutabagas resemble giant turnips except that
the leaves are smooth and bluish green and
the huge roots, which often grow half out of
the ground, have a long, leafy neck. Hardier
than turnips, rutabagas take a long time to
mature and are intolerant of hot weather, so
they are planted mostly in cooler areas of
the U.S.

How to Grow
In areas with short summers, sow seeds
6–9 in. (15–22.5 cm) apart in midsummer;
elsewhere plant in late summer. Avoid early
spring planting; prolonged temperatures of
less than 50° F (10° C) can cause plants to
bolt to seed.

Harvest
Pull the entire plant. White-rooted rutabagas
are preferred for eating fresh. The young
greens can be cooked with the roots, and the
roots can be stored in the ground for a few
weeks after frost if mulched against freezing.
Coat the trimmed roots of yellow varieties
with paraffin for extended storage.

Varieties
Laurentian is the leading yellow variety.

The milder Altasweet is good for fresh use. Wilhelmsburger Gelbe is an early, frost-resistant European variety with pink shoulders.

Salsify
Tragopogon porrifolius p. 91

Common Vegetable Oyster. This slow-growing biennial is grown as a long-season annual; it forms large clumps of broad, grasslike leaves and a heavy, deep taproot. On friable, deep soil, roots can grow to 2½ in. (6 cm) thick at the shoulder and 16 in. (40.5 cm) long. The cooked roots have a delicious taste reminiscent of oysters.

How to Grow
Direct-seed salsify 2 in. (5 cm) apart in rows 3 ft. (90 cm) apart. Cover seeds ¼ in. (6 mm) deep. Thin to 4–6 in. (10–15 cm) apart. Irrigate when 10–14 days pass without rain. Prolonged dry spells followed by soaking rains can split roots. In cool-summer areas, spring-planted salsify matures in fall just before the ground freezes. In mild-winter areas, salsify planted in early fall will produce large enough roots for harvest by late winter or early spring.

Harvest
Soak the soil with a sprinkler for an hour or two, or wait until after a rain to dig salsify. Dig roots only as you need them. If you live where winters are very cold, dig the roots before the ground freezes and sandwich them between insulating layers of straw. Cover with a rain shield of plastic sheeting held down with chicken wire.

Varieties
Mammoth Sandwich Island is the standard variety.

Black Salsify
Scorzonera hispanica p. 90

Black Oyster Plant; Scorzonera. You may have seen these roots on produce racks— long, slender, and black, in bunches of 6–12. These are the taproots of perennial plants 2–3 ft. (60–90 cm) tall, with long, narrow leaves, sometimes lobed. The flowers,

which come the second season, are yellow,
daisylike, and 2 in. (5 cm) wide.

How to Grow
Sow seeds in deep, fertile, well-prepared soil
in early spring. Late summer planting is
preferred for the Deep South and warm
West. Thin plants to stand 12 in. (30 cm)
apart.

Harvest
Harvest black salsify in late fall or winter
after cold has sweetened the roots. Roots
dug in warm weather can be placed in a
plastic bag and stored in the refrigerator for
a week to allow some of the starch to
convert to sugar. The long, slender roots are
brittle and should be dug with care. Soak
the soil deeply and use a spading fork to lift
out the roots. Scrub them and soak in
vinegar-water for 4–6 hours to eliminate
their natural bitterness. Do not peel; doing
so will diminish the flavor. The black skin
will slip off after boiling. Black salsify is less
fibrous, easier to peel, and tastes as good or
better than common salsify.

Varieties
Gigantia.

Shallot
Allium cepa pp. 108, 109

Aggregatum Group. Thought to be native
to w. Asia, shallots somewhat resemble
garlic, but the bulbs, clustered at the base of
the plant, are chestnut-brown. The plants are
smaller than those of the related onion.
Shallots reproduce only by bulb division and
do not set seeds. The cloves have a more
delicate flavor than onions.

How to Grow
Order shallot bulbs from catalogues in
spring or fall, or buy the common French
variety in gourmet food stores. Treat bulbs
with a fungicide and plant them shallow, as
you would onion sets. Space plants 6–8 in.
(15–20 cm) apart. Spring-planted shallots
will divide into numerous shoots by late
summer and can be separated and spread out
to produce more plants that will mature dry
bulbs the following summer. Shallots are
hardy except where winters are extremely
severe and snow cover is scant.

Harvest
Eat the green shallots like scallions, or dig the bulbs when the tops begin to dry. Gray shallots do not store well.

Varieties
The French variety has dark orange-brown scales, white flesh tinged with purple, and a garlicky flavor. Frogs' Legs are the same color as French but have a distinctive shape and sweet flavor. The gray variety has gray-orange scales, purple-white flesh, and a strong oniony flavor.

Skirret
Sium sisarum p. 114

Once popular in the American Colonies, skirret has slipped into obscurity despite the sweet taste of its roots. If you like root parsley and salsify, you should try skirret. This hardy perennial vegetable produces a rosette of feathery leaves and clusters of knobby roots for fall and winter harvest.

How to Grow
Poor seed germination and slow sprouting are common problems with skirret. Sow seeds in rich, deeply prepared soil in midspring, except in the South, where late summer seeding is preferable. Starting seeds indoors gives you better control over temperature and moisture; sow the seeds in peat pots to lessen transplanting shock. Set in plants or thin seedlings to stand 8–12 in. (20–30 cm) apart. Each plant will give you a cluster of roots to divide for propagation the following spring.

Harvest
Dig up the roots and prune off the tops in late fall or winter before the ground freezes. Lay the root clusters on the ground and cover them with straw held down with chicken wire. You can also store roots in moist sand in a cold (but not freezing) cellar. Skirret will overwinter in most climates, but the best roots are the young ones taken after the first growing season.

Varieties
A few seed companies, mostly European, offer skirret seeds, usually by the species. It's easy to propagate skirret vegetatively—ask friends or neighbors for "starts."

Garden Sorrel
Rumex acetosa p. 225

A frost-hardy perennial, garden sorrel is an erect, leafy plant forming large, dense clump 12–18 in. (30–45 cm) high, to 3 ft. (90 cm) high when in flower. The smooth, upright leaves are lance- or arrowhead-shaped. Garden sorrel is frequently confused with French sorrel, *R. scutatus,* a small-leaved vegetable seldom seen in North America.

How to Grow
Direct-seed, spring or fall, in full sun in ordinary garden soil. Space plants 12 in. (30 cm) apart. In a well-drained site this very sturdy plant will live for years. It can be cut to the ground once or twice during the season; feed and water to encourage new growth. Manure tea helps sorrel maintain good color. Snap off seed stalks as they start to shoot up.

Harvest
Shear or snap off leaves as needed. Sorrel has an acid, lemony taste; use it as a potherb, in leek soup, salads, or to line the vessel for baking fish. Young leaves are fragile, needing only brief cooking. Older leaves are very tart and may need 1 or 2 changes of cooking water to reduce the tartness.

Varieties
Large Belleville is the favorite.

SPINACH

Succulent, dark green leaves of spinach are a welcome ingredient in any salad and, though the bane of many a child's dinnertime, delicious cooked. Featured here is the common garden spinach (*Spinacia oleracea*), as well as 2 plants frequently grown as substitutes for it: Malabar spinach (*Basella alba*) and New Zealand spinach (*Tetragonia tetragonioides*).

Spinach
Spinacia oleracea pp. 222, 223, 224

This fast-growing, cool-loving annual is grown for salads and as a potherb. The mound of long-stemmed leaves can reach

12 in. (30 cm) high and 18 in. (45 cm) wide at maturity, but spinach is usually harvested earlier. The major differences among spinach hybrids and open-pollinated varieties are in their earliness, resistance to bolting and diseases, and leaf texture.

How to Grow
Even slow-bolting spinach varieties don't last long in warm weather, so plant seeds in the very early spring and again in early fall after the worst hot weather is past.
Wash seeds in detergent, rinse thoroughly in a tea strainer, and blot them dry before planting. Sow 3–6 in. (7.5–10.0 cm) apart in raised beds as early as the soil can be worked in spring. Where summers are cool, a succession crop planted 2 weeks later may also mature. Elsewhere, second plantings usually bolt before the leaves are large enough to eat. Wait until late summer to plant again (or until fall where winters are mild). To determine the latest safe planting date, count back 45 days from the average date of the first fall frost. Temperatures below 20° F (−6.5° C) can kill spinach.
Leaf-miner damage can be serious; watch for signs of burrowing between the top and bottom layers of leaves, and for dead tissue. Pull off affected leaves and dispose of them in the garbage, not in the compost heap.

Harvest
Snap off the outer leaves or shear the entire plant to 3–4 in. (7.5–10.0 cm) above the ground. When the central stem begins to elongate, the plant is starting to bolt; pull and eat the entire plant.

Varieties
Melody, Tyee, Indian Summer, Avon; Dixie Market for the Southeast.

Malabar Spinach
Basella alba pp. 225, 237

Indian Spinach; Malabar Nightshade; Pasali; Pu-tin-choi. One of the best hot-weather greens for cooking, Malabar spinach is a staple in tropical Africa and se. Asia, where it originated. Its glutinous texture when cooked takes some getting used to, but the strong flavor is agreeable. The low-growing plants form runners covered with sizable, succulent, thick, dark green leaves. In the North, runners can grow 2 ft. (60 cm) long by season's end. In the South, they grow much longer.

How to Grow
Where the growing season is short, start seeds indoors at 75–80°F (24.0–26.5°C) and transplant seedlings after danger of frost is past; direct-seed elsewhere. Space plants 6–12 in. (15–30 cm) apart. You can also plant seeds in 5–10-gallon (20–40-l) tubs and train runners up short trellises. Provide afternoon shade in hot climates, full sun and protection from cold winds elsewhere. The plants are quite tender to frost.

Harvest
Take tender small leaves and runner tips; older leaves are tough and fibrous. Cook alone or with meat or poultry. Mix tiny leaves sparingly with other greens in salads.

Varieties
Usually sold generically; one cultivar, Rubri, has a reddish tinge to stems and leaves.

New Zealand Spinach
Tetragonia tetragonioides pp. 234, 235

This half-hardy, short-lived perennial makes a good summer substitute for true spinach. The pretty plants have unique rhombic or triangular dark green leaves with a glistening lower surface. In the North, short runners form and the creeping plants spread to 2–3 ft. (60–90 cm) wide. In warm climates long runners can be trained up trellises.

How to Grow
Soak seeds in warm water overnight. Plant indoors in peat pots filled with sandy soil and sprout at 70–80°F (21.1–26.7°C). Transplant after frost danger is past. Or direct-seed 12 in. (30 cm) apart in rows 3 ft. (90 cm) apart. Seeds may be slow to sprout, but once plants are established, they will drop seeds and produce plenty of volunteers. New Zealand spinach prefers sandy or sandy loam soil. Although resistant to heat and dry soil, plants grow better if watered occasionally. In very hot climates, light afternoon shade helps keep them from wilting. Makes a fine container plant.

Harvest
Take only the 2 or 3 tender tip leaves;
older leaves have a strong taste. The tiny,
succulent leaves can be chopped and added
to mixed green salads. Too much can be
overpowering, though, due to the high
calcium oxylate content.

SQUASHES

These members of the cucumber family are
generally divided into 2 classes. The summer
squashes have soft skins and are eaten at
immature stages; the winter squashes have
hard shells that suit them for winter storage.
All grow on warm-weather, annual vines
with large, often lobed, leaves and yellow
flowers.

Summer Squash
*Cucurbita pepo pp. 176, 180, 181, 183,
188, 189*

Included here are warty yellow crooknecks;
smooth yellow straightnecks; white or green
top- or disk-shaped scallop or patty pan
squashes with scalloped rims; slender,
medium to dark green, club-shaped zucchini,
with golden-yellow varieties; and smooth-
skinned, variously shaped fruits
called vegetable marrows. There is little
difference in flavor among summer squash
varieties, but some difference in the texture
of the cooked flesh. Vegetable marrows are
eaten, often along with the blossoms, when
very small.

How to Grow
All squashes are grown alike. Frost-tender
annuals, they are robust and heat-resistant,
but susceptible to damage from a number of
diseases and insects. Direct-seed squash at
about the frost-free date in fertile, well-
drained soil. Use black plastic mulch in cool
climates and straw or dried grass clippings
elsewhere. Space summer squash plants 4 ft.
(120 cm) apart. You can make 2–3 plantings
of fast-maturing kinds during summer. In
early stages of growth, use spun-bonded
plastic row covers and large squares of
aluminum foil to repel vine borers, squash
bugs, and beetles.

Harvest
Summer squash is generally eaten when
immature and soft-skinned. Cut off squash
stems with a sharp knife or needle-nose
pruning shears. Fruits are most flavorful
when 4–6 in. (10–15 cm) long. Hard-skinned
mature fruits will store for a few weeks but
are not as tasty. Test the skin with your
thumbnail; if it is hard, the squash is past its
prime. Larger fruits are good if you scoop
out the seeds and peel the fruit.

Varieties
Straightneck: Early Prolific (AAS), Seneca
Prolific, Goldbar, Butterstick, Park's Creamy.
Crookneck: Sundance, Tara, Butter Swan.
Zucchini: Black Magic, Gold Rush (AAS),
Black Satin, Blackjack, Eldorado, Elite,
Gourmet Globe, Green Magic. Vegetable
marrow: Kuta, Cousa, Cocozelle, White
Bush Hybrid. Scallop or patty pan: Peter Pan
Hybrid (AAS), Yellow Bush Scallop,
Scallopini (AAS), Sunburst (AAS).

Winter Squash
Cucurbita spp. *pp. 176, 177, 178, 179, 181,
190, 191, 192, 193*

The 3 species in this group cover a wide
range of shapes, sizes, and flavors. *Cucurbita
maxima* includes several kinds: large, long
banana squashes in pink, orange, or bluish
gray; Boston marrow—medium to large,

bulbous, orange-skinned fruits shaped like a
teardrop; buttercup—medium-size, dark
green drum- or top-shaped fruits splotched
with gray; Hubbard—medium-size green,
golden, or blue-gray fruits with bumpy skin;

and Turk's turban—green, turban-shaped
fruits vividly streaked with white, red, or
orange, and with a "navel" at the blossom
end. *C. moschata* includes the tan-skinned
butternut squash—long, cylindrical fruits
with a bulbous base and orange flesh.
Cushaws resemble large, striped butternut
squash with curved necks. The deeply ribbed,

green or golden acorn squashes are small to
medium-size fruits resembling the nut; they
belong to the species *C. pepo,* as does
vegetable spaghetti, an oval squash with

ivory to golden-yellow skin and flesh that cooks to spaghettilike strands.

How to Grow
See summer squash. Winter squash needs a lot of room: Space plants 4 ft. (120 cm) apart in rows 10–15 ft. (3.0–4.5 m) apart. Only 1 planting can be made. In the South, you can plant winter squash at the same time as collards, in late summer, but diseases and insects can be especially troublesome in early fall.

Harvest
Like pumpkins, winter squash should be harvested before frost. Leave a 3-in. (7.5-cm) stem stub attached; handle fruits carefully and do not brush or wash them. Store winter squashes in a cool, dry area so that fruits don't shrivel and lose weight. In the South, spring-planted winter squash is usually harvested in late summer.

Varieties
Buttercup: Sweet Mama (AAS), Buttercup Improved, Kindred. Butternut: Early Butternut Hybrid (AAS), Waltham Butternut, Burpee's Butterbush, Hercules (large). Acorn: Jersey Golden Acorn (AAS), Table Queen, Table King (AAS), Ponca (early). Hubbard: Green Hubbard, Golden Delicious, Baby Hubbard, Baby Blue. Banana: Jumbo Pink. Cushaw: Green Striped Cushaw, Golden Nugget (AAS).

STRAWBERRIES

The small genus *Fragaria* contains only a few species of decorative or edible plants, some with runners, others with clump-forming plants. These include the various wild strawberries of cool areas of the northern hemisphere and the recently improved, mat-forming ground cover berries popular in landscaping on the West Coast. The garden strawberries incorporate several improvements over wild strawberries, not only in size and production of fruit but also in their ability to last. Some of the wild berries are so fragile that they should be eaten as they are picked.

Strawberry
Fragaria × ananassa p. 119

Garden Strawberry. Large-fruited domestic strawberries are a relatively new perennial crop, the result of a cross between native species of coastal and upland areas of both the West and East coasts. Strawberries have been greatly improved in recent years. Most modern varieties combine high sugar content with heavy production and excellent flavor. However, some cultivars developed for shipping can have odd flavor overtones. Fortunately, these are being supplanted by cultivars that taste good even in the near-ripe but firm stage seen in supermarkets. Although technically perennial, strawberry plants begin to decline somewhat in vigor after the second year, and even earlier in the Deep South, where they are often treated as annuals. Nevertheless, on fertile northern soils, plants may remain productive for as long as 5–6 years without being divided.

How to Grow
When ordering new plants, start early. Your supplier will not stock or send plants to you when it is too early or too late for your climate. Generally, plant in early spring, except in the warm South and West, where fall planting works better. Build up beds about 4 in. (10 cm) high for good drainage by transferring topsoil from aisles between rows. (This is not necessary on deep, sandy soil.) Make beds 2 ft. (60 cm) wide across the top for ease in picking. Set plants 2 ft. (60 cm) apart in rows 6 ft. (1.8 m) apart. Either mulch rows with black plastic or, in hot summer areas, with pine needles or straw. Mulching pays off in increased productivity, decreased water use, and clean fruit at harvest time. The growth of a crowded mat of runners can cause your strawberries to decline. Renewal is the solution. Either allow the runners to spread to 3 times the width of the original bed, and then till out the old center strip, or take cuttings where they root at the ends of runners, and transplant them to new beds. Nematodes, verticillium wilt, and spider mites can be troublesome, especially on lightweight soils in the South and warm West, where some strawberry growers fumigate the soil every 2 years. Yet in cool climates, using a 2-year replacement program, gardeners can often get by without spraying.

Two feedings are standard for strawberries; in spring before growth resumes and in late summer. Fall feedings can stimulate lush growth that is susceptible to winter injury.

Harvest
Pick ripe berries promptly. Be careful not to walk on the raised beds because strawberries resent compaction of soil around the roots.

Varieties
Local, state, and regional strawberry trials are conducted by various governmental agencies, and lists are published of the best modern varieties for home or commercial use. You can go very wrong by planting varieties that are not recommended for your area or are purchased from a nursery in a climate warmer than yours. Consult your County Cooperative Extension Office or a strawberry nursery. Sweetheart is a small-fruited everbearer that can be grown from seeds.

Alpine Strawberry
Fragaria vesca p. 118

Perpetual White or Yellow Fraise. This clump-forming European strawberry has hairy leaves and short plants. Some cultivars have rounded fruits, but many are elongated. Available in red, yellow, or white cultivars.

How to Grow
See strawberry. Divide every 2–3 years.

Harvest
Alpine strawberries are soft when ripe, and too fragile for shipping. They are marginal even for local marketing, and best eaten as soon as they are picked.

Varieties
Many varieties are available in Europe but only a few are propagated for gardeners on this continent. Try Baron Solemacher (red), Ruegen Improved, and Alexandria (early).

Sunflower
Helianthus annuus pp. 122, 123

Giant Sunflower; Mirasol. A warmth-loving annual for sunny locations, giant or mammoth sunflowers, to 12 ft. (3.5 m) high,

are grown principally for their nutritious seeds. Earlier-maturing, shorter hybrids for oilseed production have recently been developed and are now appearing in garden seed catalogues. The smaller-flowered sunflowers, 2–3 ft. (60–90 cm) high, are considered ornamentals and sold as garden flowers; they are favored for wild birdseed. Sunflowers are aggressive and inhibit nearby plant growth. Too large and rough for flower gardens, they look pretty against a distant fence. Smaller varieties are usually grown behind other tall annuals.

How to Grow
Direct-seed in full sun 1–2 weeks before the spring frost-free date. Seeds will sprout in only a few days and will withstand frost as seedlings. Thin plants of mammoth varieties to stand 3½–4 ft. (105–120 cm) apart; closer spacing will result in spindly plants with small heads. In windy locations, tie stalks loosely to fenceposts.

Harvest
Birds will begin pilfering seeds 1–2 weeks before they are fully dry. Wrap cheesecloth around heads to prevent loss. Test the seed coats occasionally with your thumbnail; when they are hard, cut the stem about 6 in. (15 cm) below the head, and hang the head indoors to complete drying.

Varieties
Mammoth, Mammoth Russian, Sunbird Hybrid, Sundak, Oilseed.

Sweet Potato
Ipomoea batatas pp. 102, 103

Louisiana Yam. This frost-tender, warm-weather perennial is grown for its edible roots. Perhaps native to tropical America, the sweet potato is now cultivated worldwide in warm climates. Sweet potatoes grow quickly, forming a mat of runners and dark green leaves, tinged with reddish purple in some varieties. Three classes of sweet potatoes are available—the generally earlier varieties that have yellow or orange roots with rather dry flesh; darker Louisiana yams, which are moist and very sweet when cooked; and dry, white-fleshed boniato or camote varieties.

How to Grow

Sweet potatoes grow best in sandy or sandy loam soil. Start slips (rooted cuttings) by sprouting whole tubers in warm, moist potting soil or sand. Across the South, slips of several varieties are sold in bunches of 50–100 in garden centers in late spring. Elsewhere, order by mail. You can sprout your own from store-bought roots, but you will have to guess at the variety. Sweet potatoes need only a modest initial application of 1-2-2 fertilizer; in deep sandy soils a midseason drench of liquid fertilizer may help roots to set and size up. Too much nitrogen can force vine growth at the expense of roots. Avoid double-digging; deep tillage will give you impractical, jumbo roots. Sweet potatoes dislike cool soil, so plant slips in early summer, even later than muskmelons and peppers. On heavy clay soils, work soil up thoroughly into raised beds 4 ft. (120 cm) wide and set slips 12 in. (30 cm) apart down the center. Spread 5-10-10 fertilizer, and mulch deeply around the slips with spoiled hay, rotting straw, or shredded dry leaves. Late in the season, probe beneath the vines to test root size. Let them grow as late as you can, but don't let the vines be hit by frost. Even a week or two of growth at the end of the season can add 10 percent to the weight of the crop. If an early frost is projected, cover the bed temporarily to keep vines growing through early fall.

Harvest

Be extra careful not to scrape or puncture the roots when you harvest, and don't wash them. Injured or squeaky-clean roots won't store reliably. Cure roots at 85–90° F (29.5–32.0° C) for 7–10 days in an unused cold frame or a heated room. After that, lay them in a dry, cool, well-ventilated area; keep roots from touching to prevent rot.

Varieties

Short-season cultivars will produce small to medium roots from s. New England across the s. Great Plains, and in all western gardens except cool coastal microclimates. A few "bush" cultivars with shorter runners cover a bed 4–5 ft. (1.2–1.5 m) wide. Named varieties include Nancy Hall, Centennial, Jewel, New-Jewel, Vardaman Bush, Bush Porto Rico, and Georgia Red.

Swiss Chard
Beta vulgaris pp. 242, 243

Cicla Group. Chard; Leaf Beet; Spinach Beet.
A biennial grown as an annual, Swiss chard
is a reliable, heat-resistant potherb for
summer and fall harvest. It could be
nicknamed "cut and come again" because
the deep-rooted, rugged plant will continue
to replace harvested leaves despite heavy
cutting. The leaves of chard are usually eaten
cooked. Chard takes up where the spring
greens leave off and makes a good
supplement to garden beets and other
potherbs. During midsummer, beets go out
of condition over much of the country;
chard does not.

How to Grow
Plant chard seeds as you would beets. In
mild-winter areas, plants will live over to
provide fall and winter greens but will
almost always bolt to seed late the following
spring; pull out the plants and start over.

Harvest
Few plants yield more food per square foot
of garden space with as little care. Harvest
by snapping off outer stems, leaving the
central stems to develop. When cutting large
amounts for freezing, shear off all the top
growth 3–4 in. (7.5–10.0 cm) above the soil
line. Plants will grow back if fed and
watered promptly.

Varieties
Some varieties have greenish-white or
decorative red foliage. Green varieties with
wide white leaf stems, shingled at the base
like celery, are usually better to eat than
older, narrow-stemmed varieties, such as
Lucullus. Ornamental chards are not
especially good to eat. Fordhook Giant
and Swiss Chard of Geneva have broad,
glistening white petioles. Vulcan and Ruby
Chard have ornamental red stems and
green leaves.

Tomatillo
Physalis ixocarpa p. 131

Jamberry; Mexican Husk Tomato;
Miltomate. Tomatillos are the curious fruits
seen in stores serving Hispanic trade and on

gourmet produce counters. The shiny, flattened, greenish-yellow fruits, averaging 1½–2 in. (4–5 cm) in diameter, are enclosed in papery husks. As the fruits mature and reveal a purple blush, the husks split but adhere. In Latin America, tomatillos are crushed and used in sauces; the taste is pleasant but not sweet. Plants grow to 3 ft. (90 cm) tall and spread even wider, with the branches in an unusual zigzag pattern. Leaves are heart-shaped and elongated, with long petioles.

How to Grow
Grow like tomatoes. Start from seeds; plants are rarely available. If you can't find seeds, buy ripe fruit, let it begin to decay, and mash and strain the pulp for seeds. Let the seeds dry before planting. Tomatillos are best adapted to warm, dry climates. Where rainfall and humidity are high, the plants tend to be short-lived. They can be grown as far north as the central Midwest.

Harvest
Flavor improves with maturity. Harvest after the husks split; set aside fruits that feel too hard for further ripening. Seeds from dropped fruits may volunteer and cause a weed problem.

TOMATOES

The tomato is an international favorite, and there are more varieties sold of it than of any other vegetable. It is even grown in greenhouses where the summers are too cool for pollination and fruit set in gardens. Tomatoes are related to white potatoes, peppers, eggplants, and other members of the potato family. Technically tender perennials, they are grown as warm-weather annuals. Included here are medium to large garden tomatoes and their cherry- and pear-shaped relatives.

Tomato
Lycopersicon lycopersicum pp. 132, 134, 135, 136, 137, 138, 139

Love Apple; Pomo D'Oro; Golden Apple. Garden tomatoes come in an incredible array of varieties, attesting to their popularity. Red, pink, orange, golden, yellow, striped, or white fruits exist in round, globe, oval, flattened, heart, or elongated and squarish shapes. The average garden tomato for slicing weighs 4–6 oz. (113–170 g), but some larger varieties average up to 2 lbs. (0.9 kg). High-quality slicing tomatoes have a good ratio of cell-wall to pulp, and a short, soft core. Although much is said about flavor and acidity, there is actually little variation among varieties in the pH of the ripe fruit. Most important to taste is the sugar content. Moisture content is another factor, saturated soil during the days leading up to harvest can produce bland, watery fruit.

A tomato plant can produce 10–50 lbs. (4.5–22.5 kg) of usable fruits, depending on the size and health of the plant and on whether the prevailing temperatures are favorable for pollination. Some varieties can set fruit under quite cool or quite warm conditions—or often both. Certain older varieties will set fruit only within a narrow range of temperatures.

Tomato vines fall into 3 categories. "Indeterminate" vines grow throughout the season; "large determinate" vines grow to a good size but expand little more after that point; "determinate" vines remain small to medium-size regardless of how much you feed and water them. Compact or dwarf vines are even smaller, and some are the right size for pots. Vine habit depends on the variety; plants may be upright, sprawling or with descending branches, suitable for hanging baskets. Most varieties have typical tomato foliage, but some have thick, dark green leaves resembling potato foliage. Certain midget varieties have tiny leaves.

How to Grow

If you start from seeds, use a "seed-starter mix" instead of potting soil. Plant seeds indoors 8 weeks prior to the frost-free date and germinate at 75–85° F (24.0–29.5° C). After the first true leaves appear, put seedlings in a spot where night temperatures reach 50–55° F (10–13° C); daytime temperatures can range from room temperature to 80° F (26.5° C). Cool nights keep the plants from becoming spindly. Do not overwater during early stages of growth, and maintain strong light from the sun or from fluorescent lights 2 in. (5 cm) above the plants. After 3 weeks of growth, place plants where night temperatures reach 60–65 °F (15.5–18.5 °C). After frost danger is past, set plants in the garden and protect with bottomless 1-gal. (3-l) plastic jugs for 2–3 weeks. When exposed to cold but protected from frost, the little tomato plants are "vernalized." This treatment can increase the number and quality of fruits set, especially early in the season.

Plants started very early indoors and grown to blossom or fruit stage before transplanting may languish for several days if they suffer shock or a setback in growth; some never recover fully. Smaller, cold-treated seedlings soon catch up and outproduce large, forced plants.

All tomatoes except midget varieties benefit from being grown on supports. Use cages made of large-mesh wire fencing, rolled into cylinders 2–3 ft. (60–90 cm) wide and 5–6 ft. (1.5–1.8 m) high. The mesh should be large enough to reach through for harvesting; support the cylinders with stakes. Some gardeners prune vines to 2 leader stems run up stout strings or twine. They prune off the side shoots, or suckers. These tall, slender, pruned plants are easier to spray for insects and diseases.

Tomato plants—especially varieties with small, determinate vines—are moderate feeders. Too much nitrogen or a high level of all major nutrients can overstimulate vegetative growth, delay maturity, and reduce production. Control soil pH and provide good drainage to prevent "blossom-end rot." Maintain a soil pH of 6.0–7.0 with dolomitic limestone to ensure adequate calcium and magnesium. Soils with a pH of 7.0 and higher may benefit from applications of agricultural sulfur.

Tomato diseases may prove troublesome, even in resistant hybrids. Fortunately, there are relatively safe insecticides with negligible residues for the control of soft-bodied tomato insects.

Harvest

Begin picking before tomatoes are dead ripe. Freeze them whole, or scald and skin them for canning, juicing, or freezing. Never process spoiled or mushy-ripe tomatoes; cold packing or inadequate pressure-cooking could allow dangerous organisms to survive. Partially ripe tomatoes will finish ripening satisfactorily on a windowsill, out of direct sunlight. Certain varieties keep for several weeks in a cool place. Allowing ripe tomatoes to hang on the vine decreases yield and may spread rot.

Varieties

The choice of varieties is vast; search catalogues and seed and plant displays for those that will meet your needs. No single variety or hybrid tomato will combine all the best features. Ask your County Cooperative Extension Service office for an updated list of recommended varieties. Find out which varieties are suitable for home gardens, and which tomato diseases are severe in your area; choose resistant varieties.

You will need 2 varieties in your garden, one early and one midseason or late. If space is limited, choose determinate or midget types. Read catalogue descriptions: If they mention shipping qualities or mechanical harvesting for one variety, choose another. Plant extremely early varieties in short-season gardens; avoid late varieties where seasons are short or cool.

Varieties are tested and classified according to the number of days from transplanting to the first ripe fruit. In your garden, this may vary by a few days from the catalogue listings. Summer plantings generally mature faster than spring plantings. Extra-early varieties mature in 58–63 days from transplanting; early types require 64–70 days; midseason types need 71–79 days; and late types, 80 days and up.

The foliage canopy of a tomato plant can range from heavy to open. For southern and western gardens, a dense canopy safeguards against sunburn, but in northern gardens, a heavy canopy can retard ripening. Extra-early dwarf varieties tend to have a sparse canopy; they often sunburn in the South and Southwest.

Resistance to or tolerance of specific diseases is usually denoted by an initial in the variety name: verticillium (V), fusarium (F), nematodes (N), tobacco mosaic virus (T), and alternaria (A). Look for varieties that also resist stem canker, leaf mold, gray leafspot, and blossom-end rot.

Consider fruit set. If you wish tomatoes for canning, choose a variety that produces many ripe fruits at once; if you want a long harvest season, choose a variety with extended maturity.

Here are just a few of the varieties available. Early: Siberia, Early Girl V Hybrid, Champion VFNT Hybrid, Sprint A. Midseason: Better Boy VFN Hybrid,

Burpee's Big Girl VF Hybrid, Freedom VFF,
Parks Whopper VFNT, Celebrity VFNT
Hybrid (AAS). Late: Beefmaster VFN
Hybrid, Golden Boy, Royal Ace VF.

Cherry Tomato
Lycopersicon lycopersicum var. *cerasiforme pp.*
133, 135

"Cherry" refers to the size and shape of the
fruit and has no bearing on the size of the
plant. Cherry tomatoes may be red or yellow;
large ones may be the size of a ping-pong
ball, while small varieties average ½–⅝ in.
(13–16 mm) in diameter. The fruiting
clusters, or "hands," of cherry tomatoes can
be very large and may produce 100 fruits
each. Indeed, the total production of
individual plants can equal or surpass that of
slicing tomatoes of comparable vine size.
Most varieties have high-climbing,
indeterminate vines, and the fruits of some
have comparatively tough skins. Vines can
be staked, grown in cages, or pruned to 1–2
leader stems and run up strings or arbors.

How to Grow and Harvest
Grow and harvest just as you would
standard tomatoes of comparable vine habit
and size.

Varieties
Large Red Cherry is the old standard. The
small-fruited Sweet 100 Hybrid is much
sweeter and has a high content of vitamin C,
plus fairly tender skin. Cherry Grande VF is
another variety to consider. Some midget
varieties of standard tomatoes have fruit the
same size as cherry tomatoes but generally
produce fewer fruits per hand.

Pear Tomato
Lycopersicon lycopersicum var. *pyriforme pp. 132,*
133, 134

The vines are similar to those of cherry
tomatoes—tall and indeterminate—but not
quite so productive. Pear tomatoes have
small fruits, no larger than 2 in. x 1 in.
(5.0 x 2.5 cm), and nipples on the stem ends.
"Plum" and "Peach" tomatoes are similar
but lack nipples. All 3 varieties come in red

or yellow; all have tender skins and juicy interiors. Many chefs consider pear, plum, and peach tomatoes to be the ultimate for eating. Yet some of the paste tomatoes for processing, although plum- or pear-shaped, are solid and dry.

How to Grow
Grow just as you would standard tomatoes of comparable vine size and habit.

Harvest
The vines of these varieties are so large and dense that it is difficult to find the fruits as they ripen. Try hard, because small-fruited tomatoes can drop and volunteer in your garden for several seasons thereafter.

Varieties
Red Plum, Red Pear, Yellow Plum, Yellow Pear, Roma VF Hybrid, Early Baby Boy.

Tree Tomato
Cyphomandra betacea p. 140

Tamarillo. The tree tomato is not a tomato; the plants are completely unlike tomatoes and have large, downy leaves. The rather ungainly plants are tall and treelike; the fruits resemble tomatoes only in their orange-red color and glossy skin. In semitropical climates, the frost-tender, perennial tree tomato—more a fruit than a vegetable—is widely grown for making pies and jellies. In most of the U.S., however, the tree tomato must be grown in a greenhouse or in containers brought indoors for winter protection. Thus it is unfortunate that promoters often choose this plant for advertisements full of hype and high claims. In areas with long, warm summers tree tomatoes can grow to 6 ft. (180 cm) or more, producing several pounds of glossy, orange-red, oval fruits, each about 2 in. (5 cm) long.

How to Grow
Plants grow slowly from seeds, cuttings, or small potted plants. Allow 2 years for fruiting. In semitropical areas, grow this plant as you would a papaya; elsewhere, treat it as a greenhouse plant, in a large tub that can be rolled outside during the summer. Space plants 3 ft. (90 cm) apart. Whiteflies may be a problem.

Harvest
Test the fruit, which is high in pectin, by squeezing it lightly. When fruits begin to feel soft, pick them for making jelly and fruit pies.

Turnip
Brassica rapa pp. 93, 94, 95

Rapifera Group. Turnips are multi-purpose vegetables, and varieties have been developed for their leaves, their roots, and both. The flesh may be white, white and purple, or yellow. The leaves are medium green and rough-textured, tender in young stages and ready to harvest 45–60 days after planting. Although turnips are among the most frost-hardy of vegetables, they are generally killed by hard freezes.
Spring-seeded turnips are usually harvested young because hot, dry weather causes the leaves to turn bitter and the roots to develop stringy flesh. The best turnip crops grow from direct-seeding in late summer or, in the South, early fall. Under favorable cool conditions and in moist, fertile soil, turnip roots may reach 2–3 lbs. (0.9–1.4 kg).

How to Grow
Sow turnip seeds thickly; thin plants to stand about 4 in. (10 cm) apart. The excess seedlings are fine to eat. For late summer planting in dry soil, dig a deep furrow, flood it twice with water, let it soak in, and scatter seeds in the bottom. Cover lightly with sand or sifted compost to keep the soil from crusting.

Harvest
For greens, snip off turnip plants 3–4 in. (7.5–10.0 cm) above ground. Leave roots in the ground and mulch against frost damage. Harvest only as needed by pulling up the entire plant.

Varieties
Some fast-growing hybrids between the true turnips and related brassicas are proving to be delicious and productive. Most are all-leaf cultivars, such as Just Right and All Top; these have better quality than the old Seven Top leaf turnip. For roots it is hard to beat the old Purple Top White Globe but for

novelty, try Ohno Scarlet, Gilfeather, and
Amber Ball.

Chinese Yam
Dioscorea batatas p. 236

Formerly called *D. opposita,* the Chinese yam
is grown and used much like the ubiquitous
D. alata. Its tubers are seen in Japanese and
Chinese food stores and weigh 5–10 lbs.
(2.2–4.5 kg); they are often flattened or
fanlike in shape, and selections are club-
shaped. The Chinese yam is frequently seen
as an ornamental because it will overwinter
in the Deep South and warm West, and can
tolerate cooler weather better than the
winged yam.

How to Grow and Harvest
See winged yam.

Winged Yam
Dioscorea alata p. 236

Greater Yam; White Manila Yam. Although
little grown in the United States, the winged
yam has been cultivated for centuries
throughout tropical climates and is a staple
for starch in many cultures. Because of the
recent influx of Asiatic peoples, the plant
now appears in gardens in Gulf Coast and
southwestern states. The foliage resembles
sweet potato and philodendron leaves. The
long, edible tubers may be white-skinned or
purple. Their ultimate size depends on
variety and culture—tubers of 100 lbs.
(45.5 kg) are possible.

How to Grow
A nearly frost-free climate and heavy rainfall
or irrigation are required to supply the
necessary 6–12-month warm-soil season.
Propagate yams from tubers, which can be
purchased in stores serving Asiatic clientele.
In early spring, divide the tuber into
pie-shaped pieces; include 2 or 3 buds on
each piece. Let pieces dry for a day, then
place each atop sand in an 8-in. (20-cm) pot;
sprinkle each piece with more sand until
nearly covered. Put the pots in an area with
temperatures of 75–85°F (24.0–29.5°C)
until rooting is well along; fluorescent lights

augmented with incandescent will supply
sufficient light along with gentle warmth.
Three weeks after frost danger is past, set the
plants on large piles of rooted compost
mixed with sandy soil 1–2 ft. (30–60 cm)
high. Space plants 3–4 ft. (90–120 cm) apart.
Make strong arches of wire or slender
bamboo canes and place a cover of slitted
plastic over it. Remove the plastic in early
summer or at the first sign of leaf scorch.
Feed plants occasionally with manure.
Provide tall bamboo tepees for the vines to
climb. Yams don't like heavy, waterlogged
soil. In dry, warm climates, dig a trench
around the compost pile and flood it for
maximum growth.

Harvest
Tubers store poorly; leave them in the
ground as long as possible. Dig tubers before
frost or, in nearly frost-free climates, in late
winter. Store in a cool area, no lower than
45°F (7°C). Be sure to cook yams
thoroughly; although modern cultivars are
reputedly free of the poison dioscorine, the
possibility of genetic reversion exists.
Cooking destroys the poison.

Herbs

Technically, herbs are soft-stemmed, nonwoody plants that die down at the end of the growing season, but in general usage, the term is understood to mean plants that are used for flavor or fragrance, as a dye, or in cosmetics or medicine. While herbs are often thought of as simply a means to spice up our cuisine, they are equally valuable for their aromatic properties, their delicate beauty, and their soothing and restorative effects in teas or tisanes. Herbs exist in·such a wide variety that even a small garden can accommodate many flavorful seasonings and beautiful flowers, ranging from the pungent, oniony ramp to the pretty corn poppy. In addition to such well-known favorites as rosemary, basil, and bay, herbs also include many less familiar plants: the tropical lemongrass, anise-scented sweet cicely, and alexanders, which can be eaten like celery or cooked like asparagus.

Herbs in History
Herbs were used long before the days of written history, and were so important in the life of early man that in their wanderings the Indo-Europeans undoubtedly carried them from Europe to India and eastern tribes brought others to western Europe. Magical properties were attributed to herbs because of their medicinal potency; and most herbs have many superstitions and old customs associated with them.

Early in history the fragrant thymes, rosemary, and lavender were gathered from rocky ledges on hillsides, sweet woodruff in the woods, fennel from the seacoast, and others wherever they grew wild. As people settled down into an agricultural and stationary life, they planted herbs in their gardens. Seeds of coriander were found in Egyptian tombs of the twenty-first dynasty, and of caraway among the debris of the Lake Dwellers of Switzerland. In Charlemagne's time, vegetable-and-herb gardens usually included hyssop, borage, poppies, fennel, anise, mint, sage, basil, chives, and thyme.

Many herbs have colorful common names that reveal some of the different ways—aromatic, decorative, medicinal, hallucinogenic— in which these plants have been employed through the centuries. A few examples include alecost (costmary), used to flavor beer and ale at least since the Middle Ages; catnip, a stimulant relished by those animals; bee balm (bergamot), with bright red flowers attractive to bees and hummingbirds; and herb o'grace (rue), once associated with repentance.

Growing Herbs
Anyone can grow herbs. Though every species requires some care, most herbs are tenacious by nature and will adapt to many garden conditions. Some herbs, such as basil, can even be grown indoors. Many more species, such as rue, sweet woodruff, and sage, with a little care, thrive as perennials in the North as well as in milder-climate gardens. Basil, chervil, and others are annuals. Still other

herbs, such as angelica and caraway, are biennial plants, fulfilling
their life cycle in two years.

Certain herbs are such vigorous growers—lemon balm and the
mints, for example—that they must be contained to prevent them
from overrunning the garden. Most, though, form a natural and
pleasing addition to the flower or vegetable garden, and many, such
as rosemary and Roman chamomile, are valuable as landscaping
plants.

The writeups that follow for each species contain all the
necessary information to grow healthy, productive plants. Here you
will find facts about special sun and shade requirements, soil
requirements, where to plant species with particular site preferences,
and directions for maintaining plants throughout their life
cycles.

Propagate each species as directed. Many herbs grow easily from
seeds; others, like scented geraniums, are easier to grow from
cuttings. Many of the perennials can be divided in the fall or spring.
Of course, where you live will affect your choice of herbs to grow,
but with a little imagination, there is no limit to what you can do
with herbs in your garden.

Using Herbs

Like everything else about this diverse group of plants, how you
harvest herbs and the parts you use varies from one species to
another. (Be cautious when using an unfamiliar herb; ingested in
large amounts, some plants have a toxic effect.) Coriander, for
example, yields seeds that are dried for seasoning, and its
leaves—often called cilantro, their Spanish name, or Chinese
parsley—are picked fresh for salad greens or garnishes. The flowers
of corn poppy are used to color clear syrups and wine, and
chamomile's, to make a delicious tea. Ramp, a wild onion, is
harvested to be eaten like scallions. The leaves, flowers, and seeds
of numerous other plants are often dried to scent potpourris
and sachets.

There are herbs for all seasons. When you have no fresh French
tarragon for béarnaise sauce, winter tarragon, which leafs out when
the other species is dormant, will stand in. And, of course, dried
herbs will keep the taste of summer in the kitchen through even the
longest northern winter. No matter which herbs you decide to grow,
discovering different ways to use these plants is another of the
pleasant gardening surprises in store for you.

Alexanders
Smyrnium olusatrum p. 256

Black Lovage; Horse Parsley. Alexanders is seldom seen in today's herb gardens but was at one time a major culinary and medicinal plant. This large, celerylike biennial grows 3–5 ft. (0.9–1.5 m) high. The dark stems are capped by shiny, 3-part leaves and clusters of white flowers. The leaves, stems, and flower and seed buds are all edible.

How to Grow
Start seeds outdoors in shaded beds in late summer. Transplant seedlings in fall to a sunny location. In severe winter areas, mulch seedlings. The following year, feed and water frequently.

Harvest
When plants are 12 in. (30 cm) tall, snap off outer stems and leaves and cook them like celery. In midseason, prune the stems to keep plants at a height of 2 ft. (60 cm) or lower. In fall, cover plants with tall baskets to blanch the leaves and stem tips. This makes them tender and sweet, and good in salads; the stems can be cooked like asparagus.

Angelica
Angelica archangelica p. 257

Archangel; Wild Parsnip. A biennial or short-lived perennial, angelica is large, growing 5–6 ft. (1.5–1.8 m) high and 2–3 ft. (60–90 cm) wide. The plant looks somewhat like parsnip and has twice-compound leaves and greenish flowers in huge umbels. It is grown mostly for its fragrant leaves, which are used both fresh and dried.

How to Grow
Direct-seed in late summer as soon as fresh seeds are available; seeds lose viability rapidly in storage. Transplanting is difficult. Give angelica plenty of moisture and fertilizer. Grow in full sun except in the Deep South and warm West, where afternoon shade is beneficial.

Harvest
Take foliage in spring before plants begin to flower. A light harvest can also be taken just before fall frost. The leaves, stems, seeds, and

roots are all edible, and are used in cooking, candying, teas, tisanes, and liqueurs.

Anise
Pimpinella anisum p. 251

Aniseed. This small annual grows to 2 ft. (60 cm) high and 6–12 in. (15–30 cm) wide. Plants are lanky, never lush, with finely divided upper leaves and creamy white flowers borne in flat, umbrellalike clusters.

How to Grow
Anise needs a long, cool, frost-free growing season to produce large plants, which yield the most seeds. Direct-seed in full sun as soon as the soil can be worked in spring. Thin seedlings to stand 6–12 in. (15–30 cm) apart. If planted late and hot weather sets in, plants will be tiny and spindly, and will flower and set seeds too rapidly. Transplanting usually delays flowering and reduces seed yield.

Harvest
Watch the seed heads carefully. When the first seeds begin to turn dark, cut the entire plant to the ground. Place a large paper sack over a sheaf of plants and hang them upside down; the sack will catch the dry seeds as they fall. Although yield is not high for the garden space occupied, home-grown anise seeds are superior to the imported product. They have the flavor of licorice and the aroma of sweet fennel.

Anise Hyssop
Agastache foeniculum p. 271

Blue Giant Hyssop; Fragrant Giant Hyssop. This attractive half-hardy perennial, native to North America, is of upright habit and grows to 4 ft. (120 cm) high. Its many branches are topped with short spikes of violet-blue flowers. A good landscape and bee plant, its fragrant, anise-scented foliage may be used for teas and seasoning.

How to Grow
Anise hyssop is heat-resistant and easy to grow from seeds or purchased plants. It needs well-drained soil but does not tolerate dryness. Start seedlings indoors 6–8 weeks

before the spring frost-free date. Transplant them to a sunny site when the soil is warm.

Harvest
Flowers bloom from late summer through fall. Try the beautiful fresh blossoms as a garnish on fruit or desserts. Harvest branch tips as needed for fresh use. To dry, harvest the entire plant at the early bloom stage.

Anyu
Tropaeolum tuberosum p. 261

Anyu is a half-hardy perennial nasturtium seldom seen in this country, but grown in the mountains of South America for its edible tubers. A high-climbing vine, it grows to 6–8 ft. (1.8–2.4 m) on trees and banks. The long-stemmed flowers are yellow with red spurs.

How to Grow
Seeds are very hard to find, so ask a botanical garden to send for them on your behalf. Anyu grows best in sun or light shade in mountain highlands or cool gardens. Start seeds or tubers early indoors and transplant after frost danger. Handle carefully to avoid damaging the fragile root system. Tubers may overwinter under deep snow, but store a few in a cold root cellar in case those in the garden freeze.

Harvest
Pick the edible flowers throughout the growing season. Mulch and dig tubers as late in fall as possible.

Basil
Ocimum basilicum pp. 270, 271, 272, 273, 274, 275

Most culinary basils belong to this species; the many different types vary widely in foliage size, color, aroma, and plant habit. They are all warm-weather annuals with a great ability to hybridize. Sweet or common basil is the most popular of all herbs. Plants are bright green, large, and fast growing; in warm climates they can reach 6 ft. (1.8 m) high and 4 ft. (1.2 m) wide. Leaf size ranges from 2–4 in. (5–10 cm) long. Anise basil is a tall, upright plant with purple-green sawtoothed foliage. The leaves have a strong licorice aroma and are used to flavor fruit dishes, teas, and juices, and are excellent for wreath-making. Cinnamon basil is the most ornamental; a compact plant, it has glossy, dark green leaves and lavender-white flowers. Its flavor strongly resembles cinnamon, and chopped fresh leaves are used to top pumpkin and sweet potato pies. Fine-leaf bush basil, a refined version of the French variety called Fin Vert, is favored for making pesto. Fine-leaf tall basil (also called Mexican basil) may grow to as much as 3 ft. (90 cm) high in warm climates. The thin, downy foliage of lemon basil has a tantalizing lemony taste and aroma, but the stalks of white flowers shoot up early, leaving little to harvest. Lettuce-leaved basil tastes like sweet basil; its leaves, to 7 in. (17.5 cm) long, sometimes have a seersucker or waffled texture, and are good for lining salad cups. Purple basil plants occur spontaneously in common basil, but the ornamental variety Dark Opal has won awards for its purple foliage, which is uniform in fertile soil. Leaves add color and a peppery basil taste to oils and vinegars.

How to Grow
In early summer, transplant seedlings in sunny, well-drained, fertile soil; you can also direct-seed basil later in the season, when it will sprout and develop rapidly. Give plants plenty of room, particularly in warm climates. Basil is easy to grow outdoors, but needs extra heat and light when grown indoors in winter.

Harvest
Cut leaves for fresh use as the flower buds appear; plants will regrow quickly. Trim off flowerheads before they set seeds. Freezing works better than drying, which turns leaves black unless you heat them to speed the process.

Varieties
Common sweet basil grows about the same regardless of the seed source. Spicy Globe is a good fine-leaf bush basil with small leaves; Piccolo has larger, coarser leaves. Purple Ruffles flowers later than Dark Opal; it has ruffled leaves.

Holy Basil
Ocimum canum p. 272

Hoary Basil; Tulsi. (Formerly *O. sanctum.*)
This species is so unlike sweet basil in form
and aroma that you have to look closely at
the flowers to see the relationship. Reputedl
used in Hindu religious ceremonies, holy
basil has a cloying, musky odor that
permeates the air and clings to hands and
clothing when plants are touched. The
open-growing plants reach 2 ft. (60 cm) hig
and spread wider. They have arching
branches with downy, gray-green leaves and,
in summer, numerous rough spikes of dull,
bronzy lavender-white flowers that shed
prodigious numbers of seeds.

How to Grow and Harvest
See basil. To keep plants from spreading, cli
off flower spikes before seeds set. Leaves may
be used fresh in chicken dishes, but
sparingly.

Bay
Laurus nobilis p. 275

Bay Laurel; Sweet Laurel. Bay can live for
many years as a woody houseplant; the erect,
slow-growing little trees have dark, glossy
evergreen leaves. Bay has been cultivated for
centuries.

How to Grow
Bay is best started from rooted cuttings
taken from the first flush of early summer
growth. Use a pot with a top diameter abou
(and no more than) 75 percent of the
height of the tree. Bay needs full sun and
well-drained soil. Protect from frost and cold
drafts. Feed and water sparingly during
winter. Bay trees can reach 30 ft. (9 m) high
where winter temperatures remain above
20° F (−6.7° C).

Harvest
When plants reach 12–18 in. (30–45 cm)
high, snip mature leaves occasionally for
fresh use or to dry. To keep plants vigorous,
never take more than a third of the leaves.

Sweet Bay
Magnolia virginiana p. 274

This hardy, deciduous native tree grows to
60 ft. (18 m) in the South, but remains a
bush 1–2 ft. (30–60 cm) high further north.
It has fragrant, light-colored foliage that is
downy on the underside. Very fragrant
white flowers appear beneath the leaves
simultaneously, growing to 3 in. (7.5 cm)
wide. Leaves are occasionally used fresh for
flavoring, but the taste is not at all like that
of true European bay (*Laurus nobilis*).

How to Grow and Harvest
Grow and harvest as you would bay (*Laurus
nobilis*), but note that sweet bay is found in
moist, acid soil in the wild. Dried leaves of
sweet bay retain little of their fragrance.

Bergamot
Monarda didyma p. 260

Bee Balm; Oswego Tea. This native
American perennial is often sold as an
ornamental for its spectacular blossoms.
Plants reach 3 ft. (90 cm) high and are
crowned with a rounded cluster of flowers,
each with a pincushionlike center. The wild
species has mostly red flowers, but modern
cultivars come in red, pink, purple, lavender,
or white. All have spicy, aromatic foliage,
and the flowers attract bees and
hummingbirds.

How to Grow
Grow bergamot in full sun, except in warm
summer climates, where light shade is better.
Feed existing plants twice a year. Flowering
will continue for several weeks if you remove
spent blossoms. It seldom blooms the first
year. Bergamot can become a pest in moist,
fertile soils, where the roots spread widely. It
is easy to propagate from pieces of roots:
Every 3–4 years, dig up old clumps, save a
few root tips for replanting, and discard the
old woody parts. You can also start plants
indoors in spring from seeds; flowers will be
mixed colors.

Harvest
Shear leaf tips 2–3 times during summer.
Use fresh or dried in teas, tisanes, and
potpourris.

Wild Bergamot
Monarda fistulosa p. 285

A hardy perennial, *M. fistulosa* resembles
M. didyma except that the plants are a bit
shorter and have smaller leaves. Flowers are
usually lavender, but pink, purple, or white
flowers occasionally occur in wild stands.
The individual flowers ring a pincushionlike
tuft on the tips of stems. Though not as
showy as *M. didyma,* wild bergamot makes
better tea or tisane.

How to Grow and Harvest
Grow and harvest like *M. didyma*. Wild
bergamot prefers a well-limed, rather dry soil.
Order seeds or plants from wildflower
specialists.

Borage
Borago officinalis p. 258

Talewort; Cool-tankard. To 3 ft. (90 cm)
high at maturity, borage has large, rough-
hairy, silvery leaves and blue blossoms. A
half-hardy annual, its flowers make beautiful
garnishes and the tiny leaf tips can be added
to salads or drinks for a cucumber flavor.
The leaves are edible when cooked, but there
are better summer greens.

How to Grow
Young plants are attractive and neat, but
they age ungracefully. To keep young plants
coming in, direct-seed at monthly intervals
in late spring. Do not cover: Borage seeds
need light to sprout. Transplants root
quickly and dependably. Grow in full sun,
except in the Deep South and warm West,
where afternoon shade helps.

Harvest
Borage plants are vigorous growers and can
be pruned heavily for greens and to shape up
ungainly specimens.

Salad Burnet
Poterium sanguisorba p. 262

These neat, low-growing hardy perennials
send up many gracefully-arching stems
clothed from end to end with small,
toothed, opposite leaflets. Plants reach 12 in.

(30 cm) high. Flowers are small pink tufts and not very showy. Burnet is often used as an edging in gardens or planted in groups in containers. It can be used in salads and to make a cucumbĕr-flavored vinegar.

How to Grow
Start indoors early from seeds. Transplant in the garden before the taproot begins to lengthen. Burnet prefers full sun, but will tolerate light shade where summers are quite hot. With occasional feeding and watering, the foliage color and condition will remain good all summer.

Harvest
Do not harvest until the second year. Strip off the leaflets and discard the wiry stems; use the younger leaves for salads and older leaves for vinegars, or chop and add to mixed potherbs. Plants will recover from fairly severe shearing, but leave a few blossoms to set seeds for renewing the crop.

Calendula
Calendula officinalis p. 264

Pot Marigold. Truly an edible ornamental, these hardy annuals grow 1–2 ft. (30–60 cm) high and have large, orange, yellow, cream, or white flowers that are used for flavor and coloring.

How to Grow
For winter bloom in mild areas of the country, direct-seed in early fall or set in transplants. For spring plantings, start seeds indoors early; harden off the seedlings and set them in a sunny site outdoors 3–4 weeks before the frost-free date. Calendulas live through moderate frosts, but cover them if a heavy freeze is predicted. These cool-weather plants burn out in the heat of summer. Spring-planted calendulas react to shorter nights by growing taller and setting smaller flowers.

Harvest
Snap off mature blossoms before they begin to wither. Pull off petals and soak them in water for a few minutes to float off dust and small insects. Petals are used fresh or dried to add color and a very mild flavor to soups, rice, and cookies.

Caper
Capparis spinosa p. 263

Capers are the unopened flower buds of a spiny, tender perennial shrub that grows 2–3 ft. (60–90 cm) high and sprawls 3–5 ft (90–150 cm) wide. The buds, popular for use in sauces, butters, cheese preparations, and garnishes, develop into attractive pinkish-white flowers if left on the plant.

How to Grow
Over most of the U.S. this bush is grown i containers and wintered over in a greenhou or sunny room. It can be grown as an annual, but flower buds may not form befor the first killing frost. Grow capers as perennials in mild-winter climates. Start fro seeds or root 6-in. (15- cm) cuttings from new growth. Plants grown from seeds vary; some may be erect bushes, others sprawling plants. Start seeds indoors early so plants ca be set in the garden or containers as soon a danger of frost is past. Capers need full sun and well-drained soil; they tolerate dryness. Cover the bushes if frost is predicted.

Harvest
Pinch off the flower buds before they split and show color. Capers are often pickled.

Caraway
Carum carvi p. 248

A tall, frost-hardy biennial, caraway is an ancient herb cultivated for its aromatic seeds and tender young leaves. Rosettes of carrotlike foliage form the first season, but usually no flowers. The second year, flower-stalks arise in early summer, topped by flat clusters of white blossoms that produce abundant seeds.

How to Grow
In its first year caraway needs to develop int a sturdy plant that will overwinter reliably. Where summers are short, direct-seed as earl as the soil can be worked. Farther south, direct-seed in late summer or fall for bloom the next season. To maximize seed yields, plant in full sun and fertile, well-drained soil The seed crop matures faster if you stop watering when flowers form.

Harvest
Tender young leaves impart a caraway flavor
to mixed greens and salads, and can be
plucked throughout the growing season. Cut
the flower stems when seeds start to dry and
hang them over newspapers to catch seeds as
they drop. To thresh, put dry plants into a
large cloth bag and strike the bag against a
post several times to dislodge the seeds; then
sift seeds through ¼ in. (6 mm) mesh
hardware cloth to remove the chaff.

Catnip
Nepeta cataria p. 270

This erect, durable, hardy perennial grows
2–3 ft. (60–90 cm) high and has gray-green,
felty leaves and white flowers. This is the
species cultivated as a treat for cats.

How to Grow
Start seeds indoors in early spring and
transplant to a sunny or partially shady
outdoor site after danger of frost is past.
Lime the soil well. Catnip is attractive when
young, but soon develops tall, stiff, woody
stems that become leggy. At this stage, chop
back the plants to make them look neater.
Shear off the flowers before they set seeds, or
catnip will become a garden pest.

Harvest
Snip off the flowers and spread them out to
dry in a dark, well-ventilated area. The flavor
of catnip is better than its rather rank smell.
It may be used to make a soothing tisane;
rub dry leaves lightly in a colander to
remove stems and release more flavor. Young
leaves can be chopped to give a minty flavor
to sauces. In moderation, catnip is not
dangerous, but too much catnip in any form
can have hallucinogenic effects.

Leaf Celery
Apium graveolens var. secalinum p. 255

French Celery; Chinese Celery. Leaf celery is
grown for its fancy, aromatic leaves. A
biennial grown as a long-season annual, this
herb was used centuries ago in Europe and
the Orient, where its ancestor was known as

"smallage." Its slender, rounded stalks, to 12 in. (30 cm) high, are strongly flavored and tend to become stringy with age.

How to Grow
Start seeds indoors very early to have large seedlings for transplanting. Do not transplant in early spring, since extended periods of cool weather can trigger celery to bolt to seed. Grow in full sun in fertile soil. Keep soil moist but not soggy.

Harvest
Leaf celery should be harvested when stems are 9–12 in. (22.5–30.0 cm) high, but before they develop strings and fiber. Snap off outside stems. Use the leaves as a garnish, chop and mix in salads, or add to soups, stews, and vegetable dishes. Lovage (*Levisticum officinale*) has a stronger flavor but makes an acceptable substitute.

Varieties
The leading cultivar is Dinant.

Roman Chamomile
Chamaemelum nobile p. 246

Roman Chamomile. Chamomile is a half-hardy perennial usually grown as an annual. This plant is preferred to sweet false chamomile (*Matricaria recutita*). It spreads by creeping stems, growing to 12 in. (30 cm) high and wide. Leaves are lacy and finely divided, on stems capped with small, white, daisylike flowers. The whole plant is apple-scented.

How to Grow
Start from seeds or cuttings in early spring and transplant to the garden after danger of frost is past. Chamomile does best in sun, in sandy, well-drained, slightly acid soil. It tolerates light shade. When setting out seedlings, pull out any that are unusually tall; these are probably seedlings of the aggressive and less desirable sweet false chamomile.

Harvest
The flowers are the only edible part of chamomile. When plants are in full bloom, shear off the flowers with the stem tips and let them dry. Seed-eating insects commonly infest the drying flowerheads; if insects are a

problem, spread the flowerheads on a cookie sheet and bake them at 120° F (49° C) for 30 minutes, then gently sift through a colander. Use the dried flowers for teas or tisanes.

Sweet False Chamomile
Matricaria recutita p. 247

German Chamomile. An annual to 2 ft. (60 cm) high and 6–8 in. (15–20 cm) wide, this plant has flowers that are slightly smaller than those of Roman chamomile (*Chamaemelum nobile*) and have a hollow, yellow central disk. The foliage is less fragrant but the dried flowers are less bitter than those of *C. nobile* and are often substituted in teas and tisanes.

How to Grow and Harvest
Sweet false chamomile is easy to direct-seed in spring or late fall, but plants must be controlled or they will become weedy, since seeds set in vast numbers. It prefers full sun and sandy, well-limed soil. Harvest and use like Roman chamomile.

Chervil
Anthriscus cerefolium p. 252

French Parsley. To 12 in. (30 cm) high and 18 in. (45 cm) wide, chervil resembles a fine-leaved, light green parsley. It is much used in French cuisine to add a delicate anise flavor, or as a garnish.

How to Grow
Chervil is a cool-weather annual for early spring and late summer planting, or for growing in a winter greenhouse. Always direct-seed; transplants can flower rapidly and go to seed. Thin seedlings to 6–8 in. (15–20 cm) apart. Chervil tolerates frost; if gradually hardened off, it will withstand temperatures to near 0° F (−17.8° C). Grow spring-planted chervil in full sun. In the Deep South and warm West, afternoon shade ensures larger plants with better color for fall or winter harvest.

Harvest
Shear plants off 2–3 in. (5.0–7.5 cm) above

soil level. Chervil will regrow if you leave the central leaf buds intact.

Varieties
True curled chervil is the most desirable cultivar, but many seeds sold under this name are actually the common flat-leaf selection. The flavor of flat-leaf chervil is just as good, but the leaves are not as fancy for garnishes.

Chive
Allium schoenoprasum p. 286

Chives are easy to grow and very productive over a long season. These hardy perennials produce fine, hollow, blue-green leaves that form dense, mounding clumps to 6 in. (15 cm) wide or more. In late spring and summer, small, round flower clusters in lavender, pink, white, or purple appear atop stiff stems to 12 in. (30 cm) high. As ornamental plants, chives are often used in edgings. The long leaves have a mild, oniony taste.

How to Grow
Chives grow most easily and quickly from small potted plants, but they can be direct-seeded in early spring or started from seeds indoors. Transplant the grasslike seedlings 9–12 in. (22.5–30.0 cm) apart. Plenty of water, good drainage, and occasional light feedings are essential. Young plants will gradually multiply into clumps. To divide an old clump, shear and dig it up; soak the clump in water and shake it until it pulls apart into several new plants. Replant these in clumps of 3–6 plants each. In very hot climates, chives may have to be planted each fall and grown as a winter annual. They grow well in pots: Plant 1 clump per 1-gal. (4-l) container, or several in a shallow tub.

Harvest
Begin harvesting in spring when the first flower buds appear. Shearing at this time will prevent blooming and the subsequent drain of energy on the plant. Make additional cuttings during the season, but stop harvesting in winter. Chives lose their flavor when dried, so they are usually frozen and reconstituted for use in cooking. Their flavor is milder than that of green onions. Flowe

clusters are edible when young, before seeds form. Cut the young flowering stems and hang them upside down to dry. For dried arrangements, hang flowers in a dark, well-ventilated area so that they will retain their color.

Varieties
Special greenhouse varieties are available; when grown in the garden they are indistinguishable from common chives.

Garlic Chive
Allium tuberosum p. 287

Chinese Chive; Oriental Chive. A hardy perennial, garlic chive grows to 12 in. (30 cm) high and wide. It has flat leaves and greenish-white flowerheads on stalks to 30 in. (45 cm) high. It makes a beautiful border plant, and its tender green leaves add a mild garlic flavor to foods.

How to Grow
Plant in a sunny site in average soil. Propagate by dividing clumps. Seeds planted in spring or late summer are easy to grow but slow. Cut clumps back occasionally to keep tender shoots regrowing; older leaves become coarse and weatherbeaten by the end of summer. Established plants are difficult to eradicate and yield many seeds, which must be harvested and planted as soon as they dry.

Harvest
Shear off clumps of young leaves at ground level. Chop and freeze the tender shoots for winter use. Stop harvesting in early fall to avoid weakening plants. Use dried stalks in winter arrangements.

Sweet Cicely
Myrrhis odorata p. 253

British Myrrh; Sweet Chervil. This handsome woodland perennial has fernlike leaves and bears many clusters of white flowers on grooved, hollow stems that reach 2–3 ft. (60–90 cm) high. The foliage and flowers smell and taste like anise.

How to Grow
For best results direct-seed in fall from

freshly harvested seeds. Chill seeds before
spring planting. Mix them with moist peat
moss and refrigerate at about 40°F (4.5°C)
for 30–60 days. Then start seeds indoors in
peat pots through late summer. In the fall,
transplant to fertile, organic garden soil.
Grow in light to moderate shade. Growth
starts early in spring and continues until
heavy frost. You can also divide old plants
in spring or fall. Grow as a winter annual in
mild-winter areas.

Harvest
Don't cut sweet cicely in the first year of
growth unless you are growing it as an
annual. Add the sugary fresh leaves and
tender stem tips to salads, along with the
flowers and immature seeds. Or chop and
use small amounts in soups or mixed
vegetables. You can also cook stems and
leaves and add the juice to fruit pies or
cobblers. Dried seeds give an anise scent to
potpourris.

Clove Pink
Dianthus caryophyllus p. 284

Carnation; Gillyflower. A perennial native to
s. Europe, wild clove pink reaches 1½–3 ft.
(45–60 cm) high. Plants have gray-blue
foliage and fragrant, semidouble, rose-purple
or white flowers that are abundant during
fall and early winter. In its wild form clove
pink is quite aromatic and can be used to
flavor syrups, fruit cups, and beverages. The
more ornamental carnations and pinks
developed by plant breeders have shorter
stems and extra layers of petals, but lack
much of the fragrance of the species.

How to Grow
Modern cultivars of clove pink belong in a
flower garden; set among wilder-looking
culinary herb species, the sleek, tailored
plants look out of place. Clove pink is
usually transplanted from started plants. You
should set large, budded plants in the
ground 2–3 weeks before the danger of
spring frost is past. Grow in full sun. In cool
climates, remove old blossoms so plants will
bloom continuously from midsummer to
fall. In mild-winter areas, you can also grow
plants from seedlings transplanted in early
fall; they will bloom sporadically in winter

and flourish in the spring. Plants will burn out where summers are hot and humid.

Harvest
Pluck only newly opened blossoms for fresh use; if flowers are used for flavoring, pull off the petals and snip off the bitter white bases. For potpourris and sachets, dry with a desiccant such as silica gel to preserve the natural color of the petals.

Coriander
Coriandrum sativum pp. 249, 254

Cilantro; Chinese Parsley. These alternate common names are usually applied to the plant's leaves, while the name coriander often refers just to the seeds. A hardy annual, coriander will withstand temperatures as low as 10°F (−12°C). The rounded, parsleylike leaves grow in basal rosettes and are usually harvested before plants go to bloom in summer. In flower, plants reach 2½ ft. (75 cm) high and the foliage becomes tall and lacy. Flowers are white, in an umbrellalike cluster, yielding edible seeds.

How to Grow
For best production of the heavy basal leaves, direct-seed in late summer or fall where winters are mild, in early spring elsewhere. Second plantings in early fall are usually successful. Wash seeds in dishwashing detergent, rinse thoroughly, and blot dry before planting. Plant ¼ in. (6 mm) deep in fertile soil. If you are growing only for seeds and not for the leaves, early spring seeding produces large, rugged plants that will ensure the highest seed yields.

Harvest
For leaves, shear entire plants 2–3 in. (5.0–7.5 cm) above the soil surface. Leaves will regrow with a little fertilizer and water. For seeds, let the plants grow until the first set of seeds dries enough to crack when pinched. Then cut and hang the plants to dry over a catch-cloth. Thresh and sift the seeds as described for caraway.

Costmary
Chrysanthemum balsamita p. 264

Alecost; Bible-leaf. This hardy perennial is widely adapted for garden use. Plants are sprawling and tousled-looking in the vegetative stage; stems reach 3 ft. (90 cm) high in flower. Blossoms are yellow and rather sparse. The leaves are elongated, oval, and toothed; they are leathery when dried and can be used as bookmarks. Fresh young costmary leaves are used in salads and to add a balsam flavor to beer, soups, and bread.

How to Grow
Plant in well-manured soil in full sun or partial shade. Feed and water frequently to maintain large leaves with good color. Every 3–4 years, divide old clumps; propagate plants from the outermost pieces of root.

Harvest
A single costmary plant will produce enough leaves for fresh and dried use. In late summer when the leaves look tattered, shear back half of them to the ground. Feed and water the plant; when new growth appears, shear back the remaining old leaves.

Black Cumin
Nigella sativa p. 250

Nutmeg Flower; Roman Coriander. A frost-tender annual, black cumin grows in mounds 18 in. (45 cm) high. It has lacy foliage, inflated seed pods, and attractive blue flowers that are 1½ in. (4 cm) wide. It can be grown as a substitute for the spice cumin, *cuminum cyminum,* which is slow to develop.

How to Grow
Direct-seed 2–3 weeks before the average spring frost-free date. Early seeding helps plants develop to a good size before hot weather comes, but beware of late freezes. Plant in well-drained garden soil in full sun, and fertilize to give young plants a fast start. Thin plants to 12 in. (30 cm) apart.

Harvest
Pick individual pods as they start to turn yellow. Dry in batches in the sun. Use a catch-cloth or bag to trap seeds from pods as they split, then winnow the seeds to remove chaff. Black cumin has a strong, fennel-like

flavor; grind and use the seeds as you would pepper in seasoning, but experiment first.

Dill
Anethum graveolens pp. 248, 251

Dill Weed. Native to sw. Asia and now widely naturalized in North America, dill is a half-hardy, cool-weather annual that flowers and sets seeds when nights are short and days are warm. The blue-green, lacy plants reach 3–5 ft. (90–150 cm) high and are topped with umbrellalike clusters of yellow flowers on stiff, hollow stems.

How to Grow
Dill is easy to grow; direct-seed in early spring or late summer. Transplanting is difficult. Don't plant dill during summer or it will go to seed before the plants are large enough to harvest. Dill will color best in fertile soil with ample moisture. Give it full sun; plants become spindly in semishade.

Harvest
To harvest dill leaves, shear plants when they are 6–12 in. (15–30 cm) high; plants in the vegetative stage will regrow. Once flowerheads appear, harvest for seeds: Cut and dry plants when the seed heads begin to turn brown but before seeds drop and cause dill to spread voraciously. Use fresh leaves in salads, dips, fish dishes, and with vegetables; dried seeds add flavor to pickles, vegetables, and baked goods.

Varieties
There is a slight advantage to planting late-flowering varieties, such as Hercules, in early spring. Late summer plantings timed for fall harvest are best for dill leaf crops.

Sweet Fennel
Foeniculum vulgare var. *dulce p. 250*

This half-hardy perennial or biennial looks somewhat like dill, but its finely cut, anise-scented foliage is light green rather than blue-green, and its stems are solid, not hollow like dill's. Sweet fennel reaches 4–6 ft. (120–180 cm) high in flower; the yellow clusters don't occur in quantity until the second season, when the plants are sturdy enough to support good seed yields.

How to Grow
Sweet fennel grows easily from direct-seeding. Plants tolerate a wide range of soils, but do poorly in dense, soggy clay. Sweet fennel grows very fast and needs frequent feedings to maintain vigor and good color. Prune plants to keep them dense and at a manageable height. If you are not growing sweet fennel for seeds, cut off the flowering stems.

Harvest
Spring-sown sweet fennel will grow large enough to harvest leaves by the summer of the first season. Use leaves fresh in salads or to garnish fish entrees. For fennel seeds, cut off the large individual seed heads when they begin to turn color, and dry them. If you allow too many seed heads to remain, plants will lose vigor and may die.

Scented Geraniums
Pelargonium spp. *pp. 258, 259*

Scented Pelargoniums. These half-hardy perennials are grown as annuals, principally for their marvelous fragrances, which imitate rose, lemon, cinnamon, mint, coconut, and other scents. Plant average 1½–2 ft. (45–60 cm) high. The foliage may be large and furry, or small, deeply cut, and curled. Cultivars are numerous; the blossoms of some are attractive, but secondary to the highly decorative foliage. Fresh leaves are used in baking, to flavor fruit cups, or in beverages or finger bowls to add a distinctive aroma. Dried leaves are used in teas, tisanes, potpourris, and sachets.

How to Grow
Scented geraniums are houseplants that can be plunged, pot and all, in average to dry soil, or transplanted into the garden. To grow from seeds, start indoors 8–10 weeks before the frost-free date over bottom heat of 75–80°F (24.0–26.5°C). Seeds sprout slowly and unevenly. Grow seedlings at 65–70°F (18.5–21.0°C). Before transplanting to larger pots, mix 30 percent sharp sand into the potting soil for improved drainage. You can also grow scented geraniums from cuttings taken from established plants;

cuttings should have 2–3 nodes. Snip off all except the tip leaves and let the cuttings dry in a cool spot for 2–3 days, then root them in a mixture of equal parts peat and perlite. Move plants indoors before fall frost.

Harvest
Begin pruning to keep plants in shape once they are large enough to spare a few leaves. Use the prunings fresh, or dry in a dark, well-ventilated room. Cut plants back heavily before moving them indoors.

Hyssop
Hyssopus officinalis p. 283

Though probably not the hyssop mentioned in the Bible, this plant has gained notoriety from the reference. The hardy perennial plants are dense and moundlike, covered with short, chubby spikes of blue flowers (rarely, pink or white). At maturity, hyssop reaches 2–3 ft. (60–90 cm) in height. The leaves, opposite and willowlike, have a heavy, musty odor and a strong, almost bitter flavor. Hyssop's principal uses are medicinal, but it is an attractive landscape plant.

How to Grow
Start from seeds sown indoors in early spring, 8–10 weeks before the frost-free date. Transplant seedling to pots. After they have developed a good root system, set them in the garden, 2 ft. (60 cm) apart. Where summers are long, some blooms will form the first year. Hyssop prefers full sun, well-limed, dry soil, and well-drained beds.

Harvest
Shear leaves just before plants flower, when they are most aromatic. Fresh or dried foliage can be added discreetly to herb teas.

Lavender
Lavandula spp. p. 283

Lavender has been used for centuries to give fragrance to sachets, potpourris, and linens, and to give a delicate flavor to fruit dishes, sauces, cordials, and confections. Lavender species are perennials that vary in hardiness; plants generally grow to 2½ ft. (75 cm)

high, although some may become taller with age. They have narrow leaves and dense, long-stemmed lavender or purple spikes that spring from the leaf axils. English lavender (*L. angustifolia*) is a frost-hardy species with many decorative cultivars that vary in size, habit, and blossom color. Tender species include *L. dentata*, with shorter, stubbier flower spikes than *L. angustifolia*; *L. stoechas*, a large plant with greenish-gray leaves and late-blooming flowers with a very strong aroma; *L. lanata*, with whitish foliage, and *L. pinnata*, with broad leaves. Both the leaves and the flowers of lavender are fragrant and may be used fresh or dried; they yield an aromatic oil that is extracted for commercial use. Cultivars developed especially for this purpose have a high lavender-oil content and are known as lavandins.

How to Grow
Lavender can be reproduced from seeds, cuttings, or root divisions. Plant cuttings are taken from the first flush of vegetative growth. Seeds are very difficult to start; plant indoors in late fall or winter at 70–75 ° F (21–24 ° C). Fluorescent lights are essential. Add dolomitic limestone to the soil to raise the pH to 6.5–7.5. Plant lavender in a sunny, well-drained site; sandy soil is best. Grow tender species and cultivars in containers and winter them over in a cool, sunny room.

Harvest
Fresh lavender leaves can be used along with other herbs to flavor strong game meats and fowl. Use fresh flowers to make lavender preserves. For dried use, pick flowers just as they open, along with some of the aromatic foliage. Hang them to dry in a dark, well-ventilated room.

Varieties
Some of the most popular cultivars of *L. angustifolia* are the frost-hardy Munstead, the deep purple Hidcote, and the white-flowered Alba.

Lemon Balm
Melissa officinalis p. 269

A widely adapted half-hardy perennial, lemon balm grows wild in moist, lightly shaded meadows. When mowed, it scents the air

with lemon. Plants form spreading clumps 2–2½ ft. (60–75 cm) high. The broad, toothed, opposite leaves are used in meat sauces, fruit dishes, and drinks.

How to Grow
A member of the mint family, lemon balm is easy to grow and is usually propagated by dividing root clumps or by rooting cuttings in water. It will also grow readily from seeds. Sow early indoors because the seeds are fine and can wash away in the garden. Grow in moist, fertile soil; for good color, provide full sun to light shade.

Harvest
Tender young leaves have the best flavor. Plants recover quickly from shearing; cut them back severely 2–3 times during the season to prevent seeds from setting and plants from spreading as weeds. Dried leaves lose their fragrance quickly if not promptly bottled and sealed. Try crushed leaves in teas, tisanes, and iced drinks.

Lemongrass
Cymbopogon citratus p. 286

A tropical perennial, lemongrass is grown as an annual in cooler climates. Plants form clumps of coarse, sharp-edged, grasslike leaves 4–6 ft. (120–180 cm) high. The related *C. nardus* is the source of citronella, a favorite, old-fashioned insect repellent.

How to Grow
Buy started plants or divide old clumps. After danger of frost is past, transplant to a sunny, preferably moist, location. These durable plants will tolerate a wide range of conditions. In the North, grow them in containers in a sunny corner protected from cold winds and move them indoors for winter.

Harvest
Cut off outer leaves at the base as needed. Use fresh, or dry in a dark room to preserve the green color. The lower portions of the stalks are peeled, chopped fine, and pounded to release their flavor for stir frying and fish or poultry sauces. The fibrous leaf blades are used to flavor fish stock and curries, and are removed before serving.

Lovage
Levisticum officinale p. 254

Love Parsley. Lovage looks like a tall, much-branched celery with slender stems. Plants grow 4–6 ft. (120–180 cm) high. The large flat clusters of yellow flowers make a dramatic background in the garden. These hardy perennials are widely adapted and have escaped in some areas. Once promoted as an aphrodisiac, lovage has settled down to the more prosaic and honest application as a culinary flavoring. The strong, celerylike taste and aroma will stand up to cooking.

How to Grow
Start from purchased plants; growing from seeds is slow. Clumps require 3–4 years to reach full size. When the centers start to die out, dig dormant clumps and split them with a hatchet. Lovage grows best in very rich, moist soil but does poorly in heavy, soggy clay. It prefers full sun to light shade. On sandy soil, feed plants frequently to encourage good foliage color.

Harvest
Plants will endure heavy cutting. Chop tender leaves and stem tips and use to impart celery flavor to meats, soups, and stews. Candy the stems. Dry the seeds and sprinkle them on rolls or meat.

Mallow
Malva sylvestris p. 285

An ancient herb cultivated since Roman times, mallow grows 3–4 ft. (90–120 cm) high and 2–3 ft. (60–90 cm) wide and has small round leaves and clusters of pinkish flowers. Its leaves, seeds, and flowers are still used medicinally, as decoration, and to flavor foods. Mallow is a perennial or biennial usually grown as an annual.

How to Grow
Direct-seed mallow in late spring in full sun, in moist, fertile soil with a pH of 5.5–6.5.

Harvest
The leaves add a delicate flavor to tea. Green seed capsules, called "cheeses," and flowers are chopped and added to salads.

Sweet Marjoram
Origanum majorana p. 277

Knotted Marjoram; Wurstkraut. This beautiful little gray-green plant is closely related to the oreganos. A half-hardy perennial, sweet marjoram is grown as an annual except in mild-winter climates, where it will live over. Plants reach 12 in. (30 cm) high if grown as annuals, and to 2 ft. (60 cm) high as perennials; descending branches take root and grow to form a loose, airy clump. The small, rounded leaves have a distinctly sweet aroma when crushed. Inconspicuous white flowers develop from clusters of beadlike buds.

How to Grow
Start sweet marjoram from purchased plants, since it is slow to grow from seeds. Grow in well-drained, limed soil in full sun. You can divide old plants in fall and winter them over in a greenhouse or cold frame.

Harvest
Sweet marjoram shouldn't be cut drastically. Take only a third of the top growth at a time. The flavor is best when the flower buds begin to show. Use fresh as a component of fines herbes, or alone to flavor eggs, vegetables, sausages, or stuffings. The leaves dry easily and quickly.

Apple Mint
Mentha suaveolens p. 268

A hardy perennial and aggressive grower, apple mint has distinctive downy, light green foliage. Leaves are somewhat hairy on the upper surfaces and noticeably downy on the undersides, with serrated margins. Plants can grow to 3 ft. (90 cm) high, but should be kept lower.

How to Grow
Apple mint rarely breeds true from seed and is hard to find because all the mints cross readily. Purchase plants or get mint runners from a friend. Spring plantings are best, but expect several weeks to pass before plants will increase greatly in size. Grow in full sun to light shade. Feed heavily in late summer to ensure good growth the following spring.

Apple mint tolerates dry soil but develops better color where moisture and nutrient levels are good. Mow the mint patch 2–3 times a year to encourage new growth.

Harvest
Cut mint stems flush with the ground and discard the long woody stems. Strip off and dry the whole leaves for potpourris. Save the top 2–3 sets of leaves for fresh use and garnishes. Apple mint's fragrance may vary in strength; the mild apple flavor does not hold well in dried leaves.

Curly Mint
Mentha spicata var. *crispii p. 257*

This hardy perennial is prized more for its elaborately curled, fringed leaves than for its aroma. The leaves are dark green and lightly mottled in contrasting lighter green. Plants reach 2 ft. (60 cm) high and are invasive. Commercial chefs like curly mint for garnishes, but prefer the pleasing aroma of spearmint or peppermint for everyday flavoring.

How to Grow
Transplant runners or potted plants in spring or early fall. Grow in full sun in moist, fertile soil.

Harvest
Cut the stems at ground level. Take the 2–3 sets of terminal leaves for fresh use; discard the remainder. This is not a good mint for drying or for use alone in teas. It is best suited for garnishes, or if dried, as a filler in potpourris.

Peppermint
Mentha × *piperita p. 269*

Peppermint is an invasive, hardy perennial with a sharp, penetrating yet pleasant, mint fragrance. It grows 1–2 ft. (30–60 cm) high, but can reach 3 ft. (90 cm) when flowering. Leaves are lance-shaped, and deeply notched when mature; flowers are usually purple.

How to Grow
Start in spring or fall from potted plants or pieces of runners; peppermint does not breed

true from seeds. It is aggressive and will naturalize in light shade and rich, moist soil. To prevent spreading, grow peppermint in large, shallow tubs with drainage holes. Set the tubs on bricks to keep roots from growing through the holes.

Harvest
Cut peppermint to the ground at least twice each summer. After cutting, feed and water heavily to induce fresh top growth. Use leaves and twigs fresh or dried in teas, tisanes, and iced drinks. To preserve the flavor when dried, keep leaves and twigs whole until just before use.

Pineapple Mint
Mentha suaveolens 'Variegata' *p. 267*

Pineapple mint is a variegated cultivar of apple mint with white or cream blotches on its leaves. Although it has a faint pineapple scent, the aroma is not always apparent. This mint is good for garnishes because the thick leaves are slow to wilt.

How to Grow and Harvest
Follow directions for apple mint. In rich soil, the foliage is predominately green, but in less fertile soil, the color blotches show vividly. Use pineapple mint fresh; it has no value when dried.

Spearmint
Mentha spicata p. 268

Considered the most versatile and popular garden mint, spearmint has a fruity aroma and flavor, and blends well in many edibles, including salads, teas, sauces, and dips. It is an invasive, hardy perennial that can reach 2–3 ft. (60–90 cm) high when flowering. Spearmint has bright green leaves and purple flowers that bloom from leaf axils near the branch tips. Its toothed leaves lack petioles, distinguishing it from peppermint.

How to Grow and Harvest
See peppermint. Spearmint is very aggressive and quickly overruns a garden if it is not grown in containers. The leaves are best when used fresh; for dried leaves, peppermint is superior.

Varieties
The large-leaved cultivar Scotch and the small-leaved Native contain the most mint oil. Kentucky Colonel is a strongly scented cultivar favored for juleps. Curly and variegated cultivars also exist.

Black Mustard
Brassica nigra p. 263

Black mustard is a frost-hardy annual grown for its seeds, which are dried and ground to make the familiar condiment. The coarse plant has narrow leaves and many branches of yellow flowers, followed by sickle-shaped pods of seeds. In bloom it reaches 4–6 ft. (120–180 cm) high.

How to Grow
Direct-seed in fall or very early spring in bands 12 in. (30 cm) wide. Cover seeds firmly with ¼ in. (6 mm) of soil. Thin plants to stand 6–12 in. (15–30 cm) apart. For heavy growth and seed set, plant in full sun and fertile soil. Black mustard will escape and become a weed pest if allowed to drop seeds.

Harvest
For greens, harvest entire rosettes of young plants, or use larger leaves and strip away the stringy midribs. Cut flowers and young seed pods for salads. For seeds, cut plants off at ground level after the pods on the sprays have turned brown, but before they split. Hang them to dry over a catch-cloth, and thresh as directed for caraway. To remove the chaff, rub pods through a colander or wire screen sieve. Handle the seeds carefully when crushing; the juice is a strong irritant.

Nasturtium
Tropaeolum majus pp. 260, 261

Indian Cress. The young leaves, buds, and flowers of garden nasturtiums have a delicious, nippy taste that comes from a mustard-oil component. Bush nasturtiums

grow to 2 ft. (60 cm) high in full sun; trailing kinds can be trained up supports to reach 12 ft. (3.6 m) high. They have yellow-orange flowers and round, scalloped, gray-green leaves on long, smooth, brittle stems.

How to Grow
Except in parts of Calif. where they are perennial, nasturtiums grow as frost-tender annuals. Soak seeds for 12 hours, then dry them and direct-seed in warm, well-drained soil after danger of frost is past. They prefer full sun and moderately cool weather, but make a fine, short-lived show of color in hot summer areas if grown in partial shade.

Harvest
Snip off leaves and flowering stems near ground level to keep plants neat. New growth will quickly replace the removed foliage, flowers, and buds.

Varieties
The old Gleam Hybrids have long, trailing runners that can be draped over a trellis. Modern dwarf bush nasturtiums, such as Jewel, are classified as *T. minus*. They are showier, and better for flowers because blossoms grow out beyond the foliage.

Oregano
Origanum spp. *pp. 276, 277*

Oregano is actually a flavor, and not a specific herb. The oregano sold in stores is often a blend of dried leaves of several species of *Origanum* and other genera, including *Thyme* and *Salvia*. The following is a list of the more popular oreganos that you can use individually or in combinations. Common oregano (*O. vulgare*) is a half-hardy perennial to 6 in. (15 cm) high with pink or purple flowers. The flowers are excellent for fresh or dried arrangements, but the leaves have very little flavor. The cultivar 'Aurea' has golden foliage. Italian oregano (*O. onites*) is a tender perennial with small, erect leaves; flowering stems grow to 18 in. (45 cm) high. It has a light, warm flavor, and is the preferred oregano for Italian foods. Greek oregano (*O. heracleoticum*) has coarse, ovate, hairy leaves, and grows to 18 in. (45 cm) high in flower. It has a strong, earthy aroma

and is the most flavorful. Hardiness varies in the different cultivars, but all are perennial. Spanish oregano (*O. virens*) also has a strong flavor, but is only half-hardy. It has round, bright apple-green leaves and is taller than the other oreganos.

How to Grow
Common and Greek oreganos grow well from seeds started indoors in late winter. Set seedlings out after danger of frost is past. Grow Italian and Spanish oreganos from purchased plants; Italian oregano can be propagated from cuttings or by dividing old plants. All oreganos prefer full sun and well-limed soil. They tolerate poor soil and dry conditions, but do better in moderately fertile soil with water during dry periods.

Harvest
Shear oregano back halfway when blooming starts. All oreganos dry quickly and retain their strong flavor; dry leaves whole and crush just before use.

Parsley
Petroselinum crispum pp. 255, 256

The best known of all garnishes, parsley is a frost-hardy biennial or short-lived perennial usually grown as an annual. Many arching stems form a dense mound of finely cut, dark green leaves that reach 6–10 in. (15–25 cm) high and to 16 in. (40.5 cm) wide. Several varieties exist, including curly-leaf forms, some resembling moss, and flat-leaf forms, which generally have a stronger flavor.

How to Grow
Parsley is easier to start in the garden from well-grown seedlings because seeds germinate slowly and unevenly, and young plants may take a month or more to expand. Before planting indoors or out, wash seeds in a mild detergent solution, rinse 2–3 times, and soak them overnight in warm water to improve germination. Indoors, start seeds 10–12 weeks prior to the spring frost-free date. Transplant well-hardened seedlings outdoors 2–3 weeks before the spring frost-free date, in full sun, 12–14 in. (30.0–32.5 cm) apart. Over most of the U.S., parsley is productive until killed by heavy frost. In the South and warm West, summer

heat may kill spring-planted parsley. In early
fall, you can plant a second crop in partial
shade to have parsley throughout the winter,
as long as temperatures remain above 20° F
(6.7° C).

Harvest
Shear plants 2–3 in. (5–7.5 cm) above the
soil, or pull stems off at the base. After
heavy cuttings mature plants will recover
and produce new growth if they are fed
and watered. New growth will emerge from
the central leaf buds. The fresh leaves have
innumerable uses, chopped or whole;
they can also be dried and stored in
sealed jars.

Varieties
Popular curly varieties are Moskrul, Fonvert,
Extra Curled Dwarf, Decorator, Triple
Curled, and curlina. Flat varieties include
Italian, French, and Italian Dark Green.

Pennyroyal
Mentha pulegium p. 262

A hardy, creeping perennial mint, pennyroyal
is occasionally used as a ground cover in cool
climates. It has small round to oval, dark
green leaves on many-branched stems to
12 in. (30 cm) high, and in summer bears
small, bluish-lilac blossoms in the leaf axils.
Pennyroyal has a pleasant lemony aroma
and is used to flavor meat puddings and
fish dishes.

How to Grow
Transplant potted plants or take rooted
runners from old plants. You can also sow
seeds indoors in early spring. Pennyroyal
prefers full sun and well-drained soil, but
will grow in light shade if competition with
tree roots is not too intense.

Harvest
Lift and clip off the aboveground runners
before blooming starts. Use only small
amounts of pennyroyal leaves for culinary
flavoring because too much can be toxic. It
has long been used in sachets and as an
insect repellent; patch-test it first, since some
people are allergic to it.

Corn Poppy
Papaver rhoeas p. 284

Field Poppy; Flanders Poppy; Shirley Poppy. An ornamental annual, corn poppy has dark green, hairy, irregularly lobed leaves and slender, branching stems. The flowers are usually solitary, with 4 petals, and come in red, purple, pink, or occasionally white. Plants reach 1½–2½ ft. (45–75 cm) high at bloom stage. The Shirley poppy, a popular form cultivated in flower gardens, was derived from this species and is available in several colors and with double blossoms.

How to Grow
Corn poppies need a long, cool growing season to develop to a good size before blooming. Direct-seed in fall or very early spring. The plants prefer well-drained sandy or sandy loam soil with a pH of 6.0–7.5.

Harvest
Take fresh petals at any time, but be aware that hot weather can cut the bloom period short. Watch the vase-shaped seed pods and cut them individually as they turn color and begin to dry. Store them in a paper bag until they are fully dry, then shake the seeds loose. Sieve away the chaff and sort the seeds by hand for a final cleaning. Use fresh petals for coloring wine or clear syrups, and dried seed as toppings for baked goods.

Ramp
Allium tricoccum p. 287

Wild Leek. A hardy woodland perennial native to e. North America, ramp is distinguished from other wild onions by its formidable strong smell, like that of leeks but much more potent. It was once used to flavor the strong, gamy meats eaten on the frontier. Mature plants are 12 in. (30 cm) high and usually have 2 long, wide, smooth leaves on petioles. After the leaves wither, the plant sends up flowering stems bearing rounded clusters of greenish-yellow blossoms which produce black seeds. Ramp spreads by underground rhizomes or by seeds.

How to Grow
Order seeds or plants from wildflower specialists. In early spring, plant seedlings or rhizome pieces in rich, humus soil in light

shade. Flood the patch occasionally during dry spells. In a favorable location ramp will spread, but not aggressively.

Harvest
Instead of bulbs, ramp forms slender underground stems resembling scallions. Pull these loose from the rhizomes, and discard the leaves and outer skin sheathing the stem. You won't be left with much to eat, but a little goes a long way. Use sparingly to flavor meats or greens.

Sweet Rocket
Hesperis matronalis p. 247

Dame's Rocket; Dame's Violet. A hardy biennial, sweet rocket is often grown for its fragrant lavender, purple, or white flower sprays. Plants are 3–4 ft. (90–120 cm) high and have alternate, toothed leaves. In the East, sweet rocket has escaped cultivation and naturalized in lightly shaded woodlands. It is related to mustard and has some of that plant's piquant flavor.

How to Grow
Sweet rocket dislikes hot, humid weather; direct-seed in late fall in warm-winter areas, in early spring elsewhere. The plants prefer a lightly shaded location. Thin seedlings to 12–18 in. (30–45 cm) apart. Where seasons are long, sweet rocket will often be exposed to enough spring cold to trigger flowering the first season. If not, the plants will go through the summer as leafy rosettes and will flower the second year.

Harvest
Pick stem tips, young leaves, and tender pods and use as potherbs. Use the tangy flowers in salads and fruit dishes.

Rosemary
Rosmarinus officinalis pp. 280, 281

Rosemary is a half-hardy perennial grown for its fragrant, resinous, gray-green foliage, a familiar sight and scent throughout the hills of s. France. Beyond its culinary uses, rosemary is a major landscaping plant in the Deep South and warm West. In Calif. and the Southwest, it grows as a bush 4–6 ft.

(120–180 cm) high; elsewhere it grows more slowly, to 2–4 ft. (60–120 cm) high. Ancient bushes develop picturesque twisted trunks. Creeping forms are often used as ground covers. Its leaves are small and lance-shaped. Light blue or white flowers grow in clusters from the leaf axils.

How to Grow
Rosemary is best started from potted plants grown from tip cuttings; seeds germinate slowly and poorly. Seedlings take up to 6 months to develop into pot plants. Transplant seedlings in the garden in spring after frost danger is past. Rosemary prefers full sun and dry, rocky, limy soil. Grow it on raised beds for good drainage, and in a protected corner if winters reach near-zero temperatures. In very cold climates, grow rosemary as a pot plant; in winter bring it indoors to a cool, sunny room, water sparingly, and protect from cold drafts.

Harvest
Cut 4–6 in. (10–15 cm) from the branch tips of established plants, just above the paired axillary buds; clumsy cutting results in slow recovery. Lay fresh rosemary sprigs on meats for roasting, or chop and add to fines herbes. Use the same quantity of dried rosemary as you would fresh.

Varieties
Cultivars with gold or golden-edged foliage exist, as do varieties with rich blue, lavender, purple, pink, or white flowers. The cultivars Salem and Arp are quite winter-hardy.

Cumberland Rosemary
Conradina verticillata p. 282

This beautiful, hardy native perennial is an endangered species. Although its needlelike leaves resemble those of true rosemary (*Rosmarinus officinalis*), Cumberland rosemary is supple and spreading, with many basal stems, to 12 in. (30 cm) high and 18 in. (45 cm) wide. In late spring, the plants are covered with showy lavender-pink or white flowers. The fragrant foliage suggests culinary potential.

How to Grow
Order plants from a native plant or herb specialist. Plant in full sun in well-drained

soil with a pH of 6.5–7.5, after danger of
frost is past. Cumberland rosemary
withstands heat and humidity and is hardy
to −5° F (−20.5° C). It tolerates dry soil
once established, but needs gentle watering
during dry spells. Propagate by rooting
new growth or by dividing old clumps in
early fall.

Harvest
Take branch tips starting in midsummer.
Because of its endangered status, do not
harvest wild plants.

Rue
Ruta graveolens pp. 249, 252

Herb O'Grace. This ancient medicinal plant
is a beautiful, hardy perennial that grows
erect to 2 ft. (60 cm) high and 12 in.
(30 cm) wide. It has silvery blue-green leaves
and, in early summer, sends up numerous
stalks of showy yellow flowers held well
above the foliage. The leaves can be added to
salads and sandwiches, but only in very small
amounts. Pregnant women should not eat
rue. Handling the plant, especially when it is
in flower, can cause skin irritation. Dried
leaves are often used in wreaths and other
decorations.

How to Grow
Start seeds early indoors in a mixture of 2
parts potting soil to 1 part sharp sand or
perlite. Transplant seedlings to a sunny site
after danger of frost is past. Leaves develop
an intense blue color in moist, very well
drained soil. Root tip cuttings to propagate
this herb.

Harvest
Take tender leaves and branch tips for use
anytime. Wait until just before frost to take
branches for wreaths.

Varieties
Dwarf rue and cultivars with very silvery-
blue foliage, such as Jackman's Blue, are
available. These are often used in rock
gardens and as color accents.

Sage
Salvia officinalis pp. 265, 266, 267

Garden sage is a hardy perennial with
pebbly-textured leaves that may be gray-
green, golden-edged, tricolor, or purple.
Plants range 1–2 ft. (30–60 cm) high. Often
used to season foods, sage also makes an
excellent tisane; as a medicinal plant, it is
valued for its antiseptic and antifungal
properties. It is a good landscaping and
bee plant.

How to Grow
Sage is easy to grow; sow seeds early indoors
or direct-seed after danger of frost is past.
Grow in full sun in well-drained soil at a pH
level of 6.5–7.0.

Harvest
When plants are flourishing but before
flowering shoots develop, take stem tips with
several sets of leaves. Cut in the morning,
after dew has dried but before the heat of
midday. Sage will recover from heavy
cutting. Fresh sage has better flavor than
dried. Use in either form in stuffings or with
cheese, egg, or vegetable dishes. Snip off and
dry entire flowering stems of older plants for
decorative use.

Varieties
Many variations in leaf size, color, shape, and
plant habit are available. Holt's Mammoth
sage is best for whole dried leaves.

Pineapple-scented Sage
Salvia elegans p. 259

An ornamental, pineapple-scented sage is a
half-hardy perennial usually grown as an
annual. Plants reach 4–5 ft. (1.2–1.5 m)
high and almost as wide in the South and
warm West, and only 3 ft. (90 cm) high in
the North. The leaves are dark green and
rough; the tubular flowers are vivid scarlet to
crimson and bloom for several weeks,
through fall frost. The foliage and flowers
are pineapple-scented; both can be used fresh
or dried.

How to Grow
Buy plants and set them out in well-drained
soil in full sun after danger of frost is past.

Work in preplant fertilizer, but do not feed later in the season. In northern states, where blooming starts only a few days before fall frost, you can cut back plants severely in late summer and divide and pot them to take indoors for bloom in Oct., Nov., and sporadically throughout the winter.

Harvest
Take entire branches for wreaths and potpourris. Try the fresh leaves in teas and fruit dishes, and the sweet flowers in salads, sandwiches, and desserts.

Winter Savory
Satureja montana p. 280

An attractive landscape plant, this spreading, woody, hardy perennial reaches 6–10 in. (15–25 cm) high and spreads 2 ft. (60 cm) wide when grown in hot climates in full sun. Most stems grow from the center. The small, lance-shaped, glossy leaves have sharp tips. Pink, lavender, or white flowers grow in loose whorls. The flavor of the leaves of winter savory is intensely strong, and best used to accompany sausages and salamis. The related species summer savory (*S. hortensis*), an erect, half-hardy annual with fine leaves, has a subtler flavor than *S. montana*.

How to Grow
Start seeds indoors 6–8 weeks before the spring frost-free date; sprinkle vermiculite over them in an amount that will admit enough light for plants to sprout, and stay moist. After frost danger is past, transplant seedlings in full sun in well-drained soil with a pH of 6.5–7.5.

Harvest
In the north, plants can survive only one cutting per season; in mild-winter areas, moderate cuttings can be taken in winter. Lift branches and trim them off halfway. Use leaves fresh or dried.

Shepherd's Purse
Capsella bursa-pastoris p. 282

This mustard-flavored weed, a frost-hardy annual, was introduced from Europe and has

naturalized widely. Branched stems arise from a basal rosette of leaves; white flowers on spikes 1½–2 ft. (45–60 cm) high appear in early summer, followed by triangular, purse-shaped fruits.

How to Grow
Seeds are not generally available; it is easiest to get a start from wild plants. In early fall or very early spring, direct-seed in full sun in any type of soil.

Harvest
Cut the entire plant to harvest the basal leaves. Pick the flower stems when you see the first "purses" forming. Strip off immature seeds and discard the tough end of the flower spray. The peppery leaves and flowers may be added sparingly to potherbs and spring salad greens. Cut the entire plant at early seed stage for wreath-making; they turn a lovely straw-yellow.

Tansy
Tanacetum vulgare p. 253

Over the centuries tansy has served many medicinal purposes and was traditionally used as an insect repellent. The leaves and flowers were once added to Lenten pancakes to impart a bitter flavor that was intended to remind diners of suffering and sacrifice. Tansy can be toxic: Never eat it in large amounts or drink strong tisanes made from it. A hardy perennial, this lanky plant grows 3–4 ft. (90–120 cm) high and has fernlike leaves. Flat heads of many small, buttonlike yellow flowers appear after midsummer and bloom for several weeks.

How to Grow
Start seeds indoors early in the spring. After frost danger is past, transplant seedlings to a sunny site with ordinary garden soil. Set purchased plants in the garden from late summer through fall.

Harvest
Cut off freshly opened flowers. Use dried leaves and flowers in potpourris or layered between clothes to repel insects. Or make a weak tansy tisane. Cut and hang the long flower stems for everlasting flowers.

French Tarragon
Artemisia dracunculus var. *sativa p. 281*

Estragon. Essential to fine cuisine, this anise-flavored, half-hardy perennial grows 1–2 ft. (30–60 cm) high from a burst of late spring growth. Along its slender, supple stems are narrow, dark blue-green leaves.

How to Grow
Propagate French tarragon by dividing established plants or, less usually, by tip cuttings. Divide plants in early spring before new growth begins to appear; this must be done every 3 years in the North and every 2 years in the South and warm West. Set the root divisions 3 ft. (90 cm) apart in rows 4 ft. (120 cm) apart. Grow plants in full sun in an area with good drainage, and feed them often. In warmer climates, plants usually go dormant during summer but will come back in fall if you water and fertilize them. Top growth dies back with the first heavy freeze. Because French tarragon requires winter dormancy, it is difficult to grow where winters are very mild. Where winters are severe, shear plants to the ground after frost has killed top growth, and mulch well with straw.

Harvest
French tarragon will sustain fairly heavy cutting of tip growth. Begin harvesting branch tips when the plants are 12 in. (30 cm) high. Just before the first heavy frost, harvest the entire plant. Use leaves fresh, or freeze them. Dried French tarragon is an acceptable but pale substitute for the fresh leaves. Use fresh leaves on roasted chicken and in egg or fish dishes.

Winter Tarragon
Tagetes lucida p. 265

Sweet-scented Marigold; Sweet Mace. A half-hardy perennial grown as an annual, winter tarragon is related to garden marigolds. The bushy plants grow 1–2 ft. (30–60 cm) high and have long, unbranched stems and simple, willowlike leaves that are medium green, not blue-green like the leaves of French tarragon. In fall or winter the plants bear small yellow blossoms composed of a single layer of ray flowers and a central tuft of disk flowers. The foliage has a sweet aroma with a touch of anise and is an acceptable seasonal substitute when French tarragon is dormant.

How to Grow
Winter tarragon is easy to grow indoors or out and is generally propagated from cuttings, which root easily. Transplant them to a sunny spot in the garden after danger of frost is past. Take cuttings in early fall before flowering commences and start them in pots indoors. As a houseplant, winter tarragon will yield light winter cuttings for table use.

Harvest
Winter tarragon is best used fresh; snip off the last 3–6 in. (7.5–9.0 cm) of branch tips for the tenderest leaves. Carefully dried, the leaves will retain some of their aroma.

Thyme
Thymus vulgaris pp. 278, 279

This hardy perennial is the most important of the culinary thymes and includes the classes called English thyme, French thyme, and German winter thyme. All are woody, shrubby plants with dense, upright stems that reach 12 in. (30 cm) high and 2 ft. (60 cm) wide when flowering. The tiny leaves are green or blue-green. English thyme has broad leaves, French thyme has narrow leaves, and German winter thyme has leaves with good winter color. They are popular landscape plants between stepping stones or bordering herb gardens.

How to Grow
Start French or German winter thyme from seeds indoors in early spring; start English thyme from cuttings or purchased plants. Seedlings are easily transplanted in late spring, after they have been hardened off. Thyme prefers full sun and dry soil with a pH of 6.5–7.5. In the humid South, fungus diseases may damage or kill the foliage. Old plants develop an open center; divide them every 3–5 years or replace them. Propagate by division in spring or by layering.

Harvest
Shear 2–3 in. (5.0–7.5 cm) off the branch tips. When spring blooming starts, shear

plants back halfway and feed and water them heavily. Fresh thyme has an intense, warm fragrance and mingles well with other strong herbs for flavoring meats, stews, and soups. It also dries easily and holds its flavor.

Lemon Thyme
Thymus × citriodorus pp. 278, 279

Lemon thyme is a creeping plant growing to 8 in. (20 cm) high and spreading to 2 ft. (60 cm) wide. Numerous short, soft, erect stems arise from the runners and root at the nodes. In summer the plants have pale lilac flowers. The small, shiny, dark green leaves have a marvelous lemon fragrance. Golden thyme is a cultivar.

How to Grow
Start from potted plants or rooted cuttings in late spring or early fall. Lemon thyme prefers well-drained, sandy or gravelly soil with a pH of 6.5–7.0. It may succumb to foliage diseases in the humid South and needs mulching where winters are severe.

Harvest
Lemon thyme produces a lot of branched tips for harvesting. Cut only half of the plant back, leaving at least 2 in. (5 cm) of basal growth. When that section has regrown, cut back the other half. Use fresh or dried. Add to clear broths and soups just before serving.

Lemon Verbena
Aloysia triphylla p. 273

In climates that approach the warmth of its native Latin America, lemon verbena will grow 3–5 ft. (90–150 cm) high in a single season and billow out. But in northern gardens, it grows slowly and is treated as an annual or a greenhouse plant. The woody stems have numerous apple-green, willowlike leaves that are stiff and rough to the touch. The entire plant has a strong, lemony aroma.

How to Grow
Grow lemon verbena in full sun and average to dry soil. Order plants to get a head start. If you have a greenhouse or live in a

mild-winter area, propagate plants by taking softwood cuttings from nonflowering branches in late summer. Dip cuttings in a rooting hormone and root them in moist sand. Even in a warm greenhouse, the plants will retreat into winter dormancy.

Harvest
Snip branch tips for fresh use. At the end of the season, just before frost, cut the entire plant and dry it in the dark. It is perhaps the finest of the lemon-scented herbs for drying because it retains much of its aroma and flavor; use it in teas, tisanes, and potpourris. Chefs value lemon verbena as a companion to citrus lemon because its flavor holds up in cooking.

Sweet Woodruff
Galium odoratum p. 246

Sweet Woodruff imparts the aroma of new-mown hay to May wine. Landscapers rely on it as a ground cover. A hardy, spring-blooming perennial, it grows 12–18 in. (30–45 cm) high and has white flowers and whorls of 6–8 slender, rough-edged leaves.

How to Grow
Start with purchased plants. To grow sweet woodruff successfully, moisten a bag of peat moss, spread it 2 in. (5 cm) deep, and work it into the soil. If your soil is heavy clay, also work in a 1-in. (2.5-cm) layer of sand. Turn under phosphate sources along with organic matter. Keep the soil moist, and wet it deeply if plants wilt in the afternoon sun. In hot summer areas grow in shade and maintain constant moisture.

Harvest
When sweet woodruff is flourishing, you can pick leaves and stems to make May wine. Decant dry white wine in a wide-mouth jar and add a handful of leaves and stems. Seal the jar and store it out of sunlight at room temperature. Shake the jar occasionally; after a month, strain the green matter out and serve the wine slightly chilled. Dried sweet woodruff is a fragrant addition to potpourris. Hang plants in a dark room to dry.

Appendices

Buying Guide

Seeds and plants of vegetables and herbs can be purchased in a
number of ways from dozens of companies. A list of recommended
sources follows this essay.

Ordering Seeds by Mail

Mail-order seed companies are a diverse lot. The best are full-service
firms offering a wide selection. They employ plant breeders and
horticulturists and conduct performance trials, as well as maintain
seed laboratories and air-conditioned seed storage. The worst are not
numerous, but they are visible in early spring when their gaudy ads
appear, promising the moon. Hardly a gardener alive has escaped
being bitten by one of these sharks.

The catalogue descriptions of any ethical seed company are
exuberant but accurate. They include new varieties and represent a
huge effort—performance testing, photography, accurate description,
and quality control. Unless you are a veteran gardener, it is best to
find one or two companies you trust and stick with them. Trying
to select from many catalogues can become confusing.

You will see numerous symbols on seed packets and in catalogues.
An important one is the "All-America Selections Award" symbol.
These awards are equivalent to the Oscars and Emmys of the
entertainment industry. Vegetables and flowers are judged
throughout the United States and Canada by professional
horticulturists, and the award system is above reproach. But be
aware that, once a variety has received the award, it can bear the
AAS seal for many years.

Buying Seeds off the Rack

Seed displays arrive in the stores just before the indoor planting
season for frost-hardy annuals. In the deep South and warm West
the displays arrive in early fall.

Every seed packet will give you the following information: common
name, variety name, brief description, days to maturity, directions for
starting indoors or direct-seeding, optimum spacing, best uses, name
and address of packager, gardening season for which the seeds were
packed, retail price, and a code number for internal control. There
should also be a prominent notice if the seeds have tested below
federal minimum standards for germination.

Buying Plants

The majority of vegetable plants are sold off racks in garden centers,
nurseries, hardware stores, and supermarkets. The most important
aspect of buying these plants is to get them soon after they go on
display. They are mostly greenhouse grown, in small, multiple packs
of individual pots filled with lightweight artificial growing media.
They have very little reserve nutrients, and will deteriorate if not fed
occasionally and watered frequently. Some markets display plants
indoors with no sunlight. You can imagine the stress on the plant.

More and more, growers are shipping days or weeks in advance of the frost-free date. Just because plants are displayed for sale doesn't mean it is safe to plant them.

In plants, bigger is not better. Years ago, growers delivered young "green plants" to retailers—seedlings not yet in fruit or flower. These adapted quickly and smoothly to transplanting and seldom suffered transplanting shock. Now larger, more mature plants are sold. A pepper plant loaded with fruit, for example, is greatly stressed when it is knocked out of the pot, transplanted to a harsh environment, and watered sporadically. A good guide in buying vegetable and herb plants is "Small is best."

A plant label should give not only kind and variety name in full, but also a brief description. For example, if an eggplant label reads "Dusky Hybrid, 18 inches high, dark purple, elongated fruit, 61 days," you have enough information to plant it intelligently. Most plant dealers keep catalogue sheets under the counter and will let you refer to them for descriptions. If they don't, take your business elsewhere.

Local Growers and Retailers

The prime source of a wide selection of well-grown, locally adapted vegetable varieties and common herb plants is a greenhouse grower or retailer. These are worth patronizing, because they dispense accurate advice and receive valuable feedback from customers. They stand behind their plants because they grow them themselves. For less common herb plants, try specialty grower/retailers. Some specialize in 1 genus, such as scented geraniums; others in medicinal herbs; and some in fragrant species. Most herb hobbyists make annual pilgrimages to the greenhouses of herb growers to pick up new cultivars for their collections. You can also order from price lists or catalogues.

Making Complaints

Virtually all seed companies will replace seeds that don't grow. Check their catalogues for refund policies. But remember that seeds must meet rigid germination standards in order to be offered for sale. Germination failures are more likely due to damping off, crusting of soil, bird or snail damage, or planting improperly stored leftovers than to inert seeds. In rare instances failures can be due to overheating of seed packages in transit or to packets being displayed in a warm, humid environment.

There can be mixups in the labeling of seed packets, but more often than not this occurs in the seedling flat or in the garden rather than in packing. Labeling mixups in displayed plants are common, however, and usually caused by consumers who take out labels and put them back in the wrong pot. It is a good idea to confirm that you have the correct variety by asking the seller if you are not familiar with how the seedlings should look.

Seeds & Plants

Vegetables and Herbs

Agway, Inc.
Seed Division, Box 4933, Syracuse, NY 13221
The American Seed Corp.
58233 N. Gratiot Avenue, New Haven, MI 48048
Applewood Seed Co.
833 Parfet Street, Lakewood, CO 80215
W. Atlee Burpee Co.
Warminster, PA 18974
Comstock, Ferre and Co.
263 Main Street, Wethersfield, CT 06109
Farmer Seed and Nursery Co.
Faribault, MN 55021
Ferry-Morse Seed Co.
Home Garden Division, Box 488, Fulton, KY 42041
Henry Field Seed and Nursery Co.
407 Sycamore Street, Shenandoah, IA 51602
Fredonia Seed Co.
183–185 E. Main Street, P.O. Box 180, Fredonia, NY 14063
Gurney Seed and Nursery Co.
2nd and Capitol, Yankton, SD 57079
C. C. Hart Seed Co.
304 Main Street, Box 169, Wethersfield, CT 06109
H. G. Hastings Co.
Box 4088, Atlanta, GA 30302
Jackson and Perkins
Medford, OR 97501
Johnny's Selected Seeds
Albion, ME 04910
J. W. Jung Seed Co.
Randolph, WI 53956
Northrup King and Co.
1500 Jackson Street, NE, Minneapolis, MN 55413
Chas. H. Lilly Co.
77 NE Killingsworth Street, Portland, OR 97218
Earl E. May Seed and Nursery Co.
Shenandoah, IA 51603
Harris Moran Seed Co.
3760 Buffalo Road, Rochester, NY 14624
Nichols Garden Nursery
1190 N. Pacific Highway, Albany, OR 97321
George W. Park Seed Co., Inc.
Greenwood, SC 29647
Robson Seed Farms Corp.
Hall, NY 14463
Seedway, Inc.
Hall, NY 14463

okes Seeds Ltd., Inc.
)70 Stokes Building, Buffalo, NY 14240
willey Seed Co., Inc.
O. Box 65, Trevose, PA 19047
aughan-Jacklin Corp.
00 Katrine Avenue, Downers Grove, IL 60515
ermont Bean Seed Co.
arden Lane, Bomoseen, VT 05732

pecialties

picure Seeds, Ltd.
von, NY 14414
itzawa Seed Company
56 W. Taylor Street, San Jose, CA 95110
eed Savers Exchange
ent Whealy, R.R. 2, Princeton, MO 64673
hompson and Morgan, Inc.
.O. Box 100, Farmingdale, NJ 07727

lerbs

aprilands Nursery
lver Street, Coventry, CT 06238
atnip Acres Farm
7 Christian Street, Oxford, CT 06483
ox Hill Farm
40 W. Michigan Avenue, Parma, MI 49269
lemlock Hill Herb Farm
lemlock Hill Road, Litchfield, CT 06759–0415
lilltop Herb Farm
.O. Box 1734, Cleveland, TX 77327
ogee's Greenhouses
5 North Street, Danielson, CT 06239
leadowbrook Herb Garden
oute 138, Wyoming, RI 02898
utland of Kentucky
.O. Box 16, Washington, KY 41096
he Sandy Mush Herb Nursery
oute 2, Surret Cove Road, Leicester, NC 28748
unnybrook Farm
ox 6, Chesterland, OH 44026
aylor's Herb Gardens Inc.
535 Lone Oak Road, Vista, CA 92084
Vayside Gardens
lodges, SC 29695
Vell Sweep Herb Farm
17 Mt. Bethel Road, Port Murray, NJ 07865

Pests & Diseases

Because plant pests and diseases are a fact of life for a gardener, it is helpful to become familiar with common pests and diseases in your area and to learn how to control them.

Symptoms of Plant Problems
The same general symptoms are associated with many diseases and pests, so some experience is needed to determine their causes.

Diseases
Both fungi and bacteria are responsible for a variety of diseases ranging from leafspots and wilts to root rot, but bacterial diseases usually make the affected plant tissues appear wetter than fungi do. Diseases caused by viruses and mycoplasma, often transmitted by aphids and leafhoppers, display such symptoms as mottled yellow or deformed leaves and stunted growth.

Insect Pests
Numerous insects attack plants. Sap-sucking insects—including aphids, leafhoppers, and whiteflies—suck plant juices. The affected plant becomes yellow, stunted, and misshapen. These insects produce honeydew, a sticky substance that attracts ants and sooty mold fungus growth. Other pests with rasping-sucking mouthparts, such as thrips and spider mites, scrape plant tissue and then suck the juices that well up in the injured areas.
Leaf-chewers, namely beetles and caterpillars, consume plant leaves, whole or in part. Leafminers make tunnels within the leaves, creating brown trails and causing leaf tissue to dry. In contrast, borers tunnel into shoots and stems, and their young larvae consume plant tissue, weakening the plant. Some insects, such as various grubs and maggots, feed on roots, weakening or killing the plant.

Nematodes
Microscopic roundworms called nematodes are other pests that attack roots and cause stunting and poor plant growth. They are often a problem on sandy soil in hot climates.

Environmental Stresses
Some types of plant illness result from environment-related stress, such as severe wind, drought, flooding, or extreme cold. Other problems are caused by salt toxicity, rodents, birds, nutritional deficiencies or excesses, fertilizer burn, or pesticides. Many of these injuries are avoidable if you plan and cultivate your garden wisely.

Controlling Plant Problems
Always buy healthy disease- and insect-free plants, and select disease-resistant varieties when available. Check leaves and stems for dead areas or off-color and stunted tissue. Inspect plants twice a week for signs of disease or infestation.

Routine Preventives

By cultivating the soil routinely you will expose insects and disease-causing organisms to the sun and thus lessen their chances of surviving in your garden. In the fall be sure to destroy infested or diseased plants, remove dead leaves and flowers, and clean up plant debris. Do not add diseased, infested, or herbicide-treated material to the compost pile. Spray plants with water from time to time to dislodge insect pests and remove suffocating dust. Pick off the larger insects by hand. To discourage fungal leafspots and blights, always water plants in the morning and allow the leaves to dry off before nightfall. For the same reason, provide adequate air circulation by spacing plants properly. Rotate plantings every year.

Weeds provide a home for insects and diseases, so pull them up or use herbicides. But do not apply herbicides, including "weed-and-feed" lawn preparations, too close to the garden. Herbicide injury may cause elongated, straplike, or downward-cupping leaves. Spray weed-killers when there is little air movement, but not on a very hot, dry day.

Insecticides and Fungicides

There are a number of insecticides and fungicides available, but few control diseases due to bacteria, viruses, and mycoplasma. Pesticides used on vegetables are usually "protectants," which guard uninfected foliage from insects or disease organisms. "Systemic" pesticides move through the plant and provide some therapeutic or eradicant action as well as protection. Botanical insecticides such as pyrethrum, sabadilla, and rotenone have a shorter residual effect on pests, but are considered less toxic and generally safer for the user and the environment than inorganic chemical insecticides. Biological control through the use of organisms like *Bacillus thuringiensis* (a bacterium toxic to moth and butterfly larvae) is effective and safe.

Recommended pesticides may vary to some extent from region to region. Consult your local Cooperative Extension Service or plant professional regarding the appropriate material to use. Always check the pesticide label to be sure that it is registered for use on the pest and plant with which you are dealing. Follow the label concerning safety precautions, dosage, frequency of application, and the preharvest interval—the period to wait between spraying a pesticide on food and harvesting it.

Recognizing Pests and Diseases

Learning to recognize the insects and diseases that plague plants is a first step toward controlling them. The chart on the following pages describes the most common pests and diseases that attack vegetables and herbs, the damage they cause, and control measures.

Pests and Diseases

Pest or Disease

Aphids

Cutworms

Damping-off

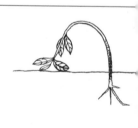

Grasshoppers

Leaf-feeding Beetles

Description	Damage	Controls
Tiny green, brown, or reddish, pear-shaped soft-bodied insects in clusters on buds, shoots, and undersides of leaves.	Suck plant juices, causing stunted or deformed blooms and leaves. Some transmit plant viruses. Secretions attract ants.	Spray with malathion or rotenone late in the day in order not to kill bees. Encourage natural predators such as ladybugs.
Smooth, wormlike, brown or green moth larvae.	Feed near soil line, cutting off stems of transplants.	Place cardboard collars around stems of transplants, extending 2 in. (5 cm) above and 1 in. (2.5 cm) below soil line.
Soilborne fungal disease that attacks seeds and seedlings.	Rotting of seeds and seedlings, resulting in failure to germinate or develop properly. Stems may become black, dry, and hard.	Start seeds in sterile perlite or vermiculite, or treat seeds with thiram or captan before planting. Don't overwater.
Elongated yellow, green, or brown insects with long hind legs and hard outer coverings.	Feed on and consume aerial plant parts.	Handpick. Spray with hot pepper and soap solution or Sevin. Protect plants with fine netting.
Hard-shelled, oval to oblong insects on leaves, stems, and flowers. Examples include Japanese, cucumber, and Mexican bean beetles.	Chew plant parts, leaving holes. Larvae of some feed on roots.	Handpick and destroy. Spray with malathion, rotenone, pyrethrum, or Sevin.

Pests and Diseases

Pest or Disease

Leaf-feeding Caterpillars

Leafhoppers

Leafminers

Leafspots

Nematodes

Description	Damage	Controls
Soft-bodied, wormlike crawling insects with several pairs of legs. May be smooth, hairy, or spiny. Adults are moths or butterflies.	Consume part or all of leaves. Flowers and shoots may also be eaten.	Handpick and destroy. Spray with *Bacillus thuringiensis,* pyrethrum, or malathion.
Small, greenish, wedge-shaped, soft-bodied insects on undersides of leaves. Quickly hop when disturbed.	Suck plant juices, causing discolored leaves and plants. Some may transmit plant virus and mycoplasma diseases.	Spray with malathion or dust plants with diatomaceous earth. The new synthetic pyrethrums are also effective.
Small pale larvae of flies or beetles. Feed between leaf surfaces.	Leaves show yellow, then brown, oval or meandering papery blotches. Leaves may drop.	Remove badly infested leaves. Spray with malathion when first mines appear.
Spots on leaves caused by fungi encouraged by humid or wet weather.	Tan, brown, or black spots on leaves. If serious, leaves may drop from plant.	Increase air circulation around plant. Remove badly diseased leaves. Spray with zineb or benomyl if serious, but not on leafy green vegetables.
Microscopic roundworms, usually associated with roots. Cause various diseases.	Stunted, off-color plants that do not respond to water or fertilizer. Minute galls may be present on roots.	Remove and destroy badly affected plants. Nematocides are available for use around valuable ornamental plants.

Pests and Diseases

Pest or Disease

Plant Bugs

Root Maggots

Root Rot

Slugs and Snails

Spider Mites

Description	Damage	Controls
Oblong, flattened, greenish-yellow insects, about ⅓ in. (8 mm) long. Some with black stripes. Wings held flat over abdomen.	Suck plant juices, causing spots on leaves. Some deform roots and shoots.	Spray with malathion or rotenone. Use sabadilla for persistent, tough bugs such as green plant bug and squash bug.
White or yellow fly larvae that feed on roots, tubers, and bulbs. Rarely a problem in warm areas.	Feed on underground plant parts, causing stunted and sickly plants. Feeding injury may lead to rot.	Place Diazinon in planting furrow; work it into soil around transplant. Or place cheesecloth on soil around base of transplant. Spun-bonded fabric covers help.
Fungal or bacterial disease, usually soilborne, often encouraged by waterlogged soil.	Wilting, off-color plants. Roots dark and dry or mushy, rather than firm and white.	Remove and destroy infected plants. Do not grow similar plants in that area. Improve soil drainage with raised beds, sand, and organic additives.
Gray, slimy, soft-bodied mollusks with or without hard outer shells. Leave slime trails on leaves; found in damp places.	Feed at night, rasping holes in leaves.	Trap slugs using stale beer in pie pans. Eliminate trash and hiding places around garden. Use metaldehyde bait, moistened, in a can so pets won't eat.
Tiny golden, red, or brown arachnids on undersides of leaves. Profuse fine webs seen with heavy infestations.	Scrape leaves and suck plant juices. Leaves become pale, rusty looking, and dry. Plant may be stunted.	Spray leaves with water or Kelthane.

Pest or Disease

Stalk Borers

Viruses

Whiteflies

Wilts, Bacterial

Wilts, Fungal

Description	Damage	Controls
Cream and brown- or purple-striped caterpillars found on or inside stems of herbaceous plants.	Burrow inside stems, plant wilts and dies.	Remove badly infested plants. Slit stems and remove borers. On squash plants, mound soil over the slit stems.
Various diseases, including mosaics, that cause off-color, stunted plants. May be transmitted by aphids.	Crinkled, mottled, deformed leaves, stunted plants, poor growth.	Remove and destroy infected plants. Control the insect vector (aphids) if present. Buy only healthy plants of resistant varieties.
Tiny flies with white, powdery wings. Fly up in great numbers when disturbed. Secrete honeydew.	Suck plant juices from undersides of leaves. Plants look yellow, sickly, and stunted. Sooty mold may be present.	Spray with malathion or pyrethrum. Sticky pest strips will trap some.
Bacterial diseases that plug plant stems. Soilborne or transmitted by insects or on cuttings.	Plants turn yellow, wilt, and die. Affected tissues may be wet and sticky.	Remove and destroy infected plants. Practice crop rotation. Use resistant varieties.
Soilborne fungal diseases that cause wilting, stunting, and eventual death of plants.	Leaves turn yellow and entire plant may wilt and die. Roots may rot.	Remove infected plants. Practice crop rotation. Use resistant varieties.

Glossary

Acid soil
Soil with a pH value of less than 7.

Alkaline soil
Soil with a pH value of more than 7.

Alternate
Arranged singly along a twig or shoot, and not in whorls or opposite pairs.

Annual
A plant whose entire life span, from sprouting to flowering and producing seeds and dying, is encompassed in 1 growing season.

Axil
The angle formed by the junction of 2 stems, or by a leafstalk and the stem to which it is attached.

Basal leaf
A leaf near the base of a stem.

Biennial
A plant whose life span extends to 2 growing seasons, sprouting in the first growing season and then flowering, producing seed, and dying in the second.

Bolting
The premature or unwanted production of flowers and seeds, often caused by starvation or excessive heat. Often applied to lettuce and spinach.

Bract
A modified and often scalelike leaf, usually located at the base of a flower, a fruit, or a cluster of flowers or fruits.

Bud
A young and undeveloped leaf, flower, or shoot.

Bulb
A short underground budlike structure, the swollen portion consisting mostly of fleshy, food-storing scale leaves.

Cloche
A glass or rigid plastic cover used to protect plants or rows from frost, wind, or rain.

Clone
A group of plants all originating by vegetative propagation from a single plant, and therefore genetically identical to it and to one another.

Compost
A blend of decomposed organic matter not yet reduced to humus; soil or sand are sometimes added.

Compound leaf
A leaf made up of 2 or more leaflets.

Corm
A solid underground stem, resembling a bulb but lacking fleshy scales; often with a membranous coat.

Cover crop
A quick-growing crop used to cover exposed ground, prevent erosion, and retard leaching. See also Green manure crop.

Creeper
Technically, a trailing shoot that takes root at the nodes; used in the text to denote vines and trailing, prostrate plants.

Crop rotation
The planting of different species in succession in 1 given area to reduce the risk of soilborne plant disease.

Cross-pollination
The transfer of pollen from one plant to another, genetically different plant.

Crown
The part of a plant between the roots and the stem, usually at soil level.

Cultivar
A man-made plant form or selection within a species.

Cutting
A piece of plant without roots; set in a rooting medium, it develops roots and is then potted as a new plant.

Dissected leaf
A deeply cut leaf, the clefts not reaching the midrib; same as a divided leaf.

Division
Propagation by separating crowns or tubers into segments that can be induced to send out roots.

Drill
A trench in which seeds are planted, or in which fertilizer is added near a row of seeds.

Forcing
The exposure of plants to warmth to induce unusually early growth.

Genus
A group of closely related species; plural, genera.

Germinate
To sprout.

Glossary

Green manure crop
A cover crop grown to be turned under for soil improvement.

Herbaceous perennial
An herbaceous plant whose top dies back seasonally but that sends out new shoots and flowers for several successive years.

Horticulture
The cultivation of plants for ornament or food.

Humus
Highly decomposed vegetable matter; an important constituent of garden soil.

Hybrid
A plant resulting from a cross between 2 parent plants belonging to different genera, species, subspecies, or varieties of the same species.

Inflorescence
A flower cluster.

Invasive
Aggressively spreading away from cultivation.

Lateral bud
A bud borne in the axil of a leaf or branch; not terminal.

Leaflet
One of the subdivisions of a compound leaf.

Legume
A member of the pea and bean family, whose fruits are pods that split in half and have the seeds attached to the lower seam. Includes alfalfa, clover, and other food, forage, and cover crops.

Loam
A humus-rich soil containing up to 25 percent clay, up to 50 percen silt, and less than 50 percent sand.

Lobed leaf
A leaf whose margin is shallowly divided.

Margin
The edge of a leaf.

Mulch
A protective covering spread over the soil around the base of plants to retard evaporation, control temperature, or enrich the soil.

Naturalized
Established as a part of the flora in an area other than the place of origin.

Neutral soil
Soil that is neither acid nor alkaline, having a pH value of 7.

Node
The place on the stem where leaves, buds, or branches are attached.

Offset
A short, lateral shoot arising near the base of a plant, readily producing new roots, and useful in propagation.

Opposite
Arranged along a twig or shoot in pairs, with 1 on each side, and not alternate or in whorls.

Peat moss
Partly decomposed moss, usually acidic, and with a high water retention, used as a component of garden soil.

Perennial
A plant whose life span extends over several growing seasons and that produces seeds in several growing seasons, rather than only 1.

Petiole
The stalk of a leaf.

pH
A symbol for the hydrogen ion content of the soil, and thus a means of expressing the acidity or alkalinity of the soil.

Plunge
To bury the pot in which a greenhouse plant is growing up to its rim in the garden; done in summer to refresh the plant.

Pollen
Minute grains containing the male germ cells of flowering plants.

Potherb
An herbaceous plant that is usually cooked in a pot; most are also used raw in salads.

Propagate
To produce new plants, either by vegetative means involving the rooting of pieces of a plant, or by sowing seeds.

Rhizome
A horizontal underground stem, distinguished from a root by the presence of nodes, and often enlarged by food storage.

Rosette
A crowded cluster of leaves; usually basal, circular, and at ground level.

Runner
A prostrate, aboveground shoot, rooting at its nodes.

Seed
A fertilized, ripened ovule, containing an embryonic plant and stored foods, and almost always covered with a protective coating.

Species
A population of plants whose members are at least potentially able to breed with each other, but that is reproductively isolated from other populations.

Spike
An elongated flower cluster in which the individual flowers lack stalks.

Subshrub
A partly woody plant.

Subspecies
A naturally occurring geographic variant of a species.

Succession planting
The planting of 1 garden crop directly after the harvest of another to increase the yield of a given area during 1 growing season.

Succulent
A plant with thick, fleshy leaves or stems that contain abundant water-storage tissue. Cacti and stonecrops are examples.

Taproot
The main, central root of a plant.

Terminal
Borne at the tip of a stem or shoot rather than in the axil.

Till
To work the soil into small fragments.

Toothed
Having the margin shallowly divided into small, toothlike segments.

Tuber
A swollen, mostly underground stem that bears buds and serves as a storage site for food.

Tufted
Growing in dense clumps or cushions.

Variety
A population of plants within a species that differ consistently from the typical form of the species.

Vegetative propagation
Propagation by means other than seed.

Volunteer seedling
A plant that sprouts from seeds formed the previous year.

Whorl
A group of 3 or more leaves or shoots, all emerging from a stem at a single node.

Photo Credits

Gillian Beckett
A well-known English horticultural photographer.
14B, 232A, 256B, 271B

W. Atlee Burpee Company
A seed and plant company in Warminster, Pennsylvania.
89A, 157A, 184A, 184B, 199A

Karen Bussolini
A nature and wildlife photographer in New York.
54

David Cavagnaro
A freelance nature photographer and author.
20A, 121B, 158B, 181A, 189A, 202A, 204A, 209A, 268B, 269B, 286B

Jack Dermid
A freelance biological photographer and retired professor.
26, 228B

Thomas E. Eltzroth
General consultant for this book and a professor of horticulture.
89B, 95A, 95B, 97B, 98A, 101B, 103A, 103B, 105B, 106B, 107A, 109B, 111B, 113A, 119B, 121A, 124B, 128B, 129A, 137A, 140A, 141A, 143B, 145A, 148B, 150A, 156B, 158A, 160B, 161B, 162B, 163A, 163B, 164B, 166A, 170A, 171A, 171B, 172A, 174B, 176B, 177B, 178B, 181B, 183B, 186A, 188B, 190A, 190B, 191A, 193B, 194A, 194B, 196, 199B, 205A, 205B, 207A, 208B, 210, 215B, 219B, 220B, 223A, 223B, 224A, 226B, 228A, 229A, 237B, 239B, 240A, 240B, 242A, 243B, 244, 248B, 254A, 256A, 260B, 264B, 265A, 265B, 266B, 267A, 273B, 277B, 278A, 278B, 280B, 283A, 284B

Derek Fell
A widely published garden writer whose photographs have appeared in numerous articles on gardening.
16, 88A, 88B, 90A, 90B, 91A, 91B, 92A, 93B, 94A, 94B, 96A, 96B, 97A, 100A, 101A, 102A, 104A, 104B, 105A, 106A, 107B, 109A, 110A, 110B, 111A, 112A, 112B, 113B, 114A, 118B, 119A, 122A, 123B, 124A, 125A, 125B, 128A, 130A, 131A, 132A, 132B, 133A, 133B, 134A, 134B, 135A, 135B, 136A, 136B, 138A, 138B, 139B, 140B, 141B, 144A, 145B, 148A, 149B, 150A, 151A, 152A, 152B, 153B, 156A, 157B, 159A, 159B, 161A, 162A, 164A, 165A, 166B, 167A, 170B, 172B, 174A, 175A, 175B, 179A, 179B, 180A, 180B, 182A, 185B, 187A, 187B, 188A, 189B, 191B, 192A, 192B, 193A, 195A, 198B, 204B, 207B, 209B, 212A, 212B, 213A, 213B, 214A, 214B, 215A, 216A, 216B, 221A, 222B, 225A, 225B, 226A, 227A, 227B, 229B, 230A, 230B, 231A, 236A, 236B, 237A, 238A, 238B, 241A, 241B, 242B, 246B, 251B, 252B, 255A, 255B, 257A, 262B, 267B, 275B, 282B, 283B, 284A

Photo Credits   *The letter after each page number refers to the position of the color plates.*   *A represents the picture at the top and B the picture at the bottom. Some pictures are also in the Visual Key.*

Charles Marden Fitch
A media specialist and horticulturist.
Cover: 'Pixie' hybrid tomato
99B, 123A, 137B, 139A, 147A, 151B, 153A, 185A, 202B, 217B, 218A, 251A, 254B, 258A, 259A, 268A, 272B, 273B, 279B

Judy Glattstein
An instructor at the New York Botanical and Brooklyn Botanic gardens.
131B, 247A, 285A

Pamela Harper
Horticultural writer, photographer, and lecturer, with an extensive library of plant and garden slides.
118A, 129B, 142A, 144B, 146A, 146B, 147B, 149A, 168, 173A, 201B, 203A, 206B, 208A, 218B, 221B, 224B, 233A, 233B, 234A, 243A, 246A, 249A, 249B, 253A, 253B, 259B, 260A, 261A, 261B, 262A, 269A, 274A, 275A, 276A, 281B, 282A

Harris Moran Seed Company
A seed wholesaler in Rochester, New York.
176A, 177A

Walter Hodge
Author of *The Audubon Society Book of Wildflowers.*
92B, 93A, 102B, 116, 120B, 160A, 173B, 178A, 198A, 219A, 235A, 235B, 247B, 279A

John A. Lynch
A photographer specializing in gardening and wildflowers.
108A, 270B, 287A

Robert E. Lyons/PHOTO/NATS
A professor of horticulture at Virginia Polytechnic Institute.
280A

Michael Philip Manheim/PHOTO RESEARCHERS, INC.
A commercial photographer in Marblehead, Massachusetts.
165B

Paul C. P. McIlhenny
Vice-president of McIlhenny Company in Louisiana.
142B

Frank Morton/ENTHEOS
A photographer and market gardener in the mountains of Washington.
222A

Richard Parker/PHOTO RESEARCHERS, INC.
A photojournalist of botany in Missouri.
43A

G. R. Roberts
High school teacher, photographer, and author in New Zealand.
98B, 99A, 100B, 108B, 115A, 130B, 167A, 186B, 206A, 250A, 263B

John J. Smith
A natural history photographer with an extensive slide collection.
15B, 232B, 248A

Steven Still
A prolific photographer and professor of horticulture.
22A, 200A, 200B, 201A, 203B, 239A, 252A, 257B, 258B, 264A, 266A,
270A, 271A, 274B, 276B, 277A, 286A, 287A

David M. Stone
A freelance nature and life science photographer.
85B

George Taloumis
Garden columnist for the *Boston Globe* and *Flower and Garden*.
234B, 272A

Mary M. Thacher/PHOTO RESEARCHERS, INC.
An urban wildlife photographer.
263A

George Whiteley/PHOTO RESEARCHERS, INC.
A retired biology teacher, presently living in Maine and Cape Cod.
250B

Jim Wilson
Author of this guide and co-owner of Savory Farms.
281A

Steven C. Wilson/ENTHEOS
A professional wildlife and landscape photographer.
217A, 220A

Marilyn T. Wood/PHOTO/NATS
Owner of PHOTO/NATS, an agency of nature photographers.
95B, 231B

Index

Chanticleer Staff

Publisher: Paul Steiner
Editor-in-Chief: Gudrun Buettner
Executive Editor: Susan Costello
Managing Editor: Jane Opper
Project Editor: Marian Appellof
Associate Editor: David Allen
Assistant Editor: Leslie Ann Marchal
Production: Helga Lose, Gina Stead,
René Schmutz
Art Director: Carol Nehring
Art Associate: Ayn Svoboda
Art Assistant: Cheryl Miller
Picture Library: Edward Douglas, John C.
Russell
Drawings: Robin Jess, Edward Lam, Sarah
Pletts, Dolores R. Santoliquido, Alan D.
Singer, Mary Jane Spring
Frost Date Map: Paul Singer

Design: Massimo Vignelli